The Closed Book
Concerning the Secret of the Borgias

by

William Le Queux

The Closed Book
Concerning the Secret of the Borgias
by William Le Queux

ISBN: 978-93-59954-02-8

Published by

DOUBLE 9 BOOKS

2/13-B, Ansari Road
Daryaganj, New Delhi – 110002
info@double9books.com
www.double9books.com
Tel. 011-40042856

ABOUT THE AUTHOR

Anglo-French journalist and author William Tufnell Le Queux was born on July 2, 1864, and died on October 13, 1927. He was also a diplomat (honorary consul for San Marino), a traveler (in Europe, the Balkans, and North Africa), a fan of flying (he presided over the first British air meeting at Doncaster in 1909), and a wireless pioneer who played music on his own station long before radio was widely available. However, he often exaggerated his own skills and accomplishments. The Great War in England in 1897 (1894), a fantasy about an invasion by France and Russia, and The Invasion of 1910 (1906), a fantasy about an invasion by Germany, are his best-known works. Le Queux was born in the city. The man who raised him was English, and his father was French. He went to school in Europe and learned art in Paris from Ignazio (or Ignace) Spiridon. As a young man, he walked across Europe and then made a living by writing for French newspapers. He moved back to London in the late 1880s and managed the magazines Gossip and Piccadilly. In 1891, he became a parliamentary reporter for The Globe. He stopped working as a reporter in 1893 to focus on writing and traveling.

CONTENTS

Chapter One
Which Mainly Concerns a Hunchback

These strange facts would never have been placed on record, nor would this exciting chapter of an eventful life have been written, except for two reasons: first, because the discovery I made has been declared to be of considerable importance to scientists, bibliophiles, and the world at large; and, secondly, because it is my dear wife's wish that in order to clear her in the eyes of both friends and foes nothing should be concealed, misrepresented, or withheld.

It was, indeed, a memorable day when I halted before the white, almost windowless house of the prior of San Sisto and knocked twice at its plain, green-painted door. The sun-blanched, time-mellowed city of Florence lay silent, glaring, and deserted in the blazing noon of a July day. The Florentines had fled to the mountains for air. The persiennes, or sun-shutters, were everywhere closed, the shops shut, the people slumbering, and the silence only broken by the heat-song of the chirping cicale in the scorched trees at the end of the Lung Arno.

Like many another Tuscan town, it stood with long rows of high, frescoed, and sculptured palaces facing the brown river, its magnificent Duomo and campanile, its quaint fourteenth-century streets, and its medieval Ponte Vecchio all forming a grim, imposing relic of long-past glory. In many places its aspect was little changed since the old quattrocento days, when it was the centre of all the arts and the powerful rival of Venice and Genoa, although its trade has decayed and its power departed. The Lion and Lily of Florence upon a flag is no longer feared, as it once was, even by the bloodthirsty corsairs, and the rich Florentine brocades, velvets, and finely tempered arms are no longer in requisition in the markets of the world.

Save for the influx of scrambling tourists, it is one of the dead towns of Europe. Modern trade passes it by unnoticed; its very name would be forgotten were it not for those marvellous works of art in its galleries and in its very streets.

I had always loved the quaint old city, ever since a boy, when my father, a retired English naval officer, lived in that ancient house with the brown frescoes in the via di Pinti in the days before the shrieking steam trams ran to Prato or the splendid Palazzo Riccardi had been desecrated by the Government. At fourteen I left those quaint, quiet streets, with their cool loggias and silent, moss-grown courtyards, for the whirl of Paris, and subsequently lived and worked in London. Then, after an absence of nearly twenty years, I found myself living again in my beloved Tuscany by the Mediterranean, at Leghorn, forty miles distant from the medieval city of my childhood. Was it, therefore, surprising that the mood often seized me to go and revisit the old places I had known as a boy? I found them all unchanged—indeed, nothing changes in "Firenza la Bella" save the fortunes of her ruined nobility and the increase of garish hotels for the accommodation of the foreigner.

I was something of an antiquary, and through many years had been collecting medieval manuscripts on vellum, ancient chapters, diplomas, notarial deeds, and such-like documents, none being of later date than the fifteenth century. To decipher the work of the old scribes is, I admit, a dry-as-dust occupation; nevertheless, it is a work that grows on one, and the palaeographist is an enthusiast always. In one's hobbies one should always join advantage to amusement, and seek to gather profit with pleasure.

My collection of musty-smelling parchments and rolls of folded vellum documents, with their formidable seals of wax or lead; of heavy vellum books bound in oaken boards and brass bosses, or tiny illuminated books of hours, so minutely written that a microscope was almost necessary to read them, appeal to very few people. Most of my friends regarded them as so many old and undecipherable books and rolls, without interest and without value. They wondered that, being continually occupied at my desk writing novels, I should take up such an essentially dry study.

Yet it was this love of collecting that first brought me into contact with Francesco Graniani, a queer little old hunchback, who was a kind of itinerant dealer in antiques. Unshaven, very shabby, and not particularly clean, he dressed always in the same faded drab suit, and, summer or winter, wore the same battered, sun-browned straw hat through all the years I knew him.

Often this strange, rather tragic figure would meet me in the sun-baked streets of Leghorn, raise his battered hat respectfully, and, taking me aside, produce mysteriously from his pocket a parchment charter with its seal, some leaves from a medieval psalter, or perhaps an illuminated codex, or a book of hours with painted miniatures. Where le obtained such gems I have never to this day discovered. None knew who the old fellow was, or where he lived; he was a complete mystery.

One morning while crossing the great square I encountered him, and he informed me in his strange, mysterious manner of the existence of a very rare and interesting manuscript in the possession of the prior of the ancient church of San Sisto, at Florence.

"If the signore goes to Firenze, Father Landini will no doubt allow him to have sight of the parchment book," he said. "Tell him that Francesco Graniani wishes it."

"But what is the character of the manuscript?" I inquired.

"I know nothing of it," he replied evasively, "except that I believe it once belonged to the Monastery of the Certosa. I heard of it only last night, and thought perhaps it might interest you."

It certainly did. Any discovery of that kind always attracted me—ever on the lookout as I was for a single folio of the original Dante.

With the object of inspecting the palaeographic treasure I next day took train to Florence, and an hour after my arrival knocked in some trepidation at the prior's green door.

The long grey church, one of the oldest in that ancient city, stood in its little piazza off the via San Gallao, and adjoining it the prior's house, a long, low, fourteenth-century building, with high, cross-barred windows, and a wonderful old-world garden in the rear.

In answer to my summons there appeared a thin, yellow-faced, sharp-tongued house-woman, and on inquiry for the father I was at once invited into a big stone hall, cool and dim after the sun-glare outside.

"Body of a thousand anchovies! Teresa, who has come to worry me now?" I heard a man demand angrily from a door at the end of a darkened corridor. "Didn't I tell you that I was not at home until after mass tomorrow? Plague you, Teresa?"

To the wizen-faced woman I stammered some apology, but at the same moment I saw a huge, almost gigantic figure in a long black cassock and biretta emerge from the room.

"Oh, signore?" he cried apologetically, the instant he caught sight of me. "Do pray excuse me. I have so many of my poor people here begging that I'm compelled to be out to them sometimes. Come in! Come in?" Then he added reproachfully, turning to his housekeeper, "Teresa, what manners you have to leave this gentleman standing in the hall like a mendicant! I'm ashamed of you, Teresa! What must the signore think—and a foreigner, too!"

In an instant the Very Reverand Bernardo Landini and I were friends. I saw that he was thoroughly genuine, a strange admixture of good-fellowship and piety. His proportions were Gargantuan. His clean-shaven face was perfectly round, fresh, and almost boyish in complexion, his dark eyes twinkled with merriment, his stomach was huge and spoke mutely of a healthy appetite, his hand big and hearty in its shake, and in his speech he aspirated his "e's," which showed him to be a born Florentine.

After I had explained that my name was Allan Kennedy, and that I was introduced by the *gobbo* of Leghorn, he took out his great horn snuff-box, rapped it loudly, and offered me a pinch.

"Ah!" he remarked. "The signore is English, yet how well he speaks our Tuscan?"

I thanked him for his compliment, and went on to explain that I had passed the years of my youth in Florence, and was at heart almost a Florentino.

This pleased him mightily, and from the moment I hinted at my antiquarian tastes he began to chatter as an enthusiast will.

The apartment wherein I sat, darkened by its closed sun-shutters, was certainly a strange one, small, and so crammed with antiques of every kind and description that one could scarcely move in it. Upon the old Empire writing-table at which he had seated himself stood a small brass crucifix of exquisite design, while all around hung ancient pictures of a religious character—saints, pietas, pictures of the Redeemer, and several great canvases reaching from floor to ceiling, evidently from church-altars. The very chairs were of the fifteenth century, heavy, massive, and covered with stamped leather; the tables were of the Renaissance; and the perfect chaos of valuable objects of art stored there was to me, a collector absolutely bewildering.

And amid it all, seated at his table, was the ponderous, beaming cleric, mopping his brow with his big red handkerchief from time to time, and leaning back in his chair to laugh and talk with me.

Yet when I mentioned that I had been sent by the mysterious old hunchback of Leghorn his face instantly grew serious, and with a low sigh he said: "Ah, poor Francesco! poor fellow?"

"You know him well, *signor priore*," I said. "Tell me about him. I'm very anxious to know who and what he really is. To me he has always been a mystery."

But the stout prior shook his head, replying in a rather hard voice: "No, signore. I regret that my lips are closed."

His response was a strange one, and led me at once to suspect that my new friend was a party to some grave secret. Therefore, seeing that his manner was firm, I dropped the subject, although more than ever interested in the queer, deformed old fellow who had so long mystified me.

My friend the priest took me around his wonderful collection, and showed me a veritable confusion of valuable antiques: a Madonna by Andrea del Sarto, a Holy Family by Tintoretto, a tiny but exquisite specimen of that lost art of della Robbia, and a quantity of old tapestries, medieval ironwork, and old, carved furniture.

In a room beyond was stored a splendid collection of Florentine armour: helmets, breastplates, gauntlets, and lances, with a heap of ancient swords, rapiers, and poniards. I took up several to examine them, and found that they were without exception splendid specimens of the Spanish armourer's work, mostly bearing upon the finely tempered blades the well-known marks of Blanco, Martinez, Ruiz, Tomas, and Pedro de Lezama.

Some of the work was wonderfully inlaid with brass and copper; and the collection appeared to be a representative one, ranging from the rusty crosshilts of the Etruscas down to the thin Spanish rapiers of the seventeenth century.

A third room, still beyond, was the priest's bedchamber, and even this was so packed with curios and bric-à-brac that there was scarcely room to enter.

Above the narrow little bed was an antique bronze crucifix, mounted upon a carved wooden background covered with old purple brocade, while the whitewashed walls were almost hidden by the profusion of religious pictures. The red-brick floor was carpetless, as were all the other apartments; but the furniture was all old, and upon the chairs were heaped quantities of silks and velvets from the Genoese looms of the seventeenth century — truly an amazing profusion of relics of Italy's past glory.

The prior smiled at my exclamations of surprise as I enthusiastically examined object after object with keen and critical eye. Then, when I remarked upon the value of the objects of art with which his unpretentious house was filled, he answered:

"I am delighted that you, signore, should feel so much interest in my few things. Like yourself, I am an enthusiast, and perhaps by my calling I am afforded unusual facilities for collecting. Here, in my poverty-stricken parish, are quantities of antiques stored in the cottages as well as in the palaces, and the *contadini* from all the countryside, even beyond Pistoja, prefer to bring me their treasures in secret rather than to offer them openly to the pawnbroker."

"But Graniani told me that you have discovered a manuscript of remarkable character. I possess a small collection; therefore may I be permitted to examine it?" I asked, carefully approaching the subject.

"Most certainly," he replied, after a moment's hesitation, it seemed. "It is in the safe in my study. Let us return there." And I followed his ponderous form back to the small apartment wherein stood his writing-table with the crucifix and heavily bound Bible and missal upon it.

But as I walked behind him, unable to see his face, I was surprised at the tone of the remark he made as though speaking to himself:

"So Francesco told you of the book, did he? Ah!"

He spoke as though in suppressed anger that the queer old hunchback had betrayed his confidence.

Chapter Two
The Priest and the Book

The prior mopped his round face again with his red handkerchief, and taking a key from his pocket fumbled at the lock of the small and old-fashioned safe, after some moments producing the precious manuscript for my inspection.

It proved to be a thick folio, bound in its original oaken boards covered with purple leather that had faded and in parts disappeared. For further protection there were added great bosses of tarnished brass, usual in fifteenth-century bindings, but the wood itself was fast decaying; the binding presented a sadly tattered and worn appearance, and the heavy volume seemed held together mainly by its great brass clasp.

He placed it before me on the table, and with eager fingers I undid the clasp and opened it. As soon as my eyes fell upon the leaves of parchment I recognised it to be a very rare and remarkable fourteenth-century manuscript, and a desire at once seized me to possess it.

Written by the monk Arnoldus of Siena, it was beautifully executed in even Gothic characters, with red and blue initials, and ornamented with a number of curious designs in gold and colours representing the seven deadly sins. Upon the first page was a long, square initial in gold; and although written with the contractions common at the time, I managed to make out the first few lines in Latin as follows:

"Arnoldus Cenni de Senis, professus in monasterio Viridis vallis canon regul. S. Augustini in Zonie silva Camerac. dioec. Liber Gnotosolitos de septem peccatis mortalibus, de decem praeceptis, de duodecim consiliis evangelicis, de quinque sensibus, de simbolo fidei, de septem sacramentis, de octo beatitudinibus, de septem donis spiritus sancti, de quatuor peccatis ad Deum clamantibus," etc.

Across the top of the first page, written in a cursive hand in brown ink of a somewhat later date, was the inscription:

"Liber canonicor. regul. monasterii S. Maynulfi in Bodeke prope Paderborn. Qui rapit hunc librum rapiant sua viscera corvi."

The introduction showed that the splendid manuscript had been written by the old Sienese monk himself in the Abbey of Saint Paul at Groenendale. The date was fixed by the "Explicit": "Iste liber est mei Fris Arnoldi Cenni de Senis Frum ordis B'te Marie carmelo. Ouem ppria manu scripsi i anno dni MoCCCoXXXIX. die. XXVIII. Maij. Finito libro Reseram' gra Xo."

I really don't know why I became so intensely interested in the volume, for the ornamentations were evidently by a Flemish illuminator, and I had come across many of a far more meritorious character in the work of the Norman scribes.

Perhaps it was owing to the quaintness of the design; perhaps because of the rareness of the work; but more probably because at the end of the book had been left fifty or so blank leaves, as was often the case in manuscripts of that period, and upon them, in a strange and difficult cursive hand, was inscribed a long record which aroused my curiosity.

As every collector of manuscripts knows, one sometimes finds curious entries upon the blank pages of vellum books. In the days before the art of printing was discovered, when the use of paper was not general, and when vellum and parchment were costly, every inch of the latter was utilise and a record meant to be permanent was usually written in the front or back of some precious volume. Therefore, the sight of this hundred pages or so of strange-looking writing in faded brown ink, penned with its many downward flourishes, uneven and difficult as compared with the remarkable regularity of the old monk's treatise upon the Seven Sins, awakened within me an eagerness to decipher it.

Horaes, psalters, offices of the Virgin, and codexes of Saints Augustine, Bernard, Ambrose, and the others are to be found in every private collection; therefore it was always my object to acquire manuscript works that were original. The volume itself was certainly a treasure, and its interest was increased tenfold by those pages of close, half-faded handwriting, written probably a century later, and evidently in indifferent ink to that used by the old monk.

"Well, signore," inquired the prior after I had been bending over the ancient volume for some minutes in silence, "what is your opinion? You are of course an expert. I am not. I know nothing about manuscripts."

His frankness was pleasing. He did not seek to expound its merits or to criticise without being able to substantiate his statements.

"A most interesting codex," I declared, just as openly. "I don't remember ever having met with Arnoldus before; and, as far as I can recollect, Quain does not mention him. How did it come into your possession?"

Landini was silent. His huge, round face, so different from the pinched, grey countenances of most priests, assumed a mysterious look, and his lips pursed themselves up in an instant. I noticed his hesitation, and, recollecting that he had told me how many people in the neighbourhood came to him in secret and sold him their most treasured possessions, saw that my question was not an exactly fair one. Instead of replying, he merely remarked that if I desired to acquire the volume he was open to an offer. Then he added:

"I think, my dear signore, that when we become better acquainted we shall like each other. Therefore I may as well tell you at once that, in addition to the holy office which I hold, I deal in antiques. Probably you will condemn me, just as half Florence has already done. But surely it is no disgrace to the habit I wear? From the sacriligious Government I receive the magnificent stipend of one thousand lire (forty pounds) annually;" and he laughed a trifle bitterly. "Can a man live on that? I have both father and mother still living, dear old souls! Babbo is eighty-one, and my mother seventy-eight; they live out at the five ways in the Val d'Ema, in the old farmhouse where I was born. With the profits I make on dealing in antiques I manage by great economy to keep them and myself, and have just a trifle to give to the deserving poor in my parish. Do you blame me, signore?"

How could I? His charming openness, so like the Tuscan priest, and yet so unlike the Tuscan tradesman, gave me an insight into his true character. The extreme simplicity of his carpetless, comfortless house, the frayed shabbiness of his cassock, and the cracked condition of his huge buckled shoes all spoke mutely for a struggle for life. Yet, on the other hand, his face was that of a supremely contented man. His collection was such that if sold at Christie's it would fetch many thousands of pounds; yet, an antiquary himself, he clung, it seemed, to a greater portion of it, and would not part with many of his treasures.

I told him that I had admiration rather than reproach at his turning dealer, when he frankly explained that his method of selling was not to regard the marketable value of an object, but to obtain a small profit upon the sum he gave for it.

"I find that this method works best," he said, "for by it I am able to render a service to those in straitened circumstances, and at the same time gain sufficient for the wants of my family. Of the real value of many things I am utterly ignorant. This manuscript, for instance, I purchased for a hundred francs. If you give me a hundred and twenty-five, and you think it is worth it, I shall be quite contented. Does the price suit you?"

Suit me! My heart leaped to my mouth. If he had suggested fifty pounds instead of five I should have been prepared to consider it. Either Quaritch in

London, Rosenthal in Munich, or Olschki in Florence would, I felt certain, be eager to give at the least a hundred pounds for it. Such manuscripts were not offered for sale every day.

"The price is not at all high," I answered. "Indeed, it is lower than I expected you would ask; therefore the book is mine." And taking my wallet from my pocket, I counted out and handed to him a dozen or so of those small, well-thumbed notes that constitute the paper currency of Italy, for which he scribbled a receipt upon a scrap of waste-paper which he picked up from the floor—a fact which showed him to be as unconventional as he was frank and honest in his dealing.

Dealers in any branch of antiques, whether in pictures, china, furniture, or manuscripts, are—except well-known firms—for the most part sharks of the worst *genus*; hence it was pleasant to make a purchase with such charming openness of purpose.

When he handed me the receipt, however, I thought I detected a strange, mysterious look upon his big, beaming countenance as he said, "I thank you, my dear Signor Kennedy, for your patronage, and I hope that you will never regret your purchase—never."

He seemed to emphasise the words in a tone unusual to him. It flashed across my mind that the manuscript might, after all, be a clever German forgery, as a good many are, and that its genuineness had already been doubted. Yet if it were, I felt certain that such a man would never disgrace his office by knowingly deceiving me.

Still, the mystery of his manner puzzled me, and I am fain to confess that my confidence in him became somewhat shaken.

His refusal to tell me anything of the ugly old hunchback whose orders he had obeyed in showing me the book, and his disinclination to tell me whence he had procured it, were both curious circumstances which occupied my mind. It also occurred to me as most probable that Graniani was merely an agent of the clerical antique-dealer, which accounted for his pockets being ever filled with precious manuscripts, bits of valuable china, miniatures, an such-like odds and ends.

Nevertheless, if the "Book of Arnoldus" were actually genuine I had secured a gem at a ridiculously low price. I did not for one moment doubt its authenticity; hence a feeling of intense satisfaction overcame everything.

He showed me several other manuscripts, including a fifteenth-century Petrarca *De Vita Solitaria*, an illuminated Horae of about the same date, and an *Evangelia quatuor* of a century earlier; but none of them attracted me so much as the heavy volume I had purchased.

Then, at my request, he took me along the dark corridor and through a side-door into the fine old church, where the light was dim and in keeping with the ancient, time-mellowed Raphaels and the dull gilding of ceiling and altar. The air was heavy with incense, and the only sound beyond the echo of our footsteps was the impudent chirp of a stray bird which had come in for shelter from the scorching sun. It was an ancient place, erected in 1089 by the Florentines to commemorate their victories on August sixth, the day of San Sisto.

For more than twenty years I had not entered there. I recollect going there in my youth, because I was enamoured of a dark-eyed little milliner from the via Dante who attended mass regularly. The past arose before me, and I smiled at that forgotten love of my ardent youth. The prior pointed out to me objects of interest not mentioned in the red guide-books, they being known to him alone. He showed me the splendid sculptured tombs of the noble houses of Cioni and of Gherardesca, whereon lay the armoured knights in stone; the Madonna of Fra Bartolommeo; the curious frescoes in the sacristy, and other objects which to both of us were interesting; then, taking me back through his house, we passed out into the tangled, old-world garden—a weedy, neglected place, with orange and fig trees, broken moss-grown statuary, and a long, cool loggia covered with laden vines.

Together we sat upon a bench in the welcome shadow, and at our feet the lizards darted across those white flagstones hollowed by the tread of generations. Father Bernardo took the long Tuscan cigar which I offered him; and, on his calling old Teresa to bring a candle, we both lit up, for the ignition of a "Virginia" in Italy is, as you know, an art in itself. He confided to me that he loved to smoke—the only indulgence he allowed himself—and then, as we lolled back, overcome by the heat and burden of the day, we discussed antiques, and he told me some strange stories of the treasures that had on various occasions passed through his hands to the national galleries or the wealthy American visitors.

A dozen times I tried to obtain from him the history of the fine old parchment codex I had just bought, but without avail. He made it a rule, he told me frankly, never to divulge from whom he obtained the objects he had to sell, and had he *not* been a cleric I should really have suspected him of being a receiver of stolen property.

Old Teresa, in blue apron and shuffling over the stones, returned to her master presently, informing him that someone was waiting for confession; therefore my friend, excusing himself, flung away his cigar, crossed himself, and hurried back to his sacred duty. He was a strange man, it was true; charming, yet at moments austere, reserved, and mysterious.

Alone, still smoking, I sat where he had left me. Opposite, the overgrown garden with its wealth of fruit and flowers was bounded by the ancient stucco wall of the church, around which, in a line above the windows, ran a row of beautiful della Robbia medallions hidden from the world.

When I had remarked upon their beauty to Landini he had sighed, saying:

"Ah, signore, if I only might sell them and pay for the restoration of my church! Each one is worth at least a thousand pounds sterling, for they are even finer specimens than those upon the Foundling Hospital. The Louvre Museum in Paris offered me a year ago twenty thousand francs for the one to the right over there in the corner." Yes; the old place breathed an air of a bygone age—the age of the Renaissance in Italy—and I sat there musing as I smoked, trying to fathom the character of the ponderous, heavy-breathing man who had that moment entered the confessional, and wondering what could be his connection with Francesco Graniani.

Across, straight before me, was a small, square, latticed window of old green glass, near which, I knew, stood the confessional-box; and suddenly—I know not why—my eye caught it, and what I noticed there riveted my attention.

Something showed white for a single instant behind the glass, then disappeared. But not, however, before I recognised that some person was keeping secret watch upon my movements, and, further, that it was none other than the forbidding-looking little hunchback of Leghorn.

In Italy one's suspicion is easily aroused, and certainly mine was by that inexplicable incident. I determined then and there to trust neither Graniani nor his clerical friend. Therefore, with a feeling of anger at such impudent espionage, I rose, re-entered the prior's house, and walked up the dark passage to the study, intending to obtain the precious volume for which I had paid, and to wish my host a hurried adieu.

On entering the darkened study, however, I discovered, somewhat to my surprise, a neat-waisted, well-dressed lady in black standing there, evidently waiting, and idling the time by glancing over the vellum pages of my newly acquired treasure.

I drew back, begging her pardon for unceremonious intrusion, but she merely bowed in acknowledgment. Her manner seemed agitated and nervous, and she wore a veil, so that in the half-light I could not well distinguish her features.

She was entirely in black, even to her gloves, and was evidently the person to whom Father Bernardo had been called, and after confession had passed through the little side-door of the church in order to consult him upon some matter of extreme importance, the nature of which I could not possibly divine. In all this I scented mystery.

Chapter Three
In which the Prior is Mysterious

The prior entered his study behind me with a hurried word of excuse, expressing regret that he had been compelled to leave me alone, and promising to join me in a few moments.

Therefore I turned, and, retracing my steps along the stone corridor wherein antique carved furniture was piled, went back again into the garden, glancing up at the window whereat I had detected the hunchback's face.

Landini had closed his study door after I had gone, thus showing that his consultation with his visitor was of a confidential nature. I regretted that I had not passed through into the church and faced Graniani, for I could not now go back and pass the closed door, especially as the keen eyes of the reverend's house-woman were upon me. So, impatiently I waited for the stout priest to rejoin me, which he did a few moments later, carrying my precious acquisition in his hand.

Perhaps you are a collector of coins or curios, monastic seals or manuscripts, birds' eggs, or butterflies? If you are, you know quite well the supreme satisfaction it gives you to secure a unique specimen at a moderate and advantageous price. Therefore, you may well understand the tenderness with which I took my treasured Arnoldus from him, and how carefully I wrapped it in a piece of brown paper which Teresa brought to her master. The priest's house-woman, shrewd, inquisitive, and a gossip, is an interesting character the world over; and old Teresa, with the wizened face and brown, wrinkled neck, was no exception. She possessed a wonderful genius for making a *minestra*, or vegetable soup, Father Bernardo had already told me, and he had promised that I should taste her culinary triumph some day.

Nevertheless, although the prior was politeness itself, pleasant yet pious, laconic yet light-hearted, I entertained a distrust of him.

I referred to my intrusion in his study while he had a visitor, but he only laughed, saying:

"It was nothing, my dear signore—nothing, I assure you. Pray don't apologise. My business with the lady, although serious, was brief. It is I who should apologise."

"No," I said; "I've been enjoying your garden. Enclosed here by the church and by your house, right in the very centre of Florence, it is so quiet and old-world, so full of antiquity, that I have much enjoyed lingering here."

"Yes," he answered reflectively; "back in the turbulent days of the Medici that remarkable figure in Italian history, Fra Savonarola, owned this garden and sat beneath this very loggia, on this very bench, thinking out those wonderful discourses and prophecies which electrified all Florence. Nothing changes here. The place is just the same today, those white walls on the four sides, only the statuary perhaps is in worse condition than it was in 1498 when he concluded his remarkable career by defying the commands of the Pope as well as the injunctions of the signoria, and was hanged and burned amid riot and bloodshed. Ah, this garden of mine has seen many vicissitudes, signore, and yonder in my church the divine Dante himself invoked the blessing of the Almighty upon his efforts to effect peace with the Pisans.'

"Your house is a truly fitting receptacle for your splendid collection," I said, impressed by his words and yet wondering at his manner.

"Do you know," he exclaimed a moment later, as though a thought had suddenly occurred to him, "I cannot help fearing that you may have acted imprudently in purchasing this manuscript. If you wish, I am quite ready to return you your money. Really, I think it would be better if you did so, signore."

"But I assure you I have no wish to return it to you," I declared, astonished at his words. If he believed he had made a bad bargain, I at least had his receipt for the amount and the book in my hand.

"But it would be better," he urged. "Better for you—and for me, for the matter of that. Here are the notes you gave me;" and taking them from his pocket he held them towards me.

I failed utterly to comprehend his intention or his motive. I had made a good bargain, and why should I relinquish it? Place yourself in my position for a moment, and think what you would have done.

"Well, *signor reverendo*," I exclaimed, "I paid the price you asked, and I really cannot see why you should attempt to cry off the deal." Truth to tell, I was a trifle annoyed.

"You have paid the price," he repeated in a strange voice, looking at me seriously. "Yes; that is true. You have paid the price in the currency of my country; but there is yet a price to pay."

"What do you mean?" I asked quickly, looking him squarely in the face.

"I mean that it would be best for us both if you gave me back my receipt and took back your money."

"Why?"

"I cannot be more explicit," he replied. "I am a man of honour," he added, "and you may trust me."

"But I am desirous of adding the codex to my collection," I argued, mystified by his sudden desire to withdraw from his word. "I asked you your price, and have paid it."

"I admit that. The affair has been but a matter of business between two gentlemen," he replied, with just a touch of hauteur. "Nevertheless, I am anxious that you should not be possessor of that manuscript."

"But why? I am a collector. When you come to Leghorn I hope you will call and look through my treasures."

"Treasures?" he echoed. "That is no treasure—it is a curse, rather."

"A curse! How can a splendid old book be a curse in the hands of a palaeographical enthusiast like myself?"

"I am a man of my word," he said in a low, distinct tone. "I tell you, my dear signore, that your enthusiasm has led you away. You should not have purchased your so-called treasure. It was ill-advised; therefore I urge you to take back the sum you have paid."

"And on my part I object to do so," I said a little warmly.

He shrugged his broad shoulders, and a pained look crossed his big features.

"Will you not listen to me—for your own good?" he urged earnestly.

"I do not think that sentiment need enter into it," I replied. "I have purchased the book, and intend to retain it in my possession."

"Very well," he sighed. "I have warned you. One day, perhaps, you will know that at least Bernardo Landini acted as your friend."

"But I cannot understand why you wish me to give you back the book," I argued. "You must have some motive?"

"Certainly I have," was his frank response. "I do not wish you to be its possessor."

"You admit that the volume is precious, therefore of value. Yet you wish to withdraw from a bad bargain!"

His lips pursed themselves for a moment, and a look of mingled regret and annoyance crossed his huge face.

"I admit the first, but deny the second. The bargain is a good one for me, but a bad one for you."

"Very well," I replied with self-satisfaction. "I will abide by it."

"You refuse to hear reason?"

"I refuse, with all due deference to you, *signor reverendo*, to return you the book I have bought."

"Then I can only regret," he said in a voice of profound commiseration. "You misconstrue my motive, but how can I blame you? I probably should, if I were in ignorance, as you are."

"Then you should enlighten me."

"Ah?" he sighed again. "I only wish it were admissible. But I cannot. If you refuse to forego your bargain, I can do nothing. When you entered here I treated you as a stranger; and now, although you do not see it, I am treating you as a friend."

I smiled. Used as I was to the subtleness of the trading Tuscan, I was suspicious that he regretted having sold the book to me at such a low price, and was trying to obtain more without asking for it point-blank.

"Well, *signor priore*," I said bluntly a moment later, "suppose I gave you an extra hundred francs for it, would that make any difference to your desire to retain possession of it?"

"None whatever," he responded. "If you gave me ten thousand more I would not willingly allow you to have it in your possession."

His reply was certainly a strange one, and caused me a few moments' reflection

"But why did you sell it if you wish to retain it?" I asked.

"Because at the time you were not my friend," he replied evasively. "You are now—I know you, and for that reason I give you warning. If you take the book from this house, recollect it is at your risk, and you will assuredly regret having done so."

I shook my head, smiling, unconvinced by his argument and suspicious of his manner. Somehow I had grown to dislike the man. If he were actually my friend, as he assured me, he would certainly not seek to do me out of a bargain. So I laughed at his misgivings, saying:

"Have no fear, *signor reverendo*. I shall treasure the old codex in a glass case, as I do the other rare manuscripts in my collection. I have a number of biblical manuscripts quite as valuable, and I take care of them, I assure you."

My eye caught the ancient window where I had seen the white, unshaven face of the old hunchback, and recollecting that there must be some mysterious connection between the two men, I tucked my precious parcel under my arm and rose to depart.

The prior knit his dark brows and crossed himself in silence.

"Then the signore refuses to heed me?" he asked in a tone of deep disappointment.

"I do," I answered quite decisively. "I have to catch my train back to Leghorn; therefore I will wish you *addio*."

"As you wish, as you wish," sighed the ponderous priest. Then placing his big hand upon my shoulder in a paternal manner, he added, "I know full well how strange my request must appear to you, my dear signore, but some day perhaps you will learn the reason. Recollect, however, that, whatever may occur, Bernardo Landini is a friend to whom you may come for counsel and advice. *Addio*, and may He protect you, guard you from misfortune, and prosper you. *Addio*."

I thanked him, and took the big, fat hand he offered.

Then, in silence, I looked into his good-humoured face and saw there a strange, indescribable expression of mingled dread and sympathy. But we parted; and, with old Teresa shuffling before me, I passed through the house and out into the white sun glare of the open piazza, bearing with me the precious burden that was destined to have such a curious and remarkable influence upon my being and my life.

Chapter Four
By the Tideless Sea

When a man secures a bargain, be it in his commerce or in his hobbies, he always endeavours to secure a second opinion. As I hurried across to hug the shadow of the Palazzo Pandolfini I glanced at my watch, and found that I had still an hour and a half before the *treno lumaca*, or snail-train, as the Florentines, with sarcastic humour, term it, would start down the Arno valley for Leghorn. Therefore I decided to carry my prize to Signor Leo Olschki, who, as you know, is one of the most renowned dealers in ancient manuscripts in the world, and whose shop is situated on the Lung Amo Acciajoli, close to the Ponte Vecchio. Many treasures of our British Museum have passed through his hands, and among bibliophiles his name is a household word.

Fortunately I found him in: a short, fair-bearded, and exceedingly courteous man, who himself is a lover of books although a dealer in them. Behind those glass cases in his shop were some magnificent illuminated manuscripts waiting to be bought by some millionaire collector or national museum, and all around from floor to ceiling were shelves full of the rarest books extant, some of the *incunabula* being the only known copies existing.

I had made many purchases of him; therefore he took me into the room at the rear of the shop, and I displayed my bargain before his expert eyes.

In a moment he pronounced it a genuine Arnoldus, a manuscript of exceeding rarity, and unique on account of several technical reasons with which it is useless to trouble those who read this curious record.

"Well, now, Signor Olschki, what would you consider approximately its worth?"

The great bibliophile stroked his beard slowly, at the same time turning over the evenly-written parchment folios.

"I suppose," he answered, after a little hesitation, "that you don't wish to sell it?"

"No. I tell you frankly that I've brought it here to show you and ask your opinion as to its genuineness."

"Genuine it is no doubt—a magnificent codex. If I had it here to sell I would not part with it under twenty-five thousand francs—a thousand pounds."

"A thousand pounds?" I echoed, for the price was far above what I had believed the manuscript to be worth.

"Rosenthal had one in his catalogue two years ago priced at sixteen thousand francs. I saw it when I was in Munich, and it was not nearly so good or well preserved as yours. Besides—this writing at the end: have you any idea what it is about?"

"Some family record," I answered. "The usual rambling statements regarding personal possessions, I expect."

"Of course," he answered. "In the fifteenth and sixteenth centuries they habitually disfigured their books in this way, as you know. It was a great pity."

Having obtained the information I desired, I repacked my treasured tome while he brought out several precious volumes for my inspection, including a magnificent French *Psalteriolum seu preces pia cum calendario*, with miniatures of the thirteenth century, which he had catalogued at four hundred and fifty pounds; and an Italian *Psalterium ad usum ord. S. Benedicti*, of two hundred leaves, written at Padua in 1428, that he had just sold to the National Museum at Berlin for fifteen thousand marks. In addition to being an expert and dealer, he was a true lover of books and manuscripts; and, knowing that my pocket would not allow me to indulge in such treasures, he would often exhibit to me his best volumes and gossip about them as every bibliophile will gossip, handling them tenderly the while.

I caught my train and returned to the white villa facing the sea, outside Leghorn, which was my bachelor home, entirely satisfied with my visit to the Tuscan capital.

Three miles beyond the noisy seaport, close down where the clear waters of the Mediterranean lazily lapped the shingly beach at the little watering-place of Antignano, stood the square, sun-blanched house, with its wide balcony, and its green sun-shutters now open to the soft breeze that came across the water with the brilliant sundown. The faithful Nello, my old Tuscan man-servant, who was cook, housekeeper, and valet all in one, had been watching for my arrival; and as I rang at the big iron gate before my garden the old fellow came hurrying to admit me, with his pleasant bow and words of welcome on his lips:

"*Ben tornato, signore; ben tornato.*"

I thanked him, carried my precious parcel to the study upstairs, and then, descending again, ate hurriedly the dinner he placed before me, anxious to examine my purchase.

My old servitor moved noiselessly in and out as I ate, fidgeting as though he wished to speak with me. But I was looking through my letters, and took but little notice of him. Italian servants are always a nuisance, being too loquacious and too ready to offer opinions or advice. I had suffered for years from a succession of unsatisfactory men, until my friend Fra Antonio of the Capuchin monastery brought old Nello to me. He had little in exterior appearance to recommend him, for his countenance was that of a Mephistopheles, and his attire neglected and shabby. He was an old soldier who had served Italy well in the days of Garibaldi, and had for years been engaged as steward on board one of the Prince line of steamers between Naples and New York.

Fra Antonio knew him well; therefore I took him on trial, and very quickly discovered that even though he had a wife and family living high up in one of the odorous back streets of Leghorn, to whom some of my provisions secretly found their way, he was a treasure of a servant.

Although old in years, he was not decrepit. His physical strength often amazed me, and after three years of service his devotion to me was often remarked by my friends. His only vice was smoking; and as he consumed the very rankest of tobacco, which clung about the house for days afterwards, I had set apart an arbour in the garden beneath the vines where he might poison the air whenever he wished.

Having dined, I ascended the wide marble staircase to my study, a big, high room, with frescoed ceiling, that looked out across the open sea. Houses are large and cheap in Italy—mine was far too large for a lonely man like myself. There were half a dozen rooms into which I never entered, and I opened my drawing-room only when I had visitors, for I have a man's dislike for silk-covered furniture, mirrors, and standard lamps.

The long windows of my study were open, and the place was at that moment filled with the crimson afterglow. I stood upon the balcony and breathed the pure air from the sea, delightfully refreshing after the stifling heat of the day. Across, in the far distance, the islands of Corsica, Capraja, and Gorgona loomed purple against the blood-red sunset, while up from the beach the evening stillness was broken by a young fisherman playing his mandolin and singing in a fine musical voice the old love-song with that chorus which every one in Italy knows so well:

"Amarti soltanto
Non basta al mio cor:
Io voglio parlarti,
Parlarti d'amor!"

Love! Ah! those words he sang brought back to me, an exile, all the bitterness of the past—all the bitterness of my own love. A lump arose in my throat when I recollected the might-have-been; but I crushed it down just as I had done a hundred times before, and re-entered the room, closing the windows to shut out the words of the song, and, sighing, seated myself at my writing-table to occupy myself with the book I had bought from the fat prior of San Sisto.

Old Nello—whose correct name was Lionello, although, as usual in Tuscany, everyone had called him Nello ever since his birth, sixty years ago—brought in my coffee and liqueur, setting it down at my elbow, and afterwards crossed to reopen the window.

"I closed it, Nello," I snapped. "Don't open it. There's too much confounded music outside."

"*Bene, signore,*" he answered. "I forgot to say that the *signor console* called at four o'clock."

"And what did the consul want?" I inquired.

"He wishes to see you tomorrow to luncheon," was the old fellow's response. "And, oh! I forgot—another man called to see the signore only a quarter of an hour before his return—the *gobbo*; Graniani."

"Graniani!" I echoed. "And what did he want, pray?"

"To sell you some more old rubbish, I suppose," was Nello's blunt reply, for he always looked upon my purchase of antiques as a terrible waste of good money. "He said he would return later."

I was very surprised at this. He had probably returned to Leghorn by an earlier train from Florence; but why he wished to see me after secretly spying upon my movements I was at a loss to know. One must, however, be clever to comprehend the ingenuity of the Italian, with all his diplomatic smiles and ingenious subtleties.

"If he comes I will see him," I responded; adding, "Do you know, Nello, I don't like that man."

"Ah, signore!" answered the old fellow, "you should never trust a hunchback."

"But when I asked you about him you knew nothing to his detriment. I look to you to make inquiries about such people."

"At the time I was in ignorance, signore," he said apologetically; "but I have learned several things since."

"Things that are not very creditable, eh?" I asked, regarding his weird, almost grotesque figure in ill-fitting black coat and crumpled shirt-front.

He hesitated as though unwilling to tell me the whole truth. He was always reserved regarding any person of bad character, and, generally speaking, a Tuscan never cares to denounce his compatriots to a foreigner.

"If I were you, signore," he said, "I'd have nothing to do with any *gobbo*."

"But I've bought several good manuscripts from him," I argued.

"The signore must please himself," he remarked. "I have warned him."

I really did not desire any warning, for the mysterious appearance of the old hunchback's face at the church window was sufficient to cause me grave suspicion. But Nello for three years past had exercised a kind of paternal care over me, seeming to regard with wonder that I could scribble piles upon piles of paper and get paid for it. It was really wonderful how I wrote roman, he often declared. He read two of them translated into Italian and published serially in the *Tribuna*, and kept the copies neatly tied in bundles, which he proudly showed to his friends as the work of his *padrone*.

"Well, had I better see the *gobbo*?" I asked.

"No, signore, I would not," was his prompt advice. "He has no business to come here. His place is in the piazza, and it is impudence to call upon a gentleman."

"Then tell him I'm engaged. I'll want nothing more tonight. Don't disturb me."

"*Benissimo, signore; buona notte.*" And old Nello went softly out well satisfied, leaving me to my coffee and my old manuscript.

I had not asked Nello to give his reason, because I knew that he would refuse to be drawn. He was a clever old fellow, and would, in argument, get the better of me.

So, the music having ceased, I reopened the window, and in the fading light settled myself to a pleasant hour with my latest acquisition.

Further acquaintance with the splendid volume was not disappointing. It was certainly a treasure; and having glanced casually at the coloured miniatures and gilt initials, I turned to the first page of the record written upon the blank pages at the end.

The cursive writing with its long flourishing was extremely difficult to decipher, and the ink much inferior to that used by the old monk Arnoldus, for it was faded and brown, having evidently been penned by one who had no acquaintance with the Gothic or book-hand. The writing was undoubtedly that of the early sixteenth century.

The first line I was able to make out read as follows:

Qui scripsit scripta manus eius sit benedicta, while, as far as I could decipher it, the record ended in the following manner:

Qui me scribebat Godefridus nomen habebat
Godefridus Lupellus
de Croylandia
me scripsit anno
domini 1542 in no
no die mensis
Janua rij.

This final page was so ill-written and half-obliterated by a great yellow damp-stain that I had not before noticed it. But by it my curiosity became further aroused, for, translated into modern English, it showed that the addition had been made to the book by one Godfrey Lupellus or Lovel, of Crowland, in Lincolnshire, probably one of the monks of that once celebrated Benedictine abbey which is now but a magnificent pile of ruins familiar to many by photographs.

The discovery that it had been penned by a person living in England caused me to set to work at once to learn what was written there, so I took a sheet of plain paper, and, assisted by that valuable little work of reference, the "Dictionary of Abbreviations," commenced to disentangle slowly the calligraphical riddle before me.

The task was extremely difficult; and, whether from the heat of the evening or owing to the fatigue I had undergone, I felt a curious, indescribable sensation slowly creeping over me.

It commenced with small shooting pains that paralysed the muscles of my jaws, gradually increasing in intensity. At first I believed that it was merely a touch of neuralgia, until all in a moment a quick, sharp pain shot down my spine, paralysing me so completely that I could neither move nor utter a sound.

My head swam. My jaws were fixed. I tried to rise, but could not; I tried to cry out for my faithful Nello, but my tongue refused to utter a sound.

A curious drowsiness seized me, and I struggled against it vainly. Never before had I experienced such a feeling. Then a second pain ran down my back far more acute and excruciating than the first, and I believe I must have fainted.

At any rate, all became an utter blank. The fat priest's solemn warning was, it seemed, no idle one.

Chapter Five
Shows Something Suspicious

Life has no labyrinth but one's steps can track it, and mind acts on mind though bodies be far divided.

Following the strange sensation that crept upon me while examining that half-faded, uneven screed came a complete blank. My muscles were paralysed, my breathing difficult, my throat contracted, and my manhood's energy utterly sapped, until I was helpless as a child. It seemed as though the unseen power had touched me with the finger of death, and I had withered and fallen.

Yet slowly and painfully I struggled back to a sense of my hapless position, and on opening my eyes, sore in their sockets, I found, to my amazement, that I was lying in a heap on the carpet beside my overturned chair, my head close to the carved leg of my writing-table. The light dazzled me, and I quickly became aware that I was lying full in the morning sunshine which streamed in at the open window.

I had fallen from my chair and remained insensible the whole night. Nello had not discovered me, as I had dismissed him, wishing to be alone.

In Tuscany it is light early in summer, and the July sun soon gathers power. I glanced at the clock, and saw that it was already a quarter to five.

Outside, a fisherman was singing a gay song as he unloaded his boat, and children were already shouting as they bathed in the sunlit water; but the brightness in the world beyond only jarred upon me, soured and embittered man that I was. Could that curious sensation be a precursory sign of some terrible malady—epilepsy or paralysis, perhaps?

I struggled to my feet and stood beside the table, dazed, unbalanced, and so weak of limb that my legs could scarcely bear me. I felt as though I had just risen from a sick-bed after months of suffering.

The book lay open at the final page whereon the writer of the record, Godfrey Lovel, had inscribed his name and date as already reproduced here. My thoughts ran back to the moment when I had experienced that sudden seizure, and I recollected how interested I had been in the few lines I had succeeded in deciphering.

The unmistakable paralysis that had stricken me down at the very moment my curiosity was aroused was certainly alarming, and even mysterious, especially after the prior's hints as to the evil that would pursue me if I determined to continue in possession of that fine old volume.

The fat priest's words recurred to me with a deep and hidden meaning, and I admit that my spirit was mightily disturbed. It seemed that I had raised a foe where I might have won a friend.

I locked the book away in my safe, and went forth upon the balcony and breathed the fresh air of morning. Across the sparkling waters of the tideless sea the islands stood grey and mysterious in the blue haze, Gorgona, peopled only by its convict-gangs, showing most distinctly of all. A veil of mystery seemed to have fallen upon everything—upon all save a mighty battleship, with black smoke belching from her three yellow funnels and flying the white ensign of England as she approached an anchorage outside the port.

A desire for fresh air seized me; therefore, feeling faint, I took a liqueur glass of neat brandy, and then descended to the big marble entrance-hall that always echoed so dismally to my lonely footsteps. Recollect that I was a man without kith or kin, self-exiled for private reasons over which I had been unable to exercise control, and although living among a people that I loved because of their sympathy and charm, I was yet homesick for England and suffering from the nostalgia that those whose lot it is to spend their lives abroad know, alas! too well.

Outside I took the old sea-road—that shadeless road that runs with so many windings away along the edge of the deadly Maremma and on to Rome. I walked it often, for it led out along the edge of the brown cliffs through a wild and uninhabited tract of country, a district which until ten years ago had been dangerous on account of a band of lawless brigands. The latter had, however, all been exterminated by the carabineers, and the loneliness of the country suited well my frame of mind.

I met no one save an old barefooted fishwife whom I knew, trudging onward with her basket poised on her head. So I lit my pipe and gave myself up to reflection, trying to account for my strange seizure. I hesitated to consult a doctor, for I entertained an Englishman's want of faith in the Italian *medico*. I longed to be able to consult my own doctor in London, and ask his opinion whether the strange stupor were an actual warning.

Although Italy possesses such distinct charm; although Tuscany was the home of my youth; although I had hosts of friends among the fishermen and honest *contadini* about me; although my friends at the white old monastery away among the olives on the side of the Black Mountain were always warm in their welcome and eager to render me the very smallest and humblest service, yet I was suddenly tired of it all. Sweet as were the pleasures of Tuscany, as Byron, Shelley, Smollett, and George Eliot had found, yet I was English, and England was my home.

I threw myself down on the grass of the cliff-top and thought it all out. Through seven long years I had led that life of utter loneliness, returning to London only for a fortnight or so each year, and then sadly leaving Charing Cross again for another twelve months of exile. I had my work, the writing of romance, to absorb my attention, it was true; but the writer of novels must live in congenial surroundings, otherwise the influence of a solitary life must show in his work.

Letters I had received from home during the past few days showed, too, that there was really no further reason why I should not return and live in England among my friends; therefore, after long reflection and carefully considering the whole question, I at length made up my mind to pack up my collection of pictures, old furniture, manuscripts, and antiques, and remove them to some country home in England.

I have a habit of acting with precipitation. My father, full of old-fashioned caution, used to chide me for it. In his day there was no such thing as smartness. But in the profession, as in business, old-fashioned stolidity has now passed away. Today, if one sees the legend, "Established 1792," over a shop, one avoids it, knowing that its proprietor is not content with up-to-date small profits. Time was when the solid professional or business man was as black-coated and serious as an undertaker; but it is all of the past. The smart, speculative man, who acts promptly and has the courage of his own convictions, is the man who succeeds in the present scramble for daily bread. In every walk of life one must keep abreast of the flood; hence, with my mind made up, I entered the consulate at eleven o'clock and announced my immediate departure to my old friend and confidant, Jack Hutchinson, one of the most popular of his Majesty's representatives abroad, and whose name with every skipper up and down the Mediterranean is synonymous with geniality of manner and kindliness of heart.

When I sank into a chair in his private room and announced to him that I was going his face fell. I knew well that he had no other English friend there, and my departure would leave him utterly alone. He was an exile, like myself; only, there was for him a comfortable pension at the end of it.

"Well," he exclaimed after a moment, "I'm awfully sorry you're going, my dear old fellow—awfully sorry. But I think you are acting wisely. You've been here too long, and have grown misanthropic. A little London life will take you out of yourself. Besides, of late you've been working far too hard."

I told him of my strange seizure; and, having heard me, he said:

"Exactly. Just what I expected. Pellegrini, the doctor, feared a collapse, and told me so weeks ago. That I'm very sorry to lose you, old chap, you know too well. But you'll be better in England. You're homesick, and that never does in Italy, you know. I and my wife both were so when I was first appointed here twelve years ago; but we've got over it—you never have." Then he added: "By the way, have you seen old Graniani today? He stopped me half an hour ago in the Corso Umberto and asked if I had seen you this morning."

It was on the point of my tongue to tell Hutchinson all that had passed in Florence on the previous day, but I thought it useless to trouble him with what seemed but vague suspicions.

"Why does he want to see me?" I inquired.

"Oh, he has got something or other to sell you, I suppose," was the consul's reply. "Somehow, Kennedy, I don't like the old fellow. Whether it's his ugliness, his deformity, or his manner, I can't tell; only, I instinctively dislike him—and more than ever when I met him just now."

"Why?"

"Well, to me his manner was as though he expected to hear some grave news regarding you."

"Grave news?" I echoed. Then it occurred to me that the old hunchback was, of course, privy to the mysterious evil following the possession of the "Book of Arnoldus."

"What grave news did he expect?"

"How do I know, my dear fellow? These Italians, and especially men of his class, are so subtle and cunning that you can never get at the bottom of their motives."

"But I've always given Graniani his price—with a little bargaining, of course. Why, I've paid him hundreds of francs. You recollect what I paid for that miniature of the missing dauphin of France?"

"But you obtained a gem, even though you had to pay heavily for it," was my friend's answer. "If it had been in old Confessini's hands you'd have had to pay double, or he would have sent it to London."

"I know that," I laughed. "Graniani has had some good things now and then, and I've been a good customer; therefore I can't see why he should entertain any hostile thought towards me."

"As I've already said, you never know the Italian character. The man who is your best friend today will be your worst enemy tomorrow. That's what makes life so insecure here and affrays with the knife so frequent. All I can say is that I noticed about the old scoundrel a distinct expectation to hear bad news of you, and I judged from his manner that he was disappointed when I told him that for aught I knew you were all right. If I were you I wouldn't have any more dealings with him. Now you're leaving Antignano, cut him. He has served your purpose well, and you can't afford to be mixed up in any quarrel with a man of his stamp."

"Yes, I will," I answered. "I don't like him myself. Of late he has been far from straight."

"And of late, it seems, he has been making secret inquiries of one of the Italian clerks here about your antecedents in England."

"Whatever for? How can my antecedents concern him?"

"Ah, that's the point, my dear Kennedy. He's forming some ingenious plot or other; therefore we must be on the alert. When a man bribes one of the clerks to obtain information about an Englishman's past, his parentage, and all the rest of it, there's something devilish suspicious about it."

"I should think so! I wonder what the old scoundrel is up to?"

"Some blackmailing business or other, most probably. If so, act with discretion, and we'll have a chat with the chief of police. The present *questore* is terribly down on blackmailers."

"But what can be the motive?"

"That's more than either of us can tell. We must watch and form our own conclusions," was the consul's reply, leaning back in his white linen suit and stretching his arms above his head. "You see now," he added, "why I am in favour of your leaving Tuscany without delay."

"Yes, I see. But there's some mystery about old Graniani, and we ought to clear it up."

"Why should we trouble to do so?" he asked.

I had told him nothing about the incident which had occurred to arouse my suspicions while I was waiting for the fat prior of San Sisto; therefore, in a few words I briefly recounted what I had witnessed.

"Strange?" he exclaimed. "Remarkably strange! We must watch him, Kennedy. It almost looks as if, for some mysterious reason, he means mischief."

We agreed as to this, and then fell to discussing the best means by which I might get rid of my house and have my collection of antiques packed for transmission to England.

Soon after noon I returned home to luncheon, and in crossing the Piazza Vittorio Emanuelle to take the electric tram my eyes caught a glimpse of a neat female figure in black, which struck me as strangely similar to that of the dark-eyed woman who had been closeted with the fat prior in Florence on the previous day. My first impulse was to turn and follow her, but not being sufficiently certain of her identity, I stepped upon the tram, although sorely puzzled. Was she in Leghorn for some secret purpose? I wondered. Somehow I felt convinced it was she.

On my arrival home, however, my suspicion became more than ever aroused, for I found old Nello in a terrible state of anxiety. On getting up he had discovered that my bed had not been slept in, and that I was absent. Being Italian, he feared that some *disgrazia* had happened to me.

Then, when I assured him that I had merely been out for a long walk instead of sleeping, he said:

"The hunchback antique-dealer is awaiting you, signore. He says it is most important that he should see you, so I have shown him upstairs to the study."

His announcement took me aback. The old scoundrel was the last visitor I expected. Nevertheless, I drew a long breath to steady my nerves, and with calm resolution mounted the stairs.

Chapter Six
The Opening of the Book

"Scusi, signore!" exclaimed the ugly, disreputable-looking old man, holding his battered straw hat behind him, and bowing with as much studied grace as his deformity would allow. The Tuscan, always the essence of politeness, is a marvellous diplomatist. "I regret to disturb the signore," he went on in his soft, musical speech; "but I was anxious to know if he met yesterday in Florence the prior of San Sisto?"

"I did," I replied, amused at his ingenious attempt to affect ignorance of our meeting.

"And did you make any purchases?"

"I bought one book—a rare Arnoldus."

"In manuscript?"

"Yes."

"Bound in original oak boards, with an old brass clasp—eh?" he inquired, with a queer smile about the corners of his mouth. "May I be permitted to see it?"

His demand aroused my suspicions at once. It was evident that the prior had regretted having sold it to me, and had sent his agent to endeavour to get it back at any cost. Therefore, knowing the unscrupulous ways of some Italians in a cosmopolitan city like Leghorn, I did not intend to give the cunning old fellow sight of it.

"Why do you wish to inspect it? I've packed it away, and it would give me great trouble to get at it again."

"Then the signore does really send things to England to sell again, as I have heard the people say?" suggested the old man somewhat rudely.

"No, I'm not a dealer," I responded angrily. "Who told you so?"

"It is common gossip, signore," replied the queer old fellow blandly. "But if you wish it, I'll take steps to correct public opinion on that point."

"Let the gossips say what pleases them," I snapped. "I've never yet sold anything I've bought. I suppose they think that by the quantity of my purchases I must be going to set up a curiosity shop. But," I added, "tell me, Graniani, why do you wish to see the manuscript I bought yesterday?"

"Oh, mere curiosity," was his quick answer. "You know I'm interested in such things, and wanted to know how the prior treated you after my recommendation."

"He treated me well enough, and I brought a bargain."

"A bargain?" he echoed, and I fancied I detected a strange curl in his lip. "The *reverendo* does not sell many bargains. How much did you pay?"

"Ah!" I laughed, "I suppose you want to charge him commission—eh?"

The hunchback grinned, displaying his toothless gums, whereupon I took up the receipt and showed him the amount I had paid.

Again he expressed a desire to be allowed to see the book; but, feeling certain that he had come to me with some hidden motive, and at the same time wondering what plot against me the evil-looking old fellow was forming, I point-blank refused. I did not tell him that I knew of his presence in Florence on the previous day, deeming it best to reserve the knowledge to myself. Without doubt he had seen the book in Landini's possession, and the desire to inspect it again was only a clever ruse.

"I think, signore, that hitherto my dealings with you have shown me to be trustworthy," he said in a tone of complaint, "and yet you refuse to allow me to see a volume that I understand is most interesting."

"And rare," I added. "It has already been valued by Olschki, who declares it to be a unique specimen, and worth very much more than I gave for it."

"I know, I know," he replied with a sly wink. "The person who sold it to the prior knew its value and told me. But it is not a bargain, signore— depend upon it that you never get a bargain from the *signor reverendo*."

"To whom, then, did it originally belong?"

"Ah, that I regret I am not at liberty to say, signore. I gave my word not to divulge the name. Our nobility who become so poor that they are compelled to sell their treasures to the rich foreigners, like yourself, are naturally very reticent about allowing themselves to be known as needy." True, I had believed that the old fellow himself was a broken-down noble, some count or marquis who had a knowledge of antiques and who had fallen upon evil times; but the events of the last couple of days had caused me to change my opinion, and to regard him rather as a clever and crafty adventurer.

I could see by his manner that he was ill at ease, and after some conversation regarding an old Montelupo plate he had offered me at a fabulous price, I waited for him to speak.

"I really wish, signore, you would show me the manuscript," he blurted forth at last. "Believe me, I have always acted in your best interests, and surely you will not refuse me such a small favour?"

"But why are you so desirous of seeing it?" I demanded.

"In order to verify a suspicion," was his response.

"Suspicion of what?"

"A suspicion which I entertain, and of which, if true, you should be warned."

I was surprised at his words. Had not the actual seller of it warned me by strange hints?

But an instant later, on reflection, I saw the cunning of the two men, who, acting in collusion, wished to repossess themselves of the book, and I resolved to combat it.

"I have no use for any warning," I laughed. "I suppose you'll tell me some fairy story or evil pursuing the man in whose possession the volume remains—eh?"

The hunchback raised his shoulders and exhibited his grimy palms, saying:

"I have come to the signore as a friend. I regret if he should seek to treat me as an enemy."

"Now, look here," I exclaimed, rather warmly, "I've no time to waste over useless humbug like this! I've bought the book at the price asked, and neither you nor the prior will get it back again. Understand that! And further," I added, "I shall not require anything more that you may have to sell. I've finished buying antiques in Leghorn. You can tell all the touts in the piazza that my purse is closed."

Again the ugly old man raised his shoulders expressively and opened out his hands—this time, however, in silence.

I rang the bell for Nello to show the fellow out. Then, when I had done this, he turned to me with knit brows and asked:

"Does the signore refuse absolutely to show me the 'Book of Arnoldus'?"

"Absolutely."

"Then it must be at the signore's peril," he said slowly, with a strange, deep meaningness and a curious expression on his brown, wrinkled face.

"I don't believe in prophecy," I cried in anger. "And if you mean it for a threat—well, only your age saves you from being kicked downstairs."

The old fellow muttered beneath his breath some words I did not catch, then bowed as haughtily as though he were a courtier born, and, turning, followed the silent Nello through the long white door.

I believe it was a threat he uttered at the moment of parting; but of that I was not quite sure, therefore was unable to charge him with it.

Still the strange warning caused me to reflect, and the old hunchback's movements and his secret inquiries about my antecedents all combined to induce within me a vague sense of anxiety and insecurity.

Through an hour in the blazing, breathless afternoon I dozed with cigarettes and my three-day-old English newspaper, as was my habit, for one cannot do literary work when the sun-shutters are closed and the place in cooling darkness. I was eager now to get back to England, and had already ordered Nello to make preparations for my departure. He was to go into town that afternoon and inform the professional packer to call and see me with a view to making wooden cases and crates for my collection of old furniture and pictures, all of which I intended to ship direct to London. Italy was a lovely country, I reflected, but, after all, England was better, especially when now, through no fault of my own, I had stumbled into a slough of mystery.

The faithful old man was heart-broken at my sudden decision to leave.

"Ah, *signor padrone*," he sighed, when he returned to report, "this is a sorry day for me! To think—the signore goes to England so far off, and I shall never see him again! I have told them in the town, and everyone regrets."

"No doubt," I answered, smiling. "I suppose I've been a pretty paying customer to the tradespeople. They must have made good profit out of me—eh, Nello?"

"They did, *signor padrone*, before I came to you; but of late it has been different. I've continually threatened to tell you when I've found them attempting to cheat. They don't like to be thought thieves by an Englishman, signore."

(A section of five lines missing, page 52.)

Faltered the white-haired old man. "Ah, signore, you don't know— indeed you don't. You have always been so good to me that somehow— well, to tell the truth, I've served you as though you were my own son. Could you not take me with you to England?"

"Impossible!" I said. "You don't know English, in the first place; besides, you have your family here. You'll be far better off in Leghorn than in England, with its grey skies and damp climate. You, a Tuscan, couldn't stand it a month."

"But Beppo Martini, from the Hotel Campari, went to London, and now he's one of the head-waiters at the Hotel Carlton—a splendid post, they say," urged Nello.

"I know. But he was younger, and he'd been in Paris years before," I answered decisively. "I regret, Nello, but to take you to England is utterly impossible. When I am gone, however, I hope to hear of you often through the *signor console*."

"But you do not know," he urged. "You can't know. All I can tell you is that when we part you will be in peril. While I am at your side nothing can happen. If you discharge me, then I fear for your safety."

I laughed at him, deeming his words but a blundering attempt to compel me to keep him. Italians are experts in threats and insinuations of evil.

"Well, Nello, I haven't any fear, I assure you," I replied. "You've been a most excellent servant to me, and I much regret that we should be compelled to part; but as for evil falling upon me during your absence, I must say frankly that I don't anticipate anything of the kind."

"But will not the *signor padrone* be warned?"

"Warned of what?" I cried, for everyone seemed to have some warning in his mouth for me. "Of what I have told you?"

"You want to go to England as my personal body-servant and guardian—eh?"

"I do," replied the old man gravely.

"And because of that you've hit upon an exceedingly clever ruse by which to induce me to let you have your way," I laughed. "No, once for all, Nello, you cannot go with me."

He stood in silence for a few minutes, as still as though he were turned to stone.

Tears stood in the eyes of the affectionate old servitor. A lump had arisen in his throat, and I saw that with difficulty he swallowed it.

"You do not know my fears, *signor padrone*," he said huskily. "It is for your own sake that I ask you to keep me as your servant—for the sake of your own future. If, however, you have decided, so it must be. Nello will leave you, signore; but he will not cease to be your humble and devoted servant."

Then he turned slowly, and went out, closing the doors after him.

I felt sorry that I had jeered at him, for I had not known how deeply he was attached to me. Still, to take a man of his age to England would be an utter folly, and I could not help feeling that the warning he had uttered was a false one, spoken with a motive.

At last I rose, and, ascending to the study, where the windows were still closed against the heat and sun-glare from the sea, took forth my treasured Arnoldus, and seated myself at my writing-table with the determination of deciphering at least some of that record written at the end.

The first line only of the uneven scrawl was in Latin, as I have already given, and for a long time I puzzled over the next, so sprawling and faded was it; but at length I discovered to my utter surprise and satisfaction that the rest was not in Latin, but in the early sixteenth-century English.

Then slowly and with infinite pains I gradually commenced to transcribe the mysterious record, the opening of which read as follows:

"For soe much as the unskilfull or the ungodly cannot of themselves conceyve the use of thys booke, I have thought it good to note unto them what fruite and comoditie they maye tayke thereof in soe plane forme of manner as I can devise.

"Fyrst, therefore, they maye here lerne who and what manner of man I am. Next, they maye knowe of mi birthe and station, of mi lyfe at the Courte of mi Lorde Don Giovanni Sforza, Tyrant of Persaro, of mi confydences wyth mi ladie Lucrezia, of my dealynges with the greate Lorde Alexandra P.P. VI., the terryble Pontiff, of mi adventures among the fayre ladyes of Pesaro and Rome, and of dyvers strange thynges in Yngolande."

Written in rather difficult sixteenth-century English, which I have modernised somewhat, it continued:

"Then may they further mark the deep significance of this my secret record, and of how with speed I made amends for my slowness beforetime. Lastly have I here noted at the request of certain that by their own labour and without instruction or help they cannot attain the knowledge of The Secret Hidden. The studious man, with small pains, by help of this book, may gather unto himself such good furniture of knowledge as shall marvellously enrich the commonplace.

"Do you, my reader, think of death? The very thoughts disturb one's reason; and though man may have many excellent qualities, yet he may have the weakness of not commanding his sentiments. Nothing is worse for man's health than to be in fear of death. Some are so wise as neither to hate nor fear it; but for my part I have an aversion to it, for it is a rash, inconsiderate thing that always cometh before it is looked for; always cometh unseasonable, parteth friends, ruineth beauty, jeereth at youth, and draweth a dark veil over the pleasures of life. Yet this dreadful evil is but the evil of a moment, and that which we cannot by any means avoid; and it is that which makes it so terrible for me, sinner that I am; for were it certain, hope might diminish some part of the fear; but when I think I must die, and that I may die every moment, and that too in a thousand different ways, I am in such a fright the which you cannot imagine. I see dangers where perchance there never were any. I am persuaded 'tis happy to be somewhat dull of mind in this case; and yet the best way to cure the pensiveness of the thoughts of death is to think or it as little as possible.

"Let him that learneth this my secret, and surviveth, seek and so gain his just reward. But if thou, my reader, hath terror of the grave seek not to learn the contents of this closed book. Tempt not the hidden power that lieth therein, but rather let the clasp remain fastened and the secret ever concealed from thy knowledge and understanding.

"I, Godfrey Lovel, one time of the Abbey of Croylande, brother of the Order of the Blessed Saint Benedict, warneth thee to stay thy curiosity, if thou fearest death as I do fear it.

"TO SEEK FURTHER IS AT THINE OWN PERIL."

Chapter Seven
Forbidden Folios

The words of warning inscribed there in large, uneven letters, shaky in places as though penned by an aged hand, stood out from the time-stained vellum page like capitals of fire.

It really seemed absurd to heed them, and yet on every side I seemed to be warned by those whom I believed to be in ignorance that any endeavour to open the Closed Book would result in disaster. Surely the manner in which the precious volume had come into my possession was romantic enough, yet why should even the faithful old Nello be apprehensive of impending evil? There was something uncanny about the whole affair—something decidedly unsatisfactory.

Italy is a land of superstition, shared alike by count and *contadino*, hence I at first put it down to some vague belief in the evil eye, of which I was in ignorance. During my residence in Tuscany I had often been surprised by the many popular beliefs and terrors. Our true Tuscan sees an omen in everything, and an exhortation to the Virgin or to good Sant' Antonio is ever upon his lips, while his first and last fingers are ever outstretched when he sees a *gobba*, or female hunchback—the harbinger of every evil.

Whether the warnings uttered to me were the outcome of mere superstition, or whether part of one of those ingenious conspiracies which he who lives among the suave Italians so often has to thwart, one fact remained—namely, that in the almost undecipherable record itself a further warning was plainly penned. And this, instead of creating fear and hesitation within me, only further aroused my curiosity.

I was determined to possess myself of the secret at all hazards.

The pale, tragic face of that dark-eyed woman whom I had discovered in the fat prior's study, and whom I had afterwards seen in the noisy, crowded city, haunted me. Yes, there was a calm sweetness in that proud and beautiful countenance, Tuscan most certainly, and yet mystery and tragedy were written there but too plainly.

How I longed to question Father Bernardo about her; for, strange as it may appear to you, my reader, her strange, subtle influence seemed upon me, and I felt myself helplessly beneath a kind of spell which, even to this day, I cannot define.

In turning those vellum leaves listlessly, I paused and gazed across my half-darkened room, deep in thought. Outside, the cicala in the dusty tamarisks kept up their cricket-like song, and in the far distance from the blue hills came the clanging of a village bell. Beyond that all was quiet—the world was hushed and gasping beneath that summer heat that ripened the maize in the fields and the grapes and oranges in my garden.

But I was sick of it all—yes, heartily sick. Italy had charmed me once; but over my heart its white dust had accumulated, and I longed for the fresh, green fields of England, longed for my own friends and my own tongue. Nostalgia had seized me badly, and I was world-weary and homesick—longing now for the day of my departure.

Presently I returned again to the study of the ill-written script before me, half-fearful of the strange warning inscribed upon the page; but slowly, and with considerable difficulty, I deciphered it as follows:

"This be the causes following why that
I, Godfrey Lovel, have made
labour to write this secret record.

"First, immediately after my birth at Winchelsea, my father, Sir Richard Lovel, baron of the King's Exchequer, died of plague, and my mother in brief time married my lord of Lincoln. The goode monks of Winchelsea learned me, but at fifteen I left their habit and religion, crossed unto France, and became a soldier of fortune with the army of the King of Navarre. Full many a strange adventure had I in those days of youth with the mercenary bande in Italy, untill, in the year of God's grace 1495, I was in Pesaro, where I entered the service of my lord Don Giovanni Sforza and his lovely lady Donna Lucrezia, who was daughter of His Holiness the Pope. At firste I was made captain of my lord duke's gentlemen-at-arms, but afterwardes my lady Lucrezia, of her gracious bounty, found me worthy to be her grace's secretary. Furthermore, pleaseth it you to understand that in the palace of the Sforza Tyrant I saw that which was not a little to my discomforte; nevertheless I must be content recording it briefly.

"But now, as touching my own part, I most humbly beseech you to bare with me, for of a verity I saw and knew what no man did; and you, my reader, who make bold sufficient after my warning and admonition, will find herein a chronicle of fact that will astound you. God be thanked there are not such thynges done in England as in Italy under the red bull of the Borgias.

"As concerning the revelations, these be the things that I have heard and have knowledge in. At the beginning thereof, the which was in the ember week of 1496, the Pope's Holiness the lord Alexander P.P. VI. sent his son the boy-cardinal to our Court at Pesaro. From the firste tyme I saw him dysmounting from hys hors in the corte-yard of the palace I dysliked hym. Although but eighteen years of age, his father had made him cardinal-deacon of Santa Maria Nuova, a vain and sinful elegaunt whose ambition knew no bounds. He had come on secret mission from the Vatican to his sister, my lady Lucrezia, and to her he spake in privy during my lord duke's absence. The lord Don Giovanni was a brutal and ill-living man, cruel to his golden-haired, beautiful wife, that I vouch; but even to my lady Lucrezia, whose life was so unhappy that she had shed tears unto me, her man of confidence and humble servitor, the object of the Cardinal Cesare's secret mission was appalling.

"At the downe of the sun on the same day my lord, having returned from a visit to the Malatesta at Rimini, welcomed the cardinal warmly and entertained him in the great banquet-hall, wherein four hundred persons supped. The revels did not end with midnight, but my lorde and his guest retired at that hour. Some tyme later I had occasion to pass along the great corridor where the chamber of my ladie Lucrezia was, and herd the sound as of a woman crying within. It was my ladie; and, obtaining permission, I entered and found her plunged in grief and remorse. Most humbly desiring her grace to accept mi poor mind towards her most noble self, I induced her to tell me the truth.

"She tore her hair in desperation as she confessed unto me, with promise of secrecy, that her brother the cardinal had been sent by her father His Holyness in order to envenom her husband the duke, because the Terrible Pontiff wished to marry her more advantagiosly for the increase of the Borgia power. Never in my life have I seene a beautiful woman in such despair, and I, her grace's confidential servitor, chamberlain, and secretarie, did I in my moste humble wise seeke to assist her, whereupon did she tell me with tears that she feared to disobey the will of His Holiness. I suggested that her grace should separate from her lord, and that the marriage should be annulled by His Holyness; but in desperation she told me that her brother Cesare had already poisoned him secretly with a certaine deadly and irrevealable compound only known to her father, her brother, and herself.

"My lord Don Giovanni Sforza, the Tyrant of Pesaro, whose reign was one of oppression, murder, bloodshed, and infamy, was doomed. In a few houres he must die. Notwithstanding that my ladie hated hys evil ways she yet wished that he should live. But she feared the wrath of His Holiness if she went unto him and told him what the lorde-cardinall his guest had done, the lord-cardinal being then wyth him discussyng the best menes of suppressing the rebellious Orsini. At last, however, my lady, makinge me give my bonde to help her, did resolve to leave Pesaro for Rome. First, being desirous of carrying wyth her the costly jewels given her on her marriage, she unlocked her jewel-chest and caused me to fill my pouch and doublet with those the most precious. Whereupon this having been done, she took from a golden caskett preserved wythin the chest a small cross-hilted poignard with perforated blade, telling me to go unto her lord the duke and strike him with it in a part not mortal. The lorde-cardinal being present, and believing that it was an assassinacion, would make no effort to secure me; therefour, having struck the blow, I was to escape at once to Rome and there await her. Within the golden caskett were three delicate tubes of greeny-white glasse, sealed carefully, the which my lady told me in confidence contained the secret and all-powerful venom of the Borgias. They had beene given her by her father as a marriage-gift, together with the poignard with thin, hollow blade containing the secret antidote.

"Concerning the Casket: This casket aforementioned, with its three glass tubes, each the length of the first joint of a man's little finger, the which place in one's hands the power of secret death, and the one tube containing the antidote, did she gyve into my safe keepinge, as well as her wondrous jewels, the like no man had before seen.

"I took the poignard, kissed my lady's hand in pledge of servitude devout, and flew to do her bidding, entering to where my lorde duke sat drinkynge with his treacherious guest, strykinge hym in the arme wyth the knife bearing the antydote—thus saveing hys life, although he believed it to be an attempt at assassination—and then escaping by the Gate of the Rocchetta under cover of night, arriving in Rome at sundown on the sixth, daye following. Wherefore wyll it be seen that not only did I carry the priceless emeralds of my ladie Lucrezia and the secret venom of the Borjas—the presence of the which cannot be detected—but I also held in my possession the antidote.

"In Rome I did hide away the treasures given into my safe keepinge in a place whereof no man knewe; while mi ladie, having fled from Pesaro, entered the convent of San Sisto; while the lorde Alexander P.P. VI., finding that his poison sent by the worshipfull cardinal had been unavailing, issued a decree annulling the marriage. Now, His Holiness had lost by death many friends in Rome, including several members of the Sacred College, and by their decease had become goodly enriched and empowered; hence the failure of the banal substance to take effect in the case of Don Giovanni must have caused him much surprise.

"Praise be to God, who, of His infinite goodnes and mercy inestimable, hath brought me out of darkness into light, and from deadly ignorance into the quick knowledge of truth, from the which through the fiend's instigation and false persuasion I have grately swerved, I was enabled to save the life of mi lord, although he be a tyrant and a man of ill-living. The lord-Cardinal Cesare returned to Rome, and six months after the divorce of my ladie His Holiness brought her forth from the convent, and gave her as wife unto the Lord Don Quadrata and Salerno, and likewise gave them the palace of the Cardinal of Santa Maria in Portico, by the Vatican, in the which to live. And here again did I return unto my ladie as her confidential chamberlain; for now, knowinge how that she were but the innocent tool in the infamous hands of the lorde Alexander and his creature the Cardinal Cesare, I resolved to devote myself unto her protection. I told unto my ladie the hiding-place of her jewels; but she would not allow me to bring them to the palace, lest they should remind her of her past unhappiness. They were best to remain where I had secreted them. Again was my unfortunate lady's marriage without love, her happiness constantly disturbed by the terror in which she lived, being compelled by the Terrible Pontiff and her ambitious brother to act in treachery and dishonour, to entice men and women to their ruine, and to place death-trappes with the secret venom."

Following this sentence was a blank space wherein was rudely drawn a curious geometrical design, some of the shaky lines—intended most probably to be straight—bearing numbers. It was almost like a plan; but careful inspection showed me that it was not, and for a long time I tried to make out its connection with the old monk's remarkable record.

Chapter Eight
Concerns a Woman's Serfdom

After long examination I came to the conclusion that the rudely executed sketch must have been placed there by another hand, as it seemed in somewhat different ink, a trifle more faded than the writing. As is so often the case in old manuscripts, blank spaces were used by subsequent posessors to note memoranda at a time when every inch of parchment or other writing surface was precious.

It apparently had no connection with the text; therefore, placing it aside for further examination, I turned the page and continued to decipher this remarkable and forbidden document regarding the perfidy of the terrible House of Borgia.

As an antiquary I had become intensely interested in the strange record, for it apparently threw an entirely new light upon the notorious Lucrezia Borgia, the woman who had brought secret poisoning to a fine art.

And as I proceeded, I found it continued as follows:

"In my most humble wise I served my ladie Lucrezia, wrapping myself, I fear, in manifold errors, and being privy to the detestable crimes of the Cardinal Cesare. Both my ladie and myself knew that it was Cesare who, with his own hand, stabbed his elder brother Giovanni Duke of Gandia and threw him into the Tiber on the night of the feast given by his mother the Madonna Giovanni at San Pietro ad Vincula. We knew, too, of many dark and foul crimes beyond those in which my lady's father and brother compelled here to partake. After the assassination of the lord of Gandia, the Cardinal Cesare threw aside his scarlet hat and became capitain-general of the Church, with the title of the Lord Duke Cesare de Valentinois. He shrank from neither sacrilege or murder, readily doffing the purple to assume the breastplate, and at head of his army crushed the feudal power of the barons in the Romagna.

"For a short space, alas! did he tarry, and brief was my lady's respite from the horrors thrust upon her. You, mi reader, who hath noe fere OF DEATH may still continue to scann this recorde; but I yet do warn and beseache of you to stay thine inquisitiveness, or the gaining of the secret, as it must be at thine own rysk and peril. Truely I affirm unto you that the thinges done in the palace of my lord Prince of Bisceglia at instigation and order of the fat-faced, double-chinned Borgia Pope were the foulest and blackest that ever man did conceive. To His Holiness's enemies the mere touch of my ladie's soft hand meant certain death, and feastes were given at the which those singled out were swept away like flies. None who dared to thwart the Borgia Pope or the lord Duke of Valentinois escaped swift and certain destruction. For them, death lurked at all times no matter how much care they took of their personal safetie. The fiendish ingenuity of Cesare Borgia showed itself in divers and sundry ways all to encompass the death of rivals that the House of Borgia became paramount, and its power overwhelming.

"Pleas it your goodness to understande that I be so bold as to put it to writing that which I have seene that you who live after me shall know and learn this my secret contained herein."

Here, again, was a second drawing, slightly more complicated than the former, and at the bottom was written, evidently in old Lovel's hand, the single and inexplicable word, in no language known to me, "*treyf.*"

At one corner was a sketch of a circle with radiating lines which might be intended to represent the sun; but so crude was the drawing that it might be meant for anything. Therefore, after a few minutes' minute examination, I came to the conclusion that my first theory was wrong, and that both had been drawn by the same hand that had inscribed the curious record.

Continuing my task of deciphering, I suddenly became seized by violent neuralgic pains in the head and back, attended by excruciating cramp in the hands, similar to that I had once experienced through writing too much. Notwithstanding this, however, I further prosecuted my investigation of the secret record which, as will be seen, proved a very remarkable one. After the inexplicable design, it continued:

"I suppose it to be the will of God that I remained the humble servante of my ladie Lucrezia obstinately determined to suffer all extremities rather than to leave her in the hands of those secret assassins. Many times did mi unhappie ladie seek my counsel, remorseful of the part she was forced to bear by His Holiness and the lord Duke of Valentinois. To mine own knowledge many who visited at the palace were envenomed in secret and went to their homes to die. Of these, one was my lord Don Ludovico Visconti, who had allied himself to the Doge and Senate of Venice, and upon the hilt of whose sword, whych he unbuckled while he sat at meat, was there placed a drop of the Borgia poison. Another was the lord Alessandro Farnese, cardinal-deaycon of San Cosina, who died suddenly after leaving the presence of His Holiness and my lady Lucrezia; a third victim was the Madonna Sancia, daughter of His Majesty Don Alonso II., to whom my lady Lucrezia was forced by her father to sende a ringe of gold, and who died one hour after plaicinge it upon her finger. Again, my lady Lucrezia was compelled to invite to a great banquet the Don Oliverotto da Femo, Don Giovanni Fogliani, Don Vitellozo of Citta di Castello, Don Paolo Orsini of Sinigaglia, Don Lorenzo Manfredi of Faenza, the white-faced cardinal-chamberlain Riarjo, and Don Juan Vera, cardinal of Santa Balbina. His Holiness and the Duke Cesare were both presente, the feaste beinge gyven in order to effect a peace with the fiefs of the Romagna. Myself I sat at the ende of the table next my lord Orsini; but a foule treachery was practised, for every guest, wythout exception, was secretely poisoned, and at breake of daye not one was alive, although no effect was felt by anyone before they left the palace. By such means as these did the Romagna fall beneath the power of the Borgias.

"Full many a woman hateful to the House of Borgia became envenomed by dainty comfits handed to her by my lady's lisping child the Duke Roderico, who was thus a poisoner at two years old, but of whose sweetemeats the ladies were unsuspecting. And be it known to you by this my record that my lady's husband, my lord Prince of Bisceglia, was but of the age of twenty and one years at this time, and helpless in the venomous hands of the Duke Cesare. Rome was filled wyth assassyns. Myself, like every man who valued his safety, put on a mail-shirt when I left my bed, and set no foote in the streetes till I had buckled a sword or at least a poignard at my side. But the red bull was rampant, for the whole power of the Borgias was contained in the deadly potency of those small phialls of glass and the impossibility of detection of the fatal *cantarella*.

"Think you, my reader, that any indifferent man, knowinge these things, and knowing also that the position of the lady Lucrezia was hateful unto her, could but suffer himselfe to remain as her faithful chamberlain, and seek to guard her from the fearsome perils that surrounded her. Forthermore, one night at nine of the clock, my ladie came to me in terror, saying that she having quarrelled with her father, His Holiness had sent for her to his private apartment in the Vatican, where he spoke unto her and took her hand in forgiveness. As she withdrewe it she saw that he wore the venome ring the which is hollow, like that in my possession, and containeth the deadly *cantarella*! Then did my lady know that she had been victym of treachery, and was doomed. Already her beautiful face was pale, and upon her were the pains in the jaws and tongue, the whych told us the truth. Not loosing a moment of time, I obtained the poignard containing the antidote, and with it struck deep into her white forearm, and whych she held for me withoute flinching untill the blood flowed, and by this meanes was her life, attempted by His Holiness the lord Alexander P.P. VI., given back unto her.

"Twyce myself was I envenomed by the Duke Cesare (accursed be his memory for ever), and twice was I able to counteract the poison with the antydote that my ladie Lucrezia had given me. The Borgia poison lurked in everything. A flower could be so impregnated that its perfume was rendered fatal; gloves were treated so that the wearer died wythin twelve hours; the hat, the boots, the staff, the mail-shirt, the woman's kirtle or the man's hose were all envenomed; nay, even unto the very chair upon the which a gueste sat. No poison was placed in the cup, it beinge always external and impossible to detect; beside which its action could be so regulated that I have known death to take place in an hour in some cases, while in others the fatal conclusion would not arrive for a week or even a month, according to the wishes of the Pope Alexander and his ambicious son. In very truth the possession of that secrete venom gave to the house of the Borgias power over both Church, state, and the riches and treasures of the world, all of whych they conquered by the vilest treachery known unto man.

"My singular good reader, my duty presupposed, pleaseth it your good readership to understande that as in the case of my lorde Sforza of Pesaro, so in the case of my lorde Prince of Bisceglia, His Holiness finding himself foiled in the attempt to kill his daughter, soon wished to rid her of her husband, seeing that to marry her again unto one of the new lords of the Romagna would support the papal power in those parts. The crisis occurred on the morrow after my lord prince had returned from Naples, the VIIIth day of August in the year of grace 1500. My lord had been secretely envenomed twice, and escaped death by meanes of the antidote; but on the night afore named, at eleven of the clock, he went forthe to Saint Peter's, but while ascending the steps was greviously stabbed by a bande of masqued men in the pay of the Duke Cesare. Weak from loss of blood, he dragged himselfe unto the Pope's apartmentes, where my ladie Lucrezia, chancing to be there, swooned at sight of him. There were fifteene wounds upon him, but his life had been saved by his mail-shirte; yet for three weekes he lay ill in the Borgia tower, my lady Lucrezia never leaving him, and, fearful of poison, preparinge his food with her own hands. None the less, before my lorde had recovered, the Duke Cesare, accompanied by one Don Michelotto, visited him one night, and havinge driven my lady and the Madonna Sancia from the room, they remained alone with him. My ladie flew down to the chamber of the Segnatura, that had been set apart for me duringe my lord's illness; and, hearinge what had transpired, I rushed up to my lord's apartment only to discover he had been foully strangled. The bravo Michelotto aimed a blow at me; but his blade turned by my mail-shirte, he made his escape. When my brave lady came and found her lord dead, her sorrow knew no bounds, for she saw that he, like unto the others, had fallen at last a victim of the Borgia treachery. Both the lord Alexander P.P. VI. and his son Cesare had the habit of saying 'That which is not done at noon can be done at sunset.'

"Reader, who darest to seek within this book, curb thy curiosity and inquisitiveness, and stay thine hand, for herein is written strange things, secrets which concern you not, and have remained hidden mysteries from the world—things the knowledge of which must render you among the greatest on earth, yet must bring evil and destruction unto you. Having gained knowledge so far, I do entreat of you, brave as thou art, to seek no further to reopen this Closed Book. Again, harken to this warning of a dead man, and save thyself."

Again those extraordinary, excruciating pains cramped my brow and limbs, while my throat once more became contracted, just as it had been on the previous night when I had commenced to make investigation.

But with my brain reeling and my senses confused I turned the time-stained page, and overleaf saw written there in capitals in the centre of one blank folio the ominous words:

"O AVARICIOUS READER
WHO HAST HEEDED NOT THE WARNING!
TRULY THOU ART ENVENOMED AND MUST
DIE. TO THEE NO POWER OF ANTIDOTE CAN
AVAIL, NO HAND CAN SAVE. THE SHARPNESS
OF DEATH IS UPON THEE."

Then, for the first time, the terrible truth flashed upon me.

The vellum leaves of that secret record were impregnated by some unknown and subtle poison, probably that secret compound of the House of Borgia that could be used to envenom any object and render it deadly to the touch; and I, disregarding the premonition, was poisoned.

I cast the heavy volume from me with a cry of horror and despair. The pain was excruciating. The sting of death was already upon me.

I had reopened The Closed Book—an action that was fatal.

Chapter Nine
Doctor Pellegrini's Opinion

I have very little recollection of what occurred immediately afterwards, for I was far too confused and full of pain.

All I remember was that I rushed downstairs to old Nello, crying that I had been suddenly taken unwell; and he, seeing my pale, distorted features, was greatly alarmed. I recollected at the moment that I had an appointment with the wife of a wine-grower, with whom I was in treaty for the purchase of an exquisite little fourteenth-century picture of St. Francis of Assisi; and, telling my faithful man that if a lady called he was to ask her to wait, I dashed out, sprang into a cab, and drove along the sun-blanched sea-road into Leghorn, where, in a high, old palace in an unfashionable quarter, I discovered my friend, Doctor Pellegrini, a short, stout, round-faced Italian, with iron-grey hair and a pair of dark eyes which had a hard and severe expression.

"Why, my dear signore," he cried in Italian as I entered his big, half-darkened study, the marble floor carpetless, and furnished barely in Tuscan style, "whatever ails you?"

"I've been poisoned, *signor dottore!*" I gasped.

"What are your symptoms? Tell me quickly," he demanded, springing towards me and taking my wrist quickly, being convinced that there was no time to lose.

"I have great difficulty in breathing," I managed to gasp. "And now there seems to be a strange, biting taste as though I'd swallowed some quinine. My neck aches and seems to be bending back, and I am in great agony."

"Very likely it is strychnine," the professor remarked. "How did you take it? Was it an accident?"

"I will explain later," I responded. "Do give me something to relieve these terrible pains. The poison, I can explain, is not strychnia, but the fatal secret compound of the Borgias."

"The Borgias! Rubbish!" he snapped. "All imagination, most probably."

"But I tell you it is. I have been envenomed by a poison, the secret of which is unknown, and the antidote was lost ages ago."

The doctor smiled in disbelief, probably remarking within himself that the English were a queer race, with all their fads, fancies, tea drinking, and smart tailoring.

"Well," he said. "I'll first give you a little chloroform, and then see what we can do. Don't upset yourself, my dear signore. We shall find an antidote somehow."

And he gave me some chloroform, which produced insensibility. Then, on recovering consciousness, I found myself on a bed in a room almost totally dark, with blankets piled upon me until they had reduced me to a state of profuse perspiration.

My head felt as though bound tightly with a band of steel, but I had no further difficulty in breathing. My limbs were no longer cramped, and my neck was again movable.

I was better, and told Pellegrini, who was seated patiently by my side watching me.

"Of course," he said, with that cool, cynical air of his which caused one instinctively to dislike him on first acquaintance.

"But I was very bad," I declared. "I've never experienced such excruciating pains before in all my life."

"And I may tell you," he said in the same calm tone, "that you've never been nearer death than you were an hour ago. I certainly thought you wouldn't pull through. I telephoned to Cassuto at the hospital, and he rushed round and helped me. I didn't believe you had really been poisoned. It certainly was not strychnia after all, although the symptoms were very like it. Tell me how it happened."

I turned on my bed towards him and briefly related how I had purchased the curious volume, and how, on two separate occasions, I had been suddenly seized while examining the secret history written at the end.

"H'm!" he grunted dubiously; "very remarkable, especially as the record mentions the unknown poison used by Lucrezia Borgia and her brother. A matter for investigation, certainly. You must allow me to submit one of the vellum pages to analysis; and perhaps we might clear up forever the ingredients of the compound which has so long remained a mystery."

"Most willingly," I answered. "We may make a discovery of the utmost interest to toxicologists. Hitherto they have declared that to produce a substance sufficiently venomous to penetrate the skin and cause death to those who touch it is impossible. Here, however, I think we have an illustration of it."

"It really seems so," he answered thoughtfully. "I should strongly advise you, when handling the book again, to wear gloves as a precaution. Having once narrowly escaped death, as you have, you cannot be too careful."

"I'll take your advice, *signore dottore*," I responded. "And I've to thank you for saving me, as you've done today."

"You had a narrow escape—a very narrow one," he remarked. "I do not think that in all my experience I have seen a man come so near death, and then recover. When you first told me that your hands had become impregnated with the Borgia poison I was, of course, sceptical. You English sometimes become so very imaginative when you live here in our climate. But I am compelled to admit that the symptoms are not those of any known poison; and if what you tell me is correct, then it really appears as though we are at last actually in possession of an object envenomed with the ancient compound about which so much has been written during the past three centuries. For my own part, I am deeply interested in the curious affair, and shall be only too happy to investigate it analytically, if you will allow me. My friend Marini, the professor of chemistry at Pavia, is at present here for the sea-bathing, and he will, I am sure, help me. As you know, he is one of the most expert analysts in Italy."

And so it was agreed that a chemical investigation should be made, in order to discover, if possible, the secret of the Borgia poison which was so subtle and could be so regulated that no effect might be felt for half an hour or for a month, as the poisoner wished, but the end was always the same—death.

By secret use of that fatal compound the Duke Caesar detto Borgia undoubtedly swept away his enemies, and more than one old chronicler alleges that his father, the Pope Alexander VI. himself, did not hesitate to use it to rid himself of obnoxious cardinals who were wealthy, or other persons who aroused his enmity. He fully lived up to his official title of Ruler of the World, and it is more than likely that by the aid of this secret compound he broke the back of the turbulent, selfish baronage which had ravaged the papal states for centuries. Certainly his reign was full of diabolical atrocities and wanton, ingenious cruelty, documentary evidence of which is still preserved in the secret archives of the Vatican and of Venice. As to the alleged crimes of the beautiful Lucrezia, a long tress of whose yellow hair is still preserved in the Ambrosian Library at Milan, those who have read Italian history know well how she has been represented as placed outside of the pale of humanity by her wantonness, her vices, and her crimes. Yet what was written in that curious record of Godfrey Lovel, soldier, courtier, and monk by turns, seemed to demonstrate that in her youth, with no initiative, no choice permitted to her, she was rather the too pliant instrument in the hands of Alexander and his son Caesar.

Anyhow, the fact remained that the writer of that secret record was absolutely in the confidence of Lucrezia Borgia, and also in possession of some of the venom, with which, in all probability, he envenomed the book in order that those who gained the secrets it contained should never live to profit by them.

Knowledge of the secret written there, he alleged, would place its possessor among the greatest upon earth. Was not that sufficient to arouse one's curiosity to proceed — to continue handling those envenomed pages, unconsciously seeking his own doom?

Surely the secret must be an important one, placed on record upon vellum, and yet so protected that the seeker after it must inevitably die ere the entire truth could be revealed.

The whole affair was most puzzling. As I sat in the swift, open cab that took me back along the sea-road to Antignano, the crimson sun was setting, and the gaily dressed Italian crowd was promenading under the ilexes and acacias beside the Mediterranean. Leghorn is a fashionable bathing-place during July and August, and from the hour when the sun sinks behind Gorgona until far into the night no fairer prospect than the Viale Regina Margherita, as the beautiful promenade is called, with its open-air cafés and big bathing establishments, can be found in the south of Europe.

Through the little wood that lies between the fashionable village of Ardenza and the sea, where the oleanders were in the full blaze of their glory, my cab sped homeward; and having left the gaiety of the outskirts of Leghorn behind, I fell to reflecting upon the future, and wondering what, after all, was the hidden truth contained in The Closed Book — the knowledge that would place its possessor among the greatest on earth?

I thought of the strange circumstances in which I had purchased the old tome, of the inexplicable manner of Father Bernardo, of the old hunchback's evil face at the church window, and, most of all, of that singularly handsome young woman in black whom I had encountered in the prior's study — the woman with whom the fat priest had spoken in private.

Why should Father Bernardo have urged me to relinquish my bargain? Why should Graniani have come to me on the same errand, and have warned me? Surely they could not be aware that the pages were envenomed, and just as surely they could have no motive in preventing my falling a victim!

If they were acting from purely humane motives, they would surely have explained the truth to me.

Besides, when I reflected, it became apparent that the vellum leaves at the end whereon was inscribed old Godfrey's chronicle had not been opened for many years, as a number of them had become stuck together by damp at the edge, and I had been compelled to separate them with a knife.

At last I sprang out, paid the driver, passed through the echoing marble hall of the *villino,* and up the stairs towards my study.

Old Nello, who followed me, greeted me with the usual *"Ben tornato, signore,"* and then added, "The lady called to see you, waited about a quarter of an hour in your study, and then left, promising to call tomorrow."

"She said nothing about the little panel of St. Francis?"

"Nothing, signore. But she seemed an inquisitive young lady—from Bologna, I should say, from her accent."

"Young lady!" I exclaimed. "Why, the wine-grower's wife is sixty, if a day. Was this lady young?"

"About twenty-six, signore," was his reply. "Hers was a pretty face—like a picture—only she seemed to wear a very sad look. She was dressed all in black, as though in mourning."

"What?" I cried, halting on the stairs, for the description of my visitor tallied with that of the woman I had seen in the priest's study in Florence and afterwards in Leghorn. "Had she black eyes and a rather protruding, pointed chin?"

"She had, signore."

"And she was alone in my study a quarter of an hour?" I exclaimed.

"Yes. I looked through the keyhole, and, seeing her prying over your papers, I entered. Then she excused herself from remaining longer, and said she would call again."

"But that's not the woman I expected, Nello?" And with a bound I rushed up the remaining stairs into the room.

A single glance around told me the truth.

The Closed Book had disappeared! It had been stolen by that woman, who had been following me, and whose face lived in my memory every hour.

I rushed around the room like a madman, asking Nello if he had placed the volume anywhere; but he had not. He recollected seeing it open upon my writing-table when he had ushered the visitor in, and had not thought of it until I now recalled the truth to him.

My treasure had been stolen; and as I turned towards my table I saw lying upon the blotting-pad a sheet of my own note paper, upon which was written in Italian, in an educated feminine hand, the axiom of Caesar Borgia as chronicled in the missing book:

"That which is not done at noon can be done at sunset."

Chapter Ten
Across Europe

The Closed Book had been filched from me at the very moment when I was about to learn the secret it contained.

I put a few well-directed questions to Nello, and became confirmed in my suspicion that the woman who had stolen it was actually the same whose face had so attracted me that it had lived within my memory every moment since our first meeting.

Curious how the faces of some women haunt us, even when we have no desire for their affection! The fascination of a woman's eyes is one of the unaccountable mysteries of life, being far beyond human ken or human control, and yet one of the most potent factors in man's existence.

In the half-open drawer of my writing-table were certain private papers that I had taken from my despatch-box two days before, intending to send them to my solicitors in London, and these the unknown in black had apparently been examining. She had called with a fixed purpose, which she had accomplished—namely, to pry into my private affairs, and to gain possession of my treasured Arnoldus, the Book of Secrets.

As I knew Tuscany and the Tuscans so well, this ingenious conspiracy was scarcely surprising. The little plots, often harmless enough, that I had detected about me during my residence by the Mediterranean had shown me what a cleverly diplomatic race they were, and with what patient secretiveness they work towards their own ends. It annoyed me, however, to think that I should thus fall a victim to that handsome woman's ingenuity. Veiled as she had been in Father Bernardo's study, I had judged her to be much older than I found she was when I had noticed her in the streets of Leghorn. Who could she be, and what could be her motive in stealing my property if she were not in league with the prior himself?

My old servant Nello, standing there beside me, knew something more than he would tell. Of that I felt convinced. Possibly he had participated in the plot, admitting her, well knowing her errand. He had warned me; therefore he must know something. What was the object of it all I utterly failed to conceive.

"That woman is a thief?" I exclaimed angrily a few moments later. "Who is she?"

"I—I do not know her, *signor padrone*," stammered the old man.

"She gave no name?"

"None. She said that you expected her."

"But she could not have taken away a big book like that without your noticing it?" I pointed out suspiciously.

"She had on a big black cloak, signore," was the crafty old fellow's response.

I closed my writing-table and locked it, for in that moment I had decided to go straight to Florence and charge Bernardo Landini with being a party to the theft. Having sold the book to me, he wished to repossess himself of it, and on my refusal, had, it seemed, put in motion a kind of conspiracy against me.

The old hunchback was undoubtedly the director of it all.

I thrust a few things into a kit-bag, placed some money in my pocket, and put on an overcoat; and telling Nello that I should not return for a couple of days, perhaps, gave orders that no one was to be admitted to the house except my most intimate friend, Hutchinson, the British consul.

At the big, bare railway station, wherein the feeble gas-jet had just been lit, I saw, lounging beside the ticket-collector, the detective attached to that post, whose duty it was to notice all arrivals and departures; and, knowing him, I called him aside and briefly described the lady who had visited me.

"Yes, signore, I saw her. She left for Pisa an hour ago; she purchased a first-class ticket for London."

"For London!" I gasped. "Had she any baggage?"

"A crocodile-leather dressing-case and a small flat box covered with brown leather."

"By what route was she travelling?"

The detective walked to the booking-office, and in response to his inquiries I learned that she had taken a direct ticket by way of Turin, Modane, Paris, and Calais. The train which caught at Pisa the express to the French frontier had left an hour ago; therefore I had no chance of overtaking her.

Still, something prompted me to take the next train to Pisa, for Italian railways are never punctual, and there was just a chance that she might have missed her connection. So half an hour later I sat in the dimly lit, rickety old compartment of that branch-line train, pondering over the events of the past day, and determined to run down the thief at all hazards.

At Pisa I quickly learned that the Leghorn train had arrived in time to catch the express; therefore the woman in black was now well on her way towards the frontier.

I purchased a railway-guide, and entering the waiting-room, sat down to study it calmly. After half an hour I decided upon a plan. The homeward Indian mail from Brindisi to London would pass through Turin at 9:10 on the following morning, and, if I caught it, would land me at Calais three hours in advance of the express by which she was travelling. But from Pisa to Turin is a far cry—half-way across Italy; and I at once consulted the station-master as to the possibility of arriving in time.

There was none, he declared. The express for the north, which left in two hours' time, could not arrive in Turin before 9:20, ten minutes after the departure of the Indian mail. Therefore it was impossible.

I paced the long, deserted platform full of chagrin and utterly bewildered.

Of a sudden, however, a thought occurred to me. I knew the manager of the Compagnie Internationale des Wagons-Lits at Turin station, a most courteous and hard-working Englishman named Nicholls. I would telegraph to him, urging him in the strongest terms to detain the Indian mail for me ten minutes.

This I did, and just before midnight stepped into the Rome-Turin express on the first stage of my stern-chase across Europe.

Through the hot, stifling July night I stretched myself out along the cushions and slept but little during the slow, tedious journey through those eighty-odd roaring tunnels that separate Pisa from Genoa, for the line is compelled to run so close to the sea in places that the waves lap the very ballast. I was excited, wondering whether I should succeed in catching the mail and arresting the woman's progress.

In those past few days I had trodden a maze of mystery. My love for the antique had brought into my life one of the strangest episodes experienced by any man, yet in those breathless moments, as I tore across Europe, I thought only of regaining possession of my remarkable treasure, and of obtaining the forbidden knowledge contained therein.

Hour after hour dragged slowly by. At Genoa, long after the sun had risen, I got out for a cup of coffee in that ugly and rather dirty buffet which travellers in Italy know so well. Then re-entering, we started off up the deep valleys and across the broad wine-lands of Asti towards Turin.

As we approached the capital of Piedmont my anxiety increased. To delay the Indian mail for ten minutes was surely a sufficient courtesy, and I knew that after that lapse of time my friend Nicholls dared not assume further responsibility. The overland mail once a week between Brindisi and Charing Cross is ever on time; a contract that must be kept whatever the cost; hence, as I frequently glanced at my watch, I grew anxious as to my success in catching it.

If I did I should arrive at Calais harbour in advance of the mysterious woman, and could on board the steamer single her out and demand the restoration of my property.

We halted at Novi, and the time lost in taking water seemed an eternity. At Alexandria we were ten minutes late—ten minutes! Think what that meant to me.

At Asti there was some difficulty about an old *contadina's* box; and when the train started at last for Turin we were nearly fourteen minutes behind time. I threw myself back with a sigh, feeling that all hope had vanished. We could never make up time on that short run; and the English mail, after waiting for me, would leave ten minutes or so before my arrival. Could any situation be more tantalising?

At last, however, we ran slowly into the great arched terminus of Turin; and as we did so I hung half my body from the carriage window, and was delighted to see the train of long, brown sleeping-cars still standing in the station.

My heart gave a bound. On the platform my friend Nicholls was awaiting me, and assisted me hurriedly to descend.

"Just in time, Mr Kennedy," he said. "Another minute and I should have been compelled to let her go. Anything serious in London?"

"Yes," I answered. "Very serious. I'll write to you all about it. But I don't know how to thank you sufficiently."

"Oh, never mind about that," he laughed. "I've got your berth for you. Come along;" and, hurrying me over to the next platform, he put me into one of the cars, wishing me *bon voyage*, waved his hand, and we moved out towards Calais—the fastest express across Europe.

Upon the result of that hard race my whole future and happiness depended. I was not, of course, aware of it at the time. I was merely consumed by curiosity regarding the strange vellum record, and was eager to obtain the knowledge that its writer had so successfully concealed—barring it with certain death to those who sought the truth.

Could I but have looked into the future, could I have realised what it all meant to me, I should never have dared to embark upon that chase; but rather should I have been pleased that this unknown woman of the sable habiliments had taken into her hands that which must sooner or later encompass her death.

But we are creatures of impulse, all of us. I found the circumstances full of romance and interest; and, beyond, I saw the woman herself as great a mystery as that written upon those envenomed pages.

My keen anxiety through those long hours while we sped through the Alps and by way of Aix, Mâcon, and Dijon to Paris need not be told. The train by which the woman I was following had travelled was before us all the way; but her delay would, I discovered, be in Paris; for while she was compelled to cross the city by cab, and wait at the Gare du Nord five hours, we travelled around the Ceinture railway, and left for Calais with only twenty minutes' wait at the French capital.

Most of my fellow-travellers were Anglo-Indians, officers and their wives home on leave, together with a few homeward-bound travellers from the Far East, everyone eager to get aboard the Dover boat and to sight the white cliffs of Old England once again after perhaps many years of exile. If you have travelled by the overland mail, you know well the excitement that commences as one nears Calais; for once beneath the British flag of the Channel steamer, one is home again. Ah! that word home—how much it conveyed to me!—how much to you, if you have travelled in far-off lands!

We swung through Boulogne around that terrible curve that generally throws over the plates and dishes of the *wagon restaurant*, and at last slackened down through Calais-Ville, and slowly proceeded to the harbour where the special boat awaited us, the train having done the long run from Brindisi four minutes under the scheduled time even though Nicholls had kept it behind for nearly a quarter of an hour.

It was now eleven o'clock in the morning, and until four o'clock in the afternoon I remained in that most dismal of all hotels, the "Terminus," at Calais, awaiting the arrival of the ordinary express from Paris. It came at last, crowded with summer tourists from Switzerland and elsewhere, business men, and that quaint, mixed set of travellers that continually pass to and fro across the Channel.

In order to discover the woman, however, I took up a position near the gangway that gave access to the steamer, and scrutinised each passenger with all the eagerness of a born detective. One after the other they passed in array, each carrying the hand-luggage, while the big, rattling cranes were at work faking aboard baggage and mails.

The stream grew thinner, until the last passenger had passed on board, and yet she did not come. My haste had been in vain. She had probably broken her journey in Paris. And yet somehow I felt that she had some motive in carrying The Closed Book to London without delay.

French porters with their arm-badges and peaked caps rushed to and fro. There was shouting in two languages, not counting the third—or bad language. They were preparing to cast off, and I was undecided whether to remain in Calais until two o'clock next morning for the arrival of the night train or to go aboard and make further search.

But just as the gangway was about to be withdrawn I distinguished among the bustling groups of passengers a face that was familiar to me, and my decision was made immediately. I rushed headlong on board, and my hopes revived as I made my way quickly across the deck.

Chapter Eleven
The Old Lady from Paris

The man with whom I shook hands heartly was about thirty-five, tall, spruce, clean-shaven, and merry-faced, wearing a black overcoat and peaked cap that gave him the appearance of a naval officer. Cross-channel passengers know Henry Hammond well, for he is one of the most popular officials in his Majesty's customs, always courteous, always lenient to the poor foreign immigrant, but always stern wherever the traveller seeks to conceal contraband goods or that thing forbidden, the pet dog; conscientious in his duty in examining the baggage of incoming passengers, and always a gentleman—different, indeed, from the prying *douaniers* of our neighbours.

With his assistant it was his duty, turn by turn, to cross from Dover by the midday service, and on the return of the steamer from Calais—the vessel on which we were now aboard—to examine all the light baggage and affix a kind of perforated stamp as certificate of examination.

As a constant traveller I had had many a pleasant chat with him during trips across. In the wildest winter tempest in Dover Straits he remained unruffled, merely turning up the collar of his overcoat, and remarking that the weather was not so bad as it might be. But nearly all of you have had your baggage examined on the boat on your return from the Continent; therefore, no doubt, you know Mr Hammond, and have answered his question whether you have "anything to declare."

"Why, Mr Kennedy," he cried, as he took my hand, "this is a surprise! I saw in the paper the other day an announcement that you were returning to live in England, but did not expect you across just yet. Look at them," he added, casting his glance around. "Big crowd this afternoon: Cook's and Gaze's weekly returns from Switzerland."

"Yes," I laughed. "You'll be busy all the way over, I suppose."

"No, I'll be done in three-quarters of an hour or so; then we'll have a chat. My assistant is already getting on with hand-baggage forward." By this time we had cast off, and were creeping slowly down the harbour.

"Well, Hammond," I said confidentially, "I'm in a dilemma;" and taking him aside into one of the unoccupied deck-cabins I briefly explained the circumstances of The Closed Book, and described its outward appearance and binding.

"By Jove!" he exclaimed, deeply interested; "it almost beats your own romances, Mr Kennedy. I've just been reading your last. Neither my wife nor I could put it down till we'd finished."

"You see, the woman ought to be on board this boat; but I've not yet seen her. I'm just going in search of her. But if you should come across any one answering the description I've given, you might tell me at once."

"Of course. You want to get this extraordinary book back again?"

"Certainly. It is a valuable piece of property, apart from the secret it contains and the mystery surrounding it;" and as I uttered those words the slow roll of the vessel showed that we were already out in the somewhat choppy sea, and warned my friend that it was time to commence his duty.

So we parted, and I started a tour around the boat, commencing tactfully at the stern, and passing in review each of the passengers. The work was by no means easy, for women when they lounge in deck-chairs assume thick wrappings and thick veils to protect their faces when the Channel is rough and the wind strong. One always feels the breeze cold after hours in a stuffy sleeping-car, and, therefore, women are prone to suffer the horrors of the ladies' cabin rather than risk catching cold.

For nearly an hour I made frantic search hither and thither throughout the whole ship, in all three classes. I gazed at the piles of heavy baggage, wondering whether my treasure were concealed there, registered through to London perhaps, in which case it might go forward without my mysterious visitor. The only place forbidden to me was, of course, the ladies' cabin, presided over by a stern stewardess; and if the woman of whom I was in pursuit was on board, she had undoubtedly concealed herself there.

She certainly had not embarked by the gangway I had watched; but there was a second gangway to the fore-part of the ship by which baggage was carried, and she might have slipped across there unnoticed, as people sometimes do.

Already Shakespeare's Cliff was showing through the evening haze, as the vessel steadily laboured in the rough sea. The passengers were mostly lying in deck-chairs *hors de combat*, and no one ventured to promenade upon the unsteady deck. I had taken up a sheltered position near the door of the ladies' cabin, determined to remain there until every passenger should have left, although I was compelled to admit that my hope was a forlorn one, and that I should have to return again to Calais by the night boat and resume my vigil on the other side.

The woman must have broken her journey in Paris, and would undoubtedly come later; but on what day or by what service she would cross I was, of course, in ignorance. And as I sat shivering upon a stool in the rough wind, with the salt spray dashing ever and anon into my face, I felt that the probabilities of regaining my treasure were very few.

I had been the victim of an ingenious conspiracy. More could not be said.

Of a sudden, however, Hammond—his coat-collar up, and walking unsteadily because of the heavy rolling of the boat—approached me, saying:

"Well, I've just finished, Mr Kennedy. Every passenger today seems to have a double amount of hand-baggage; but we've been through it all. I've seen nothing of the young lady you describe; but I've seen something else—I've found your book."

"Found it!" I cried excitedly. "Who has it? Tell me."

"Well, a few minutes ago, in the second-class, I was examining the contents of a dilapidated leather bag belonging to a little, wizen-faced old woman, very shabbily dressed, when I found down at the bottom a flat brown-paper parcel, wrapped carefully, tied with string and sealed with big blotches of black wax. I'm always suspicious of sealed packets, for they may contain anything from cigars to anarchists' bombs; therefore I ordered her to break the seals and open it. At first she refused; but on my explaining the penalty incurred, she reluctantly obeyed, and there, to my great satisfaction, I saw your old manuscript. I looked inside, and although I know little about such things, I recognised it from your description to be the stolen volume."

"Did you make any remark?"

"None," was Mr Hammond's reply. "I wished to consult you first. I did not put the usual label on the bag, so that when she passes ashore it will be stopped and again opened. What do you intend doing?"

I was puzzled. It was satisfactory to know where The Closed Book actually was, but, on the other hand, it would be difficult to regain possession of it. As my friend Hammond pointed out, I could give notice to the harbour detective on arriving at Dover, and he would detain the woman. But I should be compelled to charge her with theft. This I could not do. I could, of course, declare the book to be stolen property; but matters were the more complicated because of the theft having been committed in Italy.

For some time we discussed the situation; then I accompanied him through the second-class, where, on a chair in the gangway leading past the engines, sat a queer, dried-up looking little woman of about sixty-five, wearing a rusty black bonnet and cloak—a woman I had noticed during my tour of inspection, but whom I had never suspected of being in actual possession of my treasure.

The book had evidently been delivered to her in Paris, and she was taking it to London—to whom?

That question I put to myself decided me, and when I was out of hearing I told Hammond that I intended to follow her before claiming it, and thus ascertain, if possible, the motive of the strange international plot which was apparently in progress.

The short, wizened old lady was English: her face thin and yellow, with a pair of dark eyes that had probably once been beautiful, and hair still dark, though showing threads of grey. She wore black cloth gloves, worn out at the finger-tips, and was ponderous below the waist on account of thick skirts put on to protect herself from the cold sea-breeze.

Hammond declared that her speech was that of a well-born person, and that her frayed glove concealed a diamond ring—a circumstance which he viewed with considerable suspicion. Yet he entirely agreed with me that I should gain more by following her to her destination and watching carefully than by arresting her on landing. There was a deep, inexplicable mystery about the book and its contents; and in order to solve it I ought to be acquainted with those whom it interested.

"I can't understand the manner in which you were poisoned by touching the leaves," Hammond said reflectively. "That beats me altogether. Perhaps somebody else will have a taste of it before long."

"I shall watch," I replied determinedly.

"In any case it is a most interesting circumstance," he declared. "But it's a good job your Italian doctor was able to save you. Evidently you had a very narrow shave."

"Very," I said. "I shall never forget the agonies I suffered. But," I added, "I mean at all hazards to decipher all that the book contains. That something very extraordinary is written there I'm absolutely convinced."

"Well, it would really seem so," he agreed. "Only, don't run any risks and touch the thing with your bare hands again."

"Not likely," I laughed. And then I fell to wondering what had become of that dark-eyed, beautiful woman who had been the actual thief.

Why was the treasure wrapped and sealed so carefully? Could it be that those who had so cleverly conspired to obtain it from me were aware of the venom with which certain parts of it were contaminated? It really seemed as though they were.

We passed and repassed the short-statured old lady, talking together and appearing to take no notice of her. Evidently she was not aware of my identity; therefore I stood much greater chance in my efforts to watch her.

The examination of her bag that Hammond had made had not disturbed her in the least; but presently he returned to her, and, feigning to have forgotten to affix the necessary customs stamp, did so.

At last we slowed up beside the Admiralty Pier at Dover, and next instant all was bustle. Passengers hitherto prostrated by the voyage sprang up and pressed towards the gangway, each eager to get ashore and secure a place in the draughty and out-of-date compartments of the Joint-Railways.

With an old woman's dislike of crowds, the person we were watching slowly gathered together her belongings, folded her shabby old travelling-rug neatly, pulled her veil beneath her chin, shook out her skirts, and then, carrying her precious bag, made her way to the gangway after the first rush had passed.

Hammond's quick eye detected her to be an experienced traveller, who had crossed many times before. She sat quite unruffled and unconcerned amid all the excitement of landing.

On the pier she inquired for the train for Charing Cross, and entered a second-class compartment, where she purchased a cup of tea and a slab of that greasy bread-and-butter which seems to be all the Joint-Railways allow the jaded traveller on landing, while I took a place in the next compartment to hers, and then retired some distance away in order to consult further with Hammond.

To his astuteness and thoroughness as a searcher I owed the knowledge of where my treasure was concealed; therefore I thanked him most warmly, and just as the signal was given for departure stepped into the carriage and waved him farewell.

The run to London was without incident, but on arriving at Charing Cross I kept keen observation upon her. She clung tenaciously to the bag containing the book, refusing to let a porter handle it, and entered a four-wheeled cab. I followed to the corner of Holborn and Southampton Row, where she alighted and walked quickly across Red Lion Square until she reached a big, dingy house in Harpur Street,—a short, quiet turning off of Theobald's Road,—a house that in the old days when Bloomsbury was a fashionable quarter had no doubt been the residence of some City merchant or man of standing. The old extinguisher used by the linkmen still hung beside the big hall door, the steps leading up to it were worn hollow by the tread of generations, and under the flickering gaslight the place, with its unlighted windows, looked dark, forbidding, and deserted.

The old lady was apparently expected, for the instant she passed the lower windows the door was flung open by some unseen person, showing the big hall to be in total darkness; and she, having ascended the steps with surprising alacrity, slipped in, the door falling to quickly and quite noiselessly behind her.

Chapter Twelve
The Sign of the Bear Cub

The exterior of the house was by no means inviting.

The old lady had entered there in secret, without a doubt; otherwise she would have driven up to the door instead of alighting at the corner of Southampton Row.

I passed by on the opposite side, and as there was a street-lamp quite near was enabled to examine it fairly well, even though darkness had now set in.

All the blinds were drawn, and the inside shutters of the basement were closely barred. There was no light in any part, nor any sign of life within. In fact, the state of the windows and door-steps would lead to a conclusion that the old place was tenantless, for the exterior possessed a distinct air of neglect. Other houses in the row were of stereotyped exactness, but all more or less smarter, with steps hearthstoned and lights showing in the windows here and there. The one into which the old woman had so quickly disappeared was, however, grim, silent, forbidding.

As I strolled to the corner of Theobald's Road I wondered what next I should do. I wanted to secure possession of the book, but without litigation, and, if possible, in secret. Yet it was a very difficult matter, as Hammond had pointed out.

Rain commenced to fall, and after my long journey from the Mediterranean I felt cold and deadbeat. Therefore, my eyes catching sight of a glaring public-house nearly opposite, I crossed and obtained some brandy and the loan of the *London Directory*.

After some little search I therein found the name of the occupier of the dingy old place, as follows: "106, Gardiner, Margaret."

London's mysteries are many and inscrutable. Surely here was a strange and inexplicable one. Why, indeed, should a mere old book of no value save to a collector be stolen from me in the far-off South and spirited away at express speed across the Continent to that dark, grimy, unlit place? There was some deep, direct motive in it all, of course; but what it was I could not conceive—except that the suspicion was strong upon me that, written within The Closed Book, was some remarkable and highly profitable secret, as indeed the writer himself alleged.

Again I strolled up Harpur Street past the silent house, keenly examining its every detail.

I noticed, to my surprise, that during my brief absence the Venetian blind of one of the first-floor windows had been drawn up half-way, and that on a table quite close to it stood a small stuffed animal—a tiny bear cub I made it out to be. There was a feeble light within, as though the big room was lighted only by a single candle, and it none of the brightest.

At the end of the street I crossed and returned past the house, walking on the opposite side of the way and re-examining the windows.

Yes, it was evidently a candle burning there, and as I passed I saw a long shadow fall directly across the window, then suddenly disappear.

Could it be that the animal had been placed there as a signal to someone who would pass outside?

Somehow I became convinced that this was so. The blind had been raised just sufficiently to show the small bear cub mounted on its hind-legs and holding a card tray. I recollected having seen one very similar on the table of the Savage Club—a present from one of the members.

My natural cautiousness prompted me to wait and watch for the coming of the person for whom the silent signal was intended—if signal it were; therefore, I lit a cigarette and halted at the dark corner of East Street, the short turning at the end of the thoroughfare wherein the silent house was situated.

As I was dressed only in a thin suit of blue serge, which one generally wears in summer in Italy when not in white ducks, the steadily falling rain soon soaked me through. My straw hat hung clammily on my head, and the water dripped down my neck, rendering me most uncomfortable. There was every prospect of a soaking night—different, indeed, from that clear, rainless sky that I had just left. Ah! how dismal London seemed to me at that hour, jaded, wet, and worn-out as I was! Still, with that dogged determination which some of my enemies have said is my chief characteristic, I remained there watching for the coming of the unknown, who must be privy to the plot.

Time after time as I stood back in the shelter of a doorway, compelled ever and anon to go forth into the rain and keep my vigil, I wondered whether the conclusion I had formed was actually the right one.

The feeble light flickered in the dark room, but showed not the interior, because of the smoky lace-curtains, dingy and yellow. Yet there stood the stuffed bear cub clearly silhouetted, almost startlingly—the only object visible upon that dark, forbidding façade.

More than once I heard footsteps coming from Theobald's Road, and rushed from my hiding-place to encounter the passer-by. But each time I was disappointed. The postman came on his last delivery, but only stopped at the big offices of the Society for the Prevention of Cruelty to Children, almost opposite the house I was watching, then swung round the corner to Lamb's Conduit Street.

A policeman passed with heavy tread, flashing his bull's eye carelessly down the areas and glancing at me inquiringly; then in the roadway through the slush came a man and a woman, Italians, dragging a street-organ wearily homeward to Saffron Hill. I watched them and wondered from what part of Italy they came.

As they went by I heard the man, a strong, black-browed fellow of twenty-seven or so, exclaim, "*Accidenti!*" and knew that he was a Tuscan. The woman (old, brown-faced, and wrinkled) only sighed and dragged harder.

They went forward, turned the corner into Theobald's Road, and a few moments later the strident strains of "Soldiers of the Queen" rang out amid the bustle of the thoroughfare and the roar of traffic. They had evidently stopped before the public-house where I had borrowed the *Directory*, in the hope of earning a last copper or two before relinquishing their day's work.

Attracted by the music, I strolled back towards the spot where they had halted, and as I did so encountered two persons. One was a tall, grey-haired, rather sad-looking old gentleman, dressed somewhat shabbily, wearing an old ulster, but without umbrella; the other was an extremely pretty, fair-haired girl of perhaps twenty-two, pale-faced, and evidently agitated, for she clung to his arm and was whispering something to him as she walked. She was apparently imploring him to hear her; but he went on stolidly, heedless of her words. Her dress was plain, and, it seemed to me, betrayed the pinch of poverty. Like her companion, she had no umbrella, and her plain sailor-hat and black jacket were sodden with the rain.

Her face, however, struck me as one of the most perfect I had ever seen in all my life. That woman whom I had met in the prior's study in Florence was certainly handsome; but hers was of an entirely different type of beauty, a face about which there certainly could be no two opinions, but a face full of tragic force and energy.

This woman, however, bore a sweet expression, rendered the more interesting by that earnest, imploring look as I passed her by unnoticed. Her companion was, it struck me, a broken-down gentleman, while she herself possessed an air of refinement in face and figure, in spite of her shabby attire, that caused me to set her down as no ordinary girl.

Her extreme beauty made me turn after them.

The old man, with his thin, hard face, yet gentle eyes, was still obdurate. She held back, but without a word he closed her arm to his and pulled her forward. He seemed to walk mechanically, while she appeared bent on arresting his farther progress.

Suddenly, as I strolled on behind them, they came in full view of the window and its mysterious signal.

"Ah!" I overheard the old fellow cry in a tone of satisfaction. "See! As I hoped. At last—at last!"

"It means death—death!" the girl added in a tone more hoarse and despairing than ever I have before heard in a woman.

I had been close enough to overhear the words that confirmed my suspicion, and I must confess they held me dumbfounded. I had expected to meet some slinking thief or some hulking receiver of stolen property, who would come to look for the bear cub in the window. Certainly I had, on first encountering the pair, never for a moment believed that the signal had been placed there for them.

The man raised his head again, as though to make certain that his eyes had not deceived him, and as he did so I caught a glance of the girl's white countenance in the wind-blown light of the street-lamp.

Never, to my last day, shall I forget the terrible expression of blank despair in those wonderful eyes. All light and life had died out of her fair face. She looked as though her young heart had, at the sight of that fateful sign, been frozen by some nameless terror.

I had seen plays in which a woman's despair was depicted, but never had I witnessed real despair until that moment. Hideous is the only word that describes it.

At the end of the short thoroughfare they turned and walked back past the house, feigning, however, not to notice the lighted window. The instant I had overheard these strange ejaculations I crossed the road and hurried on round the corner out of sight, in order that they should not detect me following them; but, watching their return, I turned again and went after them into Theobald's Road.

On through the rain they trudged in the direction of Oxford Street, wet to the skin, for the down-pour still continued without cessation, and the pavements shone beneath the gaslights. Neither tram-cars nor cabs attracted them, for it seemed more than likely that their extreme poverty did not allow them the luxury of a conveyance.

The girl's hand was held to her breast as she walked, as though to stay the fierce beating of her heart, but her companion strode on steadily with fixed purpose and deep-knit brows.

I had been loath to relinquish my vigil before that silent house, fearing that the little old woman who had entered there might emerge again and carry my precious Arnoldus with her. Yet, on the other hand, this strange pair, who had come there in secret and read the signal, deeply interested me, and my curiosity impelled me to follow them.

The loud, ear-piercing runs of a street-piano suddenly recalled to my mind the pair of Italians I had noticed ten minutes before; and as we passed them playing before another public-house near Southampton Row I halted for a moment, stepped aside, and spoke to the beetle-browed young Tuscan in his own tongue.

"Listen. I want you to assist me," I exclaimed quickly. "There's no time to lose, and you'll get half a sovereign if you do as I direct. Go back alone to Harpur Street—that short turning you came up ten minutes ago—and watch a house with a stuffed bear in the upper window—Number 106. If anyone comes out, follow her—especially a little old woman. Wait there till I rejoin you. Will you do it?"

"Certainly, signore," was the young fellow's prompt reply. "Number 106, you say? Very well, trust me. My mother, here, can hire somebody to help her home with the *organino*."

"Very well. What's your name?"

"Farini Enrico," he replied, placing the surname first, in Italian style; "born at Ponte Moriano, Provincia di Lucca. The signore knows Tuscany—does he?"

"Yes," I answered. "Wait for me near that house; but don't let anyone see you are watching. I'll return as soon as possible. Lose no time." And I hurried away after the old man in the long ulster and his white-faced companion.

They had gained upon me considerably; but I soon overtook them, satisfied that in any case my watch upon the house would not be relinquished. I had lived sufficiently long in Tuscany to be able to read the Tuscan character, and I saw by the young man's manner that he was not the usual *contadino* who comes to London to grind an organ, but from his speech of quite a superior class. He wore his felt hat slightly askew, and beneath a rather forbidding exterior I detected that he possessed a keen sense of humour. His black, shining eyes laughed merrily when he mentioned his own village—a village I knew quite well, a few miles beyond the quiet, aristocratic old town of Lucca, and I saw that the very fact that I had spoken to him in his own tongue had at once secured him my servant. Italians are such children when you know them thoroughly!

I had little time for reflection, however, for the traffic of Oxford Street, although the night was wet, was considerable; and, while having some difficulty in keeping the pair in sight, I was also compelled to exercise a good deal of precaution in order to avoid recognition as the man who had encountered them in Harpur Street.

On they went at the same pace, heedless of the drenching rain, turning into Regent Street, then into Maddox Street, and across Grosvenor Square into Grosvenor Street, the centre of the West End. Suddenly, however, to my amazement, they ascended the steps of one of the best houses in the latter street; and the man, taking a latch-key from his pocket, opened the door with an air of proprietorship, and a moment later both disappeared from view, the door closing behind them.

Such a house, a veritable mansion in one of the most expensive thoroughfares in London, was the very last place I would have suspected to be their abode.

I repassed, and saw that it had been recently repainted, and presented a smart and handsome exterior. Flowers bloomed in the window-boxes, and a striped awning was spread over the portico. I noted that the number was 62A, and the next house I recognised as Viscount Lanercost's. The manner in which the shabby-genteel pair had slipped into the house showed secrecy, and yet the confident way in which the old man opened the door betrayed that he was no stranger to the place.

Again I had recourse to the pages of that book of revelation, the *London Directory*—which I obtained in a bar at the end of Park Lane, frequented mostly by gentlemen's servants—and there I found that the occupier was the Earl of Glenelg, the wealthy Scotch peer and ex-Under-Secretary, whose name had long been familiar to me, as no doubt it was to my readers, through the columns of the newspapers.

Could it be possible that the man in the shabby ulster for whom that mysterious signal had been placed in the window was actually his lordship himself?

If so, who was his white-faced companion—the beautiful woman who was terrorised?

Chapter Thirteen
What the Watchers Saw

Though utterly fagged out, I hailed a passing cab and drove back to the corner of Harpur Street, where, in the shadow, about half-way along the short thoroughfare, I discovered the young Italian keeping a watchful eye upon the house with the sign of the bear.

"No one has emerged, signore," he said to me in Italian. "I was here a few minutes after you spoke to me."

The blind was still up, and the signal still exhibited, the inmates evidently being unaware of the secret visit of the strange pair.

What connection could Father Bernardo and the old hunchback Graniani, away in Italy, have with that mysterious household?

"Has anyone passed up the street during my absence?" I asked the merry-eyed Enrico.

"Several people, signore. One man, well-dressed, like a gentleman, stood for a moment looking up at the window yonder as though he expected to see someone there. But he was apparently disappointed, and passed on."

"What kind of man?" I inquired eagerly. "Describe him."

"A signore with small, fair moustache, about forty. He carried an umbrella, so I could not see his face very well. He was tall, and walked erectly, almost like an officer. A four-wheeled cab waited for him up at the corner."

"He didn't actually pass the house?"

"No, signore. He merely walked down here sufficiently far to obtain a view of the window; then, having satisfied himself, turned back again." In reply to my question, Enrico told me that he lived with his mother in Kirby Street, Hatton Garden, the thoroughfare running parallel with Saffron Hill. They have been five years in London: five sad, despairing years. Ah, the English! they were not *cattiva*. Oh, no! It was their amazing climate that made them what they were. He pitied London people. How happy they would all be if they only lived under the blue sky of rural Tuscany! And so he went on, just as every poor Italian does who is doomed to the struggle and semi-starvation of life in our grey metropolis.

I read the young fellow's character like a book. He had served his military service at Bologna, and had been waiter in the officers' mess. Then he and his mother emigrated to London from Genoa, attracted by the proverbial richness of the *Inglese* and the report that waiters in restaurants were well paid. On arrival, however, he had soon discovered that the supply of Italian waiters was much in excess of the demand; therefore, he had been compelled to invest the ten pounds he had in a second-hand organ, and he and his mother picked up a living as best they could in the unsympathetic streets of London.

He seemed a good fellow, quite frank, and possessing that easy-going, careless manner of the true Tuscan, which never deserts him even when in circumstances of direst poverty. Your true son of the Tuscan mountains looks at the bright side of everything; a child in love, a demon in hatred, over-cautious with strangers, but easy and tractable in everything. I chatted to him for some twenty minutes, at the end of which time I resolved that he should assist me further in my investigations.

I told him how I had only arrived from Italy a few hours ago, and he grew at once excited. My train had actually passed across the rippling Serchio within a few miles of Ponte Moriano, his own village! I told him of my long residence in Tuscany, a fact which attracted him towards me; for seldom your poor Italian of the curb becomes acquainted with an Englishman who understands his ways and his language. And when I explained that I wished him to assist me in a very important and secret undertaking he at once announced his readiness to do so.

"Very well," I said, giving him the half-sovereign I had promised. "Go across to the public-house in Theobald's Road and get some supper quickly, for I want you to remain on watch here all night. I must rest and sleep for a few hours; but we must ascertain who goes and comes here. Above all, we must follow anyone carrying a parcel. A book was stolen from me in Italy, and it has been taken there."

"I quite understand," was his response; and a few moments later he left me alone while he went to obtain something to eat.

During his absence I took out a card and wrote upon it the name of the hotel to which I had decided to go because it was in the vicinity and he could call me, if necessary—the Hotel Russell.

When he returned a quarter of an hour later I gave him instructions, telling him that if he wished to call me urgently during the night he might run round to the hotel, where I would leave instructions with the night porter, who would without a moment's delay bring up to my room the card he held in his hand.

Then, jaded, wet, and hungry, I took a cab to the hotel, and sent down to Charing Cross for my bag, which I had left in the cloak-room there. In half an hour I had a welcome change of clothes and sat down to a hearty supper.

In a flash, as it were, I had returned from the charm of Tuscany into my own circle—the complex little world of literary London. That night I sat over a cigar prior to turning in, thinking and wondering. Yes, since that moment when I had bought the poisoned manuscript the world had used me very roughly. That there was a plot against me I felt certain.

Midnight came, and from my balcony on the third floor I stood watching the falling rain and the hansoms coming up from the theatres and crossing the square on their way northward. My presence in London again seemed like a dream, sick as I was of the sun-glare of the Mediterranean. My natural intuition told me that I should never return to Italy. My old friend Hutchinson would see that my collection of pictures, china, old furniture, and other antiques was packed and sent to me. He had rendered me many kindnesses in the past, and would do so again, I felt sure, for he was one of my most intimate friends.

I was soundly asleep when, of a sudden, I heard a loud rapping at the door.

"A man wants to see you, sir. He's sent up your card," exclaimed a voice in response to my sleepy growl.

I rubbed my eyes, and recollected that the voice was the night porter's.

"Very well," I replied. "I'll be down at once;" and, rising, I slipped on my things hastily, glancing at my watch and finding it to be five o'clock—four o'clock in English time, as I had not altered my watch since leaving Italy.

In the grey of dawn at the door below I met Enrico, who, speaking excitedly in Italian, said:

"Something has happened, signore. I do not know what it is; but half an hour ago a little old lady came out of the house hurriedly, and called a doctor named Barton, who has a surgery in Theobald's Road, next the fire-engine station. She seemed greatly excited, and the doctor hurried back with her. He's there now, I expect."

In an instant the truth became apparent. Someone had attempted to open The Closed Book as I had done, and had become envenomed.

I explained but little to Enrico; but together we hurried back through the dim, silent thoroughfares to Harpur Street.

I felt a certain amount of satisfaction that the thieves should suffer as I had suffered. Like myself, they had opened The Closed Book at their own risk and peril.

The house, like its neighbours, was in total darkness, save a flickering candle-flame showing through the dingy fanlight, denoting that Doctor Barton was still within. I asked the young Italian how he knew the doctor's name, and he replied that it was engraved on the brass plate on the door.

Within myself I reconstructed the whole story. An unknown inmate of the house had been poisoned, and the doctor—a friend most probably—had been hurriedly summoned. Was he aware of the antidote, as Pellegrini in Leghorn had been? Poisoning is not the usual recreation of the law-abiding Londoner, and few general practitioners, even Harley Street specialists, would care to undergo an examination upon Tanner's "Memoranda on Poisons," nearly out of date as it may be.

My chief object was to regain possession of my property. I had discovered at least two persons interested in it—namely the old gentleman and the sweet-faced young woman who had entered that smart house in Grosvenor Street. There only remained for me to fix the identity of the unknown person within that dingy old house in Harpur Street.

The doctor emerged at last when near five o'clock, and it was quite daylight. He was shown out by my fellow-passenger from Calais, who thanked him profusely for his efforts, evidently successful.

For an hour or two I saw nothing could be done; therefore we both relinquished our vigil: Enrico returning to his home behind Saffron Hill to snatch an hour's sleep and some breakfast, and I back to the hotel.

In thinking over all the curious events, I resolved that it was necessary to confide in one or other of my friends in London. At present no one knew that I was back in town; but when they did I knew that a flood of invitations would pour upon me.

As I have already said, it was now my intention to settle down in England, and I was eager to begin house-hunting, so as to have a fitting place ready to receive my antiquarian collection when it arrived from Italy. Some months must elapse before I could be settled in a country house, which I intended; therefore, on reflection, I resolved to accept the hospitality of one of my best friends of the old London days, Captain Walter Wyman, the well-known traveller and writer. He was about my own age, and had earned success and popularity by dint of perseverance and intrepid exploration. Inheriting an ample income from his father, the late Sir Henry Wyman, Knight, the great Wigan ironmaster, he had after a bitter disappointment in love devoted himself to the pursuit of geographical knowledge, and as a result of his travels in Asia and Africa the world had been considerably enriched by information. Fever, however, had seriously impaired his health, and he was at present back in his comfortable chambers in Dover Street, where he had only a few weeks ago invited me to stay if I came to town.

I decided to accept his hospitality in preference to the comfortless hotel life, which, after some years of it in various places on the Continent, I abominate. Of all men in whom I might confide, Walter Wyman would be the best. He lived for adventure, and as the world is well aware had had a considerable amount of it during his travels.

At ten o'clock that morning his white-headed old valet Thompson admitted me.

"Why, my dear Allan!" my friend cried, jumping from his chair, where he was enjoying his after-breakfast cigarette, "this is a surprise! You're back, then?"

"Yes," I replied. "I came back suddenly last night, and am going to accept your invitation to stay."

"Of course. You know we wouldn't be friends any longer if you went elsewhere. How long are you over for?"

"For good. I'm going to look out for a cottage or something in the country. I'm sick of Italy at last."

Wyman smiled, offered me a cigarette, and ordered Thompson to bring brandy and soda. Careless, easy-going cosmopolitan that he was, it never struck him that strong drink so early in the morning was unusual.

He was dark, with a rather reddish complexion, tall, well-groomed, well-dressed in a suit of dark-blue, and well set-up altogether. Although several touches of fever had played havoc with him, he nevertheless looked the pink of condition—a fine specimen of English manhood.

When I had lit my cigarette I spoke to him confidentially, and he listened to my story with the utmost attention. In that cozy room, the walls of which were hung with savage arms and trophies of the chase, and the floor covered with the skins of animals that had fallen to his gun, I told him the whole of the strange circumstances, relating briefly the incomplete story as written in The Closed Book and the remarkable conspiracy that was apparently in progress.

When I had described the mysterious visit of the tall old gentleman and the young woman to Harpur Street, and had related how I had followed them to the Earl of Glenelg's house in Grosvenor Street, he jumped up, exclaiming:

"Why, from your description, my dear fellow, he must have been the Earl himself, and the girl was evidently his daughter, Lady Judith Gordon! They've been abroad this two years, and to half London their whereabouts has been a mystery. I had no idea they had returned. By Jove! what you tell me is really most puzzling. It seems to me that you ought to get back that book at any cost."

Chapter Fourteen
The Counsel of Friends

We discussed the best mode of regaining possession of the book, but our conclusions were not very clear.

My friend Walter set about giving old Thompson orders to prepare my room, for he was one of the few bachelors who could afford to keep a spare guest-chamber in his flat. It was a hobby of his that his chambers should remain in just the same order during his absence as when at home. He had been travelling sometimes for two years at a stretch, and yet when I had called there I found old Thompson just as prim as usual, merely replying to callers, "Captain Wyman is not at home, sir." Thompson was a wonderful servant, and had been old Sir Henry's right hand until his death. Indeed, he had been in the service of the Wymans for a trifle over fifty years, and appeared to treat Walter more as a son than as master.

My friend fully agreed with me that I had done right in engaging Enrico as watcher. He would be useful, and could act as spy in places where we could not afford to be seen. That there was some remarkable conspiracy in progress Wyman was, like myself, convinced; but what it was he failed to comprehend.

We carefully discussed the curious affair, and after an hour of anxious discussion formed a plan of campaign which we promptly proceeded to carry out.

While I remained there resting, he took a cab and called on the doctor named Barton.

When he returned, he explained that he consulted the doctor, and feigning the symptoms of poisoning which I had explained, the unsuspecting medico had at once remarked that only a few hours before he had been called to a similar case. He suggested to Wyman that perhaps both had eaten something unsound purchased at a shop in the neighbourhood.

Then, after receiving a dose, and being compelled to swallow it in order to keep up the fiction, my friend had commenced to chat with the doctor, and learned that the patient he had been called to was a clean-shaven, middle-aged man who had apparently about nine months ago come to live in Harpur Street. The name he gave was Selby, no profession—at least as far as the doctor knew. He had been struck by his rather mysterious bearing. The little old lady was probably a relation, but of that he was not quite sure. The name I had found in the *Directory* was that of the present tenant. Wyman had also approached the subject of The Closed Book; but it was apparent that neither Selby nor the doctor suspected that its leaves were envenomed. The patient had made no remark to the doctor about the book. Barton had found him suffering acutely, and betraying all the symptoms of poisoning; but beyond that he knew nothing.

Yet Wyman's visit had cleared up one or two points, and had given us the name of the man into whose possession The Closed Book had passed.

Presently we went forth again in company, and at the corner of Theobald's Road found the young Italian still vigilant, although palpably worn out and very hungry. Nothing had transpired, we learned. No one had come out of the house; but the little old lady had come to the door and taken in the milk and bread from the baker. She apparently acted as housekeeper.

We dismissed Enrico for four hours, and I took his place, while Walter Wyman went down to the Naval and Military Club, where he declared he was certain to meet a friend of his who was intimate with Lord Glenelg, and from whom he might obtain some information.

"What connection they have with this affair is a profound mystery," he remarked; "just as much of a mystery as the fact they are in London when believed to be abroad. Colonel Brock, my friend, only told me the night before last that they were with friends up at Mussooree, in the north of India."

"Well, it seems they're back again now," I remarked.

"So it appears," was his reply, and he stepped into a hansom and drove down to the club to gather information, leaving me to lounge in the vicinity of that rather dark and cheerless London street.

The weather was damp and muggy, and the continuous traffic in Theobald's Road jarred upon my nerves. Even in the broad daylight the exterior of the house in Harpur Street was dingy, with an air of distinct mystery. The shutters of the area window remained closed; but the stuffed bear cub had now been removed from the upper window, having served its purpose, whatever that might be.

Soon after noon Wyman met me again. He had been active every moment, had seen his friend, and had moreover called at Grosvenor Street under some pretext, only to discover that the Earl and his daughter, having returned unexpectedly from abroad two days ago, had left again that very morning.

Was it that inexplicable signal that had caused the pair to flee from London again?

The reason why they had been both dressed shabbily was now obvious. They were in London in secret, and feared recognition. Walter Wyman's interest was now thoroughly aroused, and he declared his intention of sifting the matter to the bottom.

The question now arose as to the means by which we should get back the book stolen from me. In the bar of the public-house where I had taken refreshment on the previous night we further discussed the matter. To attempt to regain it by interviewing the man Selby would, we felt assured, be in vain, for of such value was it and so widespread the conspiracy that he would probably either deny that it was in his possession or openly defy us. On the other hand, it would be a dangerous matter to commit a burglary there, and more dangerous still to enter forcibly and demand my property. Even Doctor Barton had confessed that there was something puzzling and forbidding about the blustering man's manner and antecedents.

Therefore, we found ourselves at a complete deadlock.

I wished heartily that I had ordered the old woman to be stopped on landing at Dover pier.

Could the police assist us? Wyman thought not, at least not in their official capacity. We should frighten this Mr Selby, and if so would probably lose the precious volume altogether.

We both saw that it was a matter in which there must be no bungling. My friend Wyman was as shrewd a man as any in London, and this fighting with conspirators was work just to his liking. He was one of those men who, in whatever tight corner they find themselves, either at home or abroad, always managed to wriggle out of it.

In the first place, we had no knowledge of the character of the man with whom we had to deal; while, in the second, we were utterly in the dark as to the motive of the conspiracy against me from the moment when the rare Arnoldus had passed into my hand.

That we should act promptly and with firm determination was imperative; but what line to take we knew not.

The more we discussed it the more determined I became to act fearlessly and go straight to the point by going to the police station and demanding the little old woman's arrest. Such a course would bring matters to a head, and yet I still hesitated to show our enemies our hand. At present they were unaware of my presence in London, and surely their ignorance of this would be to our advantage, inasmuch as the looker-on sees most of the game.

I felt that I wanted an expert opinion, and suddenly recollected that in the old days, when I had lived in London before, I had been on friendly terms with a detective-sergeant of the Criminal Investigation Department named Noyes, who had been attached to the Hunter Street Police Station. I had several acquaintances in the Metropolitan police, as most literary men have; but to Noyes I had been indebted more than once for showing me certain phases of unknown London. Therefore I knew that if I sought his advice he would willingly give it.

Leaving Wyman to watch, I therefore took a cab to Hunter Street, and inquired of the inspector on duty for my friend, who, I was informed, had been promoted to the rank of inspector, and was posted at the chief station of the T Division at Hammersmith.

I returned in the cab to Wyman, and then lost no time in following out my quest by going out to Hammersmith.

I found my friend, a loosely built, heavy-jawed man of middle-age, sitting in his upstairs office; and when I entered he rose to welcome me warmly. Then, on telling him that I had come to seek his advice, he settled himself at his plain writing-table to listen.

The story I related interested him just as much as it had Wyman; but now and then he pencilled a note upon the sheet of paper he had instinctively placed before him. I related the whole facts from first to last, concealing nothing. The secret poisoning appealed to him, clever detective that he was, for every man attached to Scotland Yard will tell you that a good many more people die in London of poison annually than ever doctors or coroner's juries suspect.

"Now, what I want is to get my property back again without these people knowing," I explained at last.

"I quite see," he said. "If they knew you had followed them up so quickly it might put an end to their game without you ever knowing what their motive has been. Yes, you want that book back at all costs, but in a secret way. You can easily lay information before the magistrate; and I could, on that, go and search for the stolen property. But that's hardly your game, Mr Kennedy. We must use methods a trifle more—well, artistic, shall we call it?" and his big face broadened into a grin.

"Well now, what do you suggest?" I asked.

But, instead of responding, he asked me for a detailed description of the rare and interesting volume. Then, when I had given it to him, he raised his eyes from the paper whereon he had made some memoranda, and with a mysterious smile asked:

"Would you be willing to leave the affair entirely in my hands, Mr Kennedy? I have an idea that I might, with the assistance of a friend, be able to get hold of the book without this person Selby knowing that it has gone back into your possession. If I attempt it, however, you must not be seen anywhere in the vicinity. Any observation kept upon the old lady or upon this fellow Selby must be done by your friend, Captain Wyman. Would you be inclined to act under my directions and lie low until I communicate with you?"

"Certainly," I answered, although not yet understanding his point.

"If there is a conspiracy, you'll very quickly be spotted if you remain hanging about Harpur Street," he said. "I think, if you're prepared to pay a sovereign or two, that I can get hold of the book for you. Only it will have to be done secretly; and, in order that you should not be suspected of regaining possession of it, you must go away into the country and wait until you hear from me. We don't want them to suspect anything, otherwise we may not be able to solve the mystery of it all."

"I'll leave the whole affair in your hands, Noyes, of course," I responded. "When shall I go into the country?"

"Today. Go where you like, to some place within easy reach of town, and stay there till you hear from me. Don't go back to Harpur Street, because it's too dangerous. You must be recognised sooner or later. I'll find Captain Wyman and explain matters to him. Why not run down to somewhere on the Great Northern, to Peterborough, for instance. It's on the main line, and the first stop of the expresses to the north—an hour and a half from King's Cross. You see I could get down quickly if I wanted to see you, or you could run up if necessary. There's a good old-fashioned hotel—the 'Angel.' I stopped there once when I was after a German bank-note forger, and was very comfortable."

"Very well. I'll go there. That will be my address till I hear from you. Tell it to Captain Wyman, as he may want to write to me."

After some discussion, in which he steadily refused to enlighten me further upon his scheme for getting hold of The Closed Book, we returned together by the underground railway to Charing Cross, where we parted, he to seek my friend Wyman, and I to hide myself in the small provincial town of Peterborough, where I arrived that afternoon about half-past four.

As Noyes had declared, the "Angel" was replete with old-fashioned comfort, a relic of the bygone posting-days and a centre of agricultural commerce on market-days. Except the cathedral, there is very little of interest in the town of Peterborough; for of late years it has been modernised out of all recognition. In itself it is ugly, although situated in the centre of the rich green pasturage of the Nene Valley, a busy place, where the hand of the vandal has been at work everywhere save perhaps in Narrow Street, the small, old-fashioned thoroughfare wherein the "Angel" is situated.

I spent the evening examining the interior of the cathedral, afterwards taking a stroll as far as the village of Longthorpe, and after dinner retired early, for I had not yet recovered from my swift journey across Europe.

The following day passed, and still the next, yet I could only idle there, chafing and anxious regarding the success of Noyes's undertaking. Letters from Wyman showed that, aided by Enrico, he was still keeping observation upon the house, although he had seen nothing further of my friend the detective after his announcement of my departure.

I began to wonder if Noyes had broken faith with me. Yet we had been the best of friends in the old days when I had lived and worked in London; and I thought I knew him well enough to be confident that he would assist me in every way within his power.

Therefore I wandered the streets of Peterborough or lounged in the bar of my hotel, in hourly expectation of some message from him.

His silence was ominous, and my uneasiness increased until, on the third day, I determined to remain inactive no longer.

Chapter Fifteen
The Old Monk's Secret

To idle in a provincial town without friends and without occupation is neither pleasant nor profitable. In London one can always amuse one's self and pass the time; but in dull Peterborough my principal excitement, in addition to visiting the much-restored cathedral and the local museum in the Minster Precincts, was to watch fat stock being sold by auction.

Anxiety consumed me as to what had occurred at Harpur Street, and whether The Closed Book was actually lost to me. I had telegraphed twice to Noyes, Hammersmith Police Station, but had received no response. His silence was in no way reassuring, therefore I resolved that if I heard nothing by nine o'clock that night I would return to London by the last train.

I dined at seven after a dismal day, and while at table the waiter entered the coffee-room where I sat alone, saying that a gentleman wished to see me. Next moment Noyes, dressed like a commercial traveller in dark-blue suit and bowler hat, entered the room.

There was a smile of triumph on his face, from which I gathered instantly that he had been successful. He carried a black leather bag in his hand, and this he opened as soon as the waiter had gone out, saying, as he produced a brown-paper packet:

"I'm glad to say, Mr Kennedy, that I've been able to do the trick. It was a very delicate matter, and the affair presented features and difficulties I had never anticipated."

"Then you've actually got it?" I cried eagerly, opening the parcel and displaying the precious volume.

"There it is, as you see," he laughed. "Only please don't ask how I got possession of it, because I'd rather not say—you understand."

Detectives are apt to be mysterious sometimes, therefore I did not question him further. For me it was sufficient that he had been able to secure it without the thieves knowing into whose possession it had passed. I was well aware of the great circle of criminal acquaintances Noyes had in

London, and I suspected that it was through one of them that the book had been obtained.

"I wired twice to you," I said, when at my invitation he seated himself at the table to join me at dinner.

"I know," was his response. "It was not necessary to reply. In such a case as this patience is everything. You were just a trifle too impatient, Mr Kennedy—if you'll pardon me saying it. I had promised to do what I could, and did so, with the result you see."

I know I deserved this quiet reproof, and admitted it, for patience is one of the many good qualities I do not possess.

He would explain nothing of the means by which he had obtained my property, although he told me one or two strange facts concerning Selby and the little old lady who had travelled from Paris.

"I've seen Selby," he said. "At first I seemed to have a faint idea that I'd seen his face before, and that he was wanted for something. But I've searched at the Yard, and found no photograph resembling him, so I suppose I must be mistaken. The old woman's name is Mrs Pickard. She knows several foreigners living at different places, mostly people in good circumstances."

"You haven't seen anything of a tall, dark, and very handsome young woman—Italian probably?" I hazarded, wondering if the actual thief had arrived in London.

"No. Captain Wyman is still on the watch. He's as good as any man I've ever had under me—quite professional in his methods. And that young Italian, too, seems a smart sort of chap. You picked him up quite accidentally, I think you said?"

I explained how I had sought Enrico's aid, and what opinion I had formed of him.

"Well," Noyes remarked, as he gulped down a glass of Bass with evident gusto, "I shall return tonight, but you'd best remain here, Mr Kennedy; or, if not here, somewhere in the country. You must not be seen in town. Bury yourself away from there, and leave all the watching to us. You've got the book, therefore be careful it don't go out of your possession again."

"Trust me," I laughed. "When I've gone through it all I shall put it in a bank for safe keeping."

"It ain't the sort of thing to leave about if the leaves are really poisoned, as you say. I've been afraid to open the thing," he remarked, half apologetically.

"I'm tired of this place," I said, longing to return to London.

"Then go somewhere else—to the seaside, for instance. You're quite near the east coast places here."

"A good idea," I exclaimed. "I'll go to Sheringham tonight. I stayed at the 'Grand' once, and will go there again."

"Very well," he said, and we concluded our meal and lit cigars afterwards, chatting over the various remarkable features of the mystery. My decision to go to the little watering-place, now becoming so popular, pleased him. My absence from London was imperative, he declared, and at Sheringham, if dull, I could at any rate get some golf. How long I would be compelled to remain there he had no idea.

"Let me complete my inquiries," he said. "They are very difficult; but I don't despair as long as Captain Wyman will continue to assist me. Perhaps, when you've deciphered the whole of the book, a further clue will be furnished to the motive of all this secrecy and conspiracy."

"I shall resume at Sheringham tomorrow," I replied. "I expect to discover some secret which will throw further light on recent events."

At nine o'clock, after an exchange of expressions of confidence, we drove together to the Great Northern station, and after seeing him into the up-express. I took the slow night train, *via* Wisbech and South Lynn, to the clean little fishing-village of Sheringham, which Harley Street has recently discovered to be so healthy, and which society is now commencing to patronise.

I took a private sitting-room at the "Grand," overlooking the promenade, an expensive luxury to be sure, but I wanted quiet and privacy in my investigations; and next morning, after my breakfast had been cleared, I first assumed a pair of thick driving-gloves, and then reopened The Closed Book at the page where my reading had been so abruptly broken off.

I think, in order to reproduce the record plainly, it will be best to give the transcript just as I copy it from the time-stained poisoned pages now before me, with all its quaintness of expression and orthography, only eliminating the contractions and some obscurities.

What I further deciphered, then, was as follows:

"Reader who darest to seeke within this BOOK, I commend me unto you as heartily as I may think, trusting in God that you be (the which Jesu continue) in good prosperity. It is not out of your remembrance that my lord of Valentinois had sworn to kill me because I had given help unto my lady Lucrezia, and had more than once used the knife contayning the antidote, striking as I had stricken my lord of Pesaro those whom he attempted to poison. Hence my lady, seeing that her lord was dead, and right knowing her helplessness, induced me to recover her jewels and flie to England with them, there to await her ladyship's arrival, her intention being to seeke the gracious intercession of our lord Cardynal Wolsey, who had befriended her when in Rome. Loth as I was to leave my lady alone in the Vatican, that place of so many black deeds, I saw that to serve her I must obey, hence did I at once repair unto the spot near unto the village of Monte-Compatri, where I had concealed my lady Lucrezia's wondrous jewels within a strong casket of wood and iron. The Borgia emeralds, be it knowne unto you, were the finest the world had ever seen, and were once the property of the Great Turk, the Sultan Muhammed, who is said to have obtained them from the ruins of ancient Babylon. They were set in the forme of a neck-collar, each stone as large as a mann's thumb. And preserved with them were diamonds, pearls, and rubies of value enormous, and with the which was the sealed phiall of the secret venom and the antidote. All these did I recover securely, and having bade farewell unto my lady, journeyed to England after many adventures that need not be herein recounted. Arrived in London, I again took up my lyving in the house of my friend Sir George Goodrick, in East Chepe, on the iij. daye of January in the yeare of our Lord 1501.

"For the space of one year and two monthes I remained in London, until a messenger came from my lady with the amazing news that she had become wedded unto the lord Don Alfonso D'Este, heir of the lord Duke Ercole of Ferrara, and, having removed to Ferrara, did not intend travellynge to England at that presente. In her letter she told me how that at last she had wedded a man she loved, and that with her confessor she was seeking the forgiveness of her God for the black deedes her brother Cesare had compelled her to commit. Furthermore, she tolde me that knowing her jewels were in safe keeping in my hands she wished me to still retaine them in their secret hyding-place until such time as she should arrive to see mi lord Cardynal Wolsey at Hamton. She pointed out that I, well knowing of the terrible deedes commited by her, and therefore havying been more than once her assistant in her murderous treachery, was as guiltie as she. The blood of many of those who had been envenomed was upon my hands, therefore it was for me to make penance and seek forgiveness.

"Her words were those of a penitent woman, and they caused me to think. She was happy with her husband, but uneasy on account of her guiltiness of mind. She was repentant, and wished me to be so. For a long time I thought over her words, until at last becoming convinced that being privy to those foul poison-plots wherein death was dealt secretly to every enemy, I was also an assassin and accursed. Wherefore, after much reason, I resolved to hide mi lady's treasure and enter as a novice the order of Saint Benedict at their great abbey of Croylande in Lincolnshire, hoping that the rigours of a monastic life would open up to me the glories and comforts of religion, of the which I stood sorely in need.

"Please it you, reader, to understand that I repaired to Croylande, and having sunk the casket of my lady's jewels in the fish pond one hundred and thirty and one paces south-east of the grand altar of the abbey, midway between the shores, I entered as novice of the sacred order, Roberte de Deepynge then being abbot. Through eighteen full years did I make penance, leading a religious life and making peace with my God. Our abbey was one of the finest and well-favoured in all England, and my lyfe was spent mostlie in religious work among the people. At times I visited the abbeys of Peterborough, Thorney, Fynshed, Fountance (Fountains), St. Albans, and our great Glassynburie (Glastonbury), travelling much, and making many and long pilgrimages. Much that I did see at Glassynburie was indeed of a scandal; but my bounden duty most humbly remembered, I speak not of the evil deeds of those supposed to live in sanctitie. One day in April, when I passed across the tryangular bridge at Croylande towardes the Abbeye, having been to the priory of Castor to visit the beadsman Willyam Petre, a monk, my friend named Malcolm Maxwell, brought unto me a travel-stained messenger from Ferrara, who tolde to me the death of my lady Lucrezia, and gave unto me a letter written to me an hour before she died. She urged me to continue my lyfe of religion and peace with God, and sente me as her dying wish that her pryceless jewels should remain concealed because a curse rested upon them. She wished that no man should see or touch them, but her will was that they might only be used in the cause of the holy Catholic church. And for that purpose she left the treasure in mi hands, together with the poison-phiall and the secrete antidote to be used if occasion warranted in the same cause, these also beynge concealed with the marvellous gems in the mud of the fish pond. This news overburdened my heart with greefe, and I vowed unto God (praised be Him) that I would faithfully fulfil my lady's commandments, and still continue in my unfained fidelity of my allegiance. Wherein reducing to remembrance the prised memories and perpetual renowned facts of the famous Duchess, yet having the reader's most benign and gracious favour, I resolved to still remain in the sanctuarie of the abbey, although I hadde in mi possession some of the finest jewells known unto the world, and the whych, if solde, might keepe me in prosperity all my days."

Chapter Sixteen
Continues the Record

Pausing in my work, I rose and looked out across the sunlit sea. Then, eager to gain further knowledge, returned and continued the deciphering, as follows:

"Of the years I remained at Croylande, growing old in years, and often visiting with my friend Malcolm Maxwell the beadsman Petre of Castor, beyond the town of Peterborough, I speak not, save to say that much happened in London of the king's marriages and or our lord-Cardynall Wolsey's disfavour with his majesty.

"But now, reader, another thing did happen in the year 1537 that unquieted our abbot and all of us—namely, that the king intended to suppress and seize our abbey, as his majesty had seized the houses of Romburgh, Fyneshed, Walsinghame, and Bury St. Edmonds. Whereupon our abbot, John Welles, a holy and well-beloved man, wrote unto Thomas Cromwell, chief secretary to the king's highness, this letter:

"'With due reverence I command me unto your honourable lordship, humbly asserteing the same that I send your lordship by this bearer part of our fen fish, right meekly beseeching your lordship favourably to accept the same fish, and to be good and favourable, lord, unto me and my poor house, in such cause as I hereafter shall have cause to serve unto your good lordship, and I with my bretheren shall daily pray to our Lord God for the long continuance of your lordship in health.—At Croylande the xxv. day of March, by your daily orator, John, abbot there.'

"But it pleased not the King's Secretary that our splendid abbey should be spared, and the gift of our fish was unavailing. The king's highness recognised not the good and true service done to his grace, and gave not his favour unto us. Because of its isolation our abbey became a place of refuge in those black days of the king's wrath against us. Through those years I had lived a quiet life in the cloister, mostly employed in prayer and meditation, for of a vertie I was penitent, and prayed for the repose of the soul of my Lady Lucrezia. Alas, the secular spirit prevailed in our land, and we received worde at the first daybreak in December 1538 that the commissioners, William Farre, Robert Southwell, and Thomas Myldemay, who had seized the monastery of St. Androse in Northampton for the king's use, intended to seize likewise our house and lands. Therefore did our good abbot John take me aside with Malcolm Maxwell and held counsel with us how best to conceal owr altar plate and jewels, of the which we held a goodly quantitie. Secretly, knowing how safe a place was the fish ponde, wherein I had already hidden the Borgia treasure, I suggested it, and that night, leaving sufficient silver to satisfy his majesty's commissioners, the three of us took the great silver altar and a goodlie number of the Abbey treasures, and, placing the latter in three chests bound with iron, sank them deep in the mud in the centre of the pond. Only Maxwell and myself were privy to the secret that we had taken from the abbey treasury the things that follow."

In Old English the list read:

"i. greate altar of sylver, mayde by the Abbat Richard in 1281.
i. great chalyce of golde gyven by Thomas de Bernack in the yeere 1356.
iiij. large chalyces of sylver.
iiiij. patens.
i. alms bason.
viij. cuppes of sylver.
iii. cuppes of golde.
ii. golde candelsticks.
iiij. golde crucifixes.
viij. cuppes of sylver.
ii. sylver boxes full of the precious stones tayken from the altars and
robes. Some of great syze.
iii. small boxes of other jewells."

Continuing, the record stated:

"Of the rest, we left two chalices and other things for the king's highness, the Abbot knowing well that our house must be destroyed and desecrated, and that we must be scattered. The night was dark, with thicke fen-mist, when we carried forth the heavy chests and let them down noiselesslie into the water at a spotte at the opposite end to where through many years my own treasure lay well concealed. The ponde was deepe, and dried not in summer, beinge fed by many springs, and well fylled wyth good carp for Fridays. Malcolm kept watch by the south door while I, wyth the Abbot, sank owr treasure in the deepest parte of the lake. Then, when we returned in silence, we all three went into the Abbot's chamber and there swore to Almighty God to ever preserve the secret, tayking oath that neither should seeke to recover the hidden treasure withoute the consent of the other two. We knew that our glorious abbey was doomed, and wished to save what we could for the Church's benefit. And we were not mistaken, for three dayes later the Commissioners came with Thomas Cromwell himself, and our good Abbot was forced to surrender unto them everything. Thus we monks, to the number of one hundred and sixty and four, were dispersed; and the king's men stripped our great church, seized all that was of value, sold the bells and the lead, and then broke and battered down the walls. Seeing their ill-intentions, some of us still remayned in refuge in houses of the people in the neighbourhood, I finding hospitality at an inn called The Oak Branch at Eye, while Malcolm was at Thorney, owr abbot having departed to London.

"Through a full month we watched the destruction of owr magnificent Abbey, how that Southwell's men did break owr statues and tore down the very tower, I lingering there because of my own treasure concealed and unable to recover it lest my actions should be noted. Once I heard rumour that Southwell intended to pump out the lakes, and surely the pump was sette up. Then did I tremble, well knowinge that all that we had hidden must be discovered. Cromwell, however, considered that they had seized all of which we were possessed, and luckily gave orders for the work of pumping to be stopped, an order which pleased me mightily, for every other hole and corner was well searched for anything hidden, especially for books and proclamations against the king's actions.

"On the fifth of February 1539, my friend Malcolm Maxwell, who like miself had been compelled by the king's commissioners to discard his habit, came to me, saying that he had decided to return to Scotland, his own country, and offered me asylum in his brother's house, the castel of Treyf, in Galloway. His invitation accepted, I managed one night by the light of the moon to drag the fish pond, and after many attempts succeeded in recovering the casket of wood and iron that I had brought from Italie, no one knowinge of my actions. To Malcolm, who was older than myself, I declared that my casket contained my Booke of Hours and a relic of Saint Peter—the which I had brought from Rome—for he knew not that it really contained my dead lady's jewels and her secrete phials. As touching our journey north by the great roade through Stamford and York to Carlisle I will not speak, save to say that we hadde manie adventures, and more than once I was in imminent peril of losing mi precious casket. On the borderlandes all was in disorder, and the moss-troopers were ever ready to steal and kill. While passing by the high road through Dumfries and Dalbeatie we went into the great Abbey of Dundrennan, and prayed before the silver image of Our Lady there; and also we made a pilgramage to St. Ninian's shrine, afterwards passing across the hills and glens by Auchencaim and over Bengairn, and thence to the river Dee, where, upon an island, stood the greate grim castle of Treyf, once the impregnable fortalice of the Black Douglas, but now in the possession of my Lorde Maxwell of Terregles, an ancient baron of great landes, and brother of Friar Malcolm.

"In this, the wildest part of Galloway, we were received warmly by my lord of Treyf, who on the nighte of our arrival was entertaining in the great banquetting-hall John Gordon of Lochinvar, who had juste been to France with the Scottish King incognito in search of a wife; Gylbert Earl of Cassilis; David Vaus, abbot of Soulseat; his brother John Vaus of Bambarrock; with the lairds of Garlies and Sorby. The talk as we ate our venison with wheat bread was of how the two Galloway lairds the Macdowalls of Freuch and of Mindork were invadinge Arran with fire and sword, and how they had burned the castle of Brodick to the ground. By their conversation I knewe well that although my lord Maxwell was steward of Kilcudbricht (Kirkcudbright) and keeper of Treyf, which the kinge had wrested from the Douglas; he was, however, not truly loyal, and that there was conspiracy against the king just as there had been in that same stronghold in the days of the Black Douglas.

"Still far from it that I, a houseless fryar, should utter complaints, for mi lord, not havynge seen his brother for fifteen years, treated us both with greatest courtesy, and gave us asylum for as long as we wished, assigninge to us rooms in the tower that commanded the sweep of the river lookynge up towards Greenlaw. Through a full year I remained with my lorde Maxwell, riding often against the Gordons of Kenmuir, the Douglases of Drumlanrig, and the Agnews of Locknaw, having well concealed my treasure-casket in a safe spot upon the island. Old in yeares, yet much fierce warfare did I see across the hills and treacherous mosses of Galloway, often ridinge over the border against the English with Malcolm, who, like myself, had readilie doffed the habit for the breastplate. We besieged the castle of Kenmuir, and took its lord prisoner to Stirling, as also we did the lord of Orchardton, Willyam Cairns.

"At this time our King Henry of England had shaken off the Holy Father's authority, and the doctrines of the reformed religion were widelie spreading among the people. In Scotland, too, a greate national change was unavoidably approachinge; for religious reformation had been long advancing, and doctrines in opposition to the Romish Faith had been propagated in Galloway by the Gordons of Airds. The Bible, which had been locked up from the laity by the clergy, was now procured in numbers, and secret meetings were beinge held in the woods to read it, for even possession of a copie of the sacred book was a penal offence. Of a verity the persecution was terrible, for many were imprisoned or committed to the flames.

"Treyf was a goodly stronghold, square, surrounded by a barbican and flanked at each angle by a circular tower, secured in front by a deep fosse and vallum, while the island itself was surrounded by the rapid waters of the Dee; and my lord Maxwell, with the kinge's authority behind him, was the most powerful of the lords of Galloway. One night, however, we returned from ridyng against the English from Lochmaben. Our Galloway troopers, with Lochinvar at their head, had utterly routed a large body of Somerset's men, and as in the sundown my charger's heels clattered on the drawbridge of Treyf, Malcolm, who had remained, came forward to greet me with pale face, and took me up into my chamber where we could speak privately. He told me that the conspiracy against the kinge, formed by his brother, had been discovered, and that a mounted messenger had arrived from Helen Lady of Torhouse, who was with the Court in Edinburgh, to warn him that his majesty had sent an armed force on his way to us. My lord Maxwell's intentions regarding an alliance with Somerset to the detriment of the Scottish king had been betrayed by one of the conspirators, Johnston of Lockwood, and the messenger alleged that five thousande men were already at Dumfries wyth orders to storm and take Treyf, with my lord Maxwell, his brother Malcolm, and myself, who, cominge from England as we dyd, were beleeved to have been in the plot, and to also arrest young Gordon of Lochinvar, Abbot Vaus of Soulseat, and Gylbert Earl of Cassilis, at their various houses. My lord Maxwell was absent wythe James Earle of Bothwell at Earlston, but a messenger was sent in hot haste to him, while Malcolm and myself tooke counsel as to how we should act. My lord's fair daughter Margaret was in the castle, and we saw that to save her and ourselves we must all three flie. They were hastily preparinge while I had gone in secret to secure my precious casket, when the guard suddenly announced that the advance guard of the kinge's army was already at Treyf Mains. Not an instant was to be lost, therefore, compelled to leave my ladie Lucrezia's jewels in their safe hiding-place, I sprang into the saddle of a fresh charger, which one of the troopers led to me, and, following Malcolm and the fair Margaret, dashed across the drawbridge and along the frail wooden brydge that connected the island wyth the opposite banke. Scarce had my horse's hoofs touched the road than the weak supports of the bridge were knocked away, fell in pieces in the river, and were swept down the stream, while at the same instant the portcullis fell, and the rattling of chains told that the drawbridge was drawn up and the stronghold isolated and rendered impregnable.

"The fair daughter of Maxwell proved a good horsewoman, and through the long dark night we all three rode our hardest, well knowinge that capture meant either death or imprisonment in the dungeons of Edinburgh. Indeed, our departure was noted, and for some hours we were hotly pursued; but Margaret Maxwell knew the countrie as well as any moss-trooper, and she led us safely through the Glenkens into the giant solitudes of Carsphairn; then, after a rest, taking a circular route, we rode along the wild shore of Loch Doon, over the Rhinns of Kells, and across to Auchenmalg Bay, where we arrived in sadde plight and exhausted on the second night. Through the whole of Galloway the kinge's men were searchinge for us, and we heard that my lord Maxwell had already fallen into their hands near Loch Ken, while Treyf was holding out against the besiegers. To remain in Scotland longer was impossible, although I grieved in secrete that I had no means by which to recover my precious casket. Ours was truly a position of gravest peril."

Chapter Seventeen
Contains Forbidden Knowledge

I had read almost to the end of old Godfrey's record, and paused for a cigarette. I had written so much that my hand was tired; but it was certainly a highly interesting story, and threw a new light upon Lucrezia Borgia and her crimes, as well as presenting us with a secret chapter of the history of the dissolution of the monasteries by Henry VIII. From an antiquarian point of view the record was, therefore, a most valuable find.

Eager to learn the whole I flung away my cigarette when only half consumed, and again turned to, penning each word as I puzzled it out, and as I now copy it out for you:

"Wyth a sum of gold did I bribe a fisherman to take us in his boat to Maryport, in England, where the wrath of Kyng James could not reache us. In company we travelled to York, where I left Malcolm and his neice with their kinsmen who lived close by the city, and continued my way to London, filled with regret that I had been competed to leave my treasure in hiding on account of a false suspicion against me, and yet not daring to return to Treyf, now that it was in possession of the hateful king's men. What towardness or intowardness I saw while at that castle on the Dee I need not inform you, or what adventures occurred to me in London, except to say that I soon became seized by a desire to return to Italy, the which I did, journeying to Florence, and there reassumynge the religious habyt and enteringe the monastery of Certosa, and am now ending my dayes within the cloister there.

"Please it you to understand, my reader, that on enteringe this monastery aforesaid I became so troubled with the past that I have penned in brief, this ninth day of February, 1542, all that happened to me, in order to leave on recorde the fiendish crimes of the Borgia; to show how my Lady Lucrezia was but the unwilling agent of His Holiness and the Duke Cesare; to affirm that my connection wyth the secret envenoming was in my poor lady's interests and for her protection; and, lastly, to leave on record the exact place within Treyf's grim walls where lie concealed my lady's jewels, together with the secret phials, the small casket that contains emeralds, the worth of which be sufficient to found the fortune of a great house. As touching the family of Borgia, the evil they have done is herein written in this Closed Book, just as it is written in the solemn booke above the which no man can observe.

"A curse resteth upon all the Borgia, save my lady Lucrezia, so also there resteth a curse upon him who shall attempt to take my lady's jewells for his own uses. Already the knowledge gained by you from my record must prove fatal, as I have by preface forewarned you, inquisitive reader, therefore it were best if you sought no further to understand the spot where the treasure lieth hidden. Still, as I perceive that it is my bounden duty to place on record the spot where the casket lieth concealed now that my life is so short a span, in order that the jewels may rot be lost for ever, I write these instructions which, before actinge upon, you must note very carefully, otherwise the secret place of concealment can never be discovered. And further, be it recollected that the jewels have upon them the blood of innocent victims, and that a curse will fall upon the finder providing they are not sold and half the proceeds given to the poor. Heed ye this!

"Item: Directions for recovering the casket:

"Go unto the castle at half-past three of the clocke when the sun shines on September the sixth, and followe the shadow of the east angle of the keep forty and three paces from the edge of the inner moat, then, with the face turned straight towardes Bengairn, walk fifty and six paces. Seek there, for my lady Lucrezia's treasure is hidden at a playce no man knoweth save Malcolm Maxwell; but the secret of whych thou mayest discover if thou wilt again face death.

"But heed thys my warning, ye who hast gayned this knowledge. Evil be upon ye and eternal purgatory if ye dare take my lady's treasure for your own uses without devoting one-half to actes of charity.

"Seek both at Treyf and in the lake at Croylarde, and thy diligence shall be well rewarded by that which thou shalt find.

"Item: How to discover the place at Treyf:

"First find a piece of ruined wall of greate stones, one bearinge a circle cut upon it as large as a manne's hande. Then, measuring five paces towards the barbican, find—"

The next page contained the quaint ending which I have already reproduced.

A page of The Closed Book was missing—the most important page of all!

The folios containing the secret record were not numbered like the rest of the volume; but on closely examining the place I found that the important folio of vellum had been torn out.

I wondered if it was possible that Selby had read the book just as I had done, and having gained the secret had abstracted the leaf whereon minute directions for the recovery of the treasure had been written. That he had been seized with symptoms of poisoning was a clear proof that he had been examining the envenomed pages.

Suddenly recollecting, I turned back to the two roughly drawn plans in the centre of the record, wondering if either would give a clew to the whereabouts of the treasure. The reason of the word "treyf" that was scrawled in the margin of one of them, and had so puzzled me, was now rendered plain. The plan no doubt concerned the ancient castle of Treyf, and it seemed more than likely that by its aid I might succeed in discovering the hiding-place of the Borgia emeralds and the vial of Lucrezia's secret poison.

The other plan, bearing no name and no distinguishing mark, told me nothing.

I rose, and, standing at the open window, looked out upon the sunlit sea. It was different from the blue, tideless Mediterranean, in sight of which I had passed those seven years of my life, but the breeze from it was more invigorating and the surf whiter and heavier than the watery highway of southern Europe. I stood there, lost in thought.

The secret of the hidden treasure was what old Godfrey Lovel, soldier, courtier, and monk, had written and yet endeavoured to hide, first by his terrible warnings, and secondly by poisoning the pages of the record with that deadly secret substance of the Borgias. Malcolm Maxwell had died; and he, being the only person aware of the place of concealment of the casket and its priceless contents, had conceived it to be his duty to leave that record, yet so to guard it that any who sought to open The Closed Book would die mysteriously.

I recollected the very narrow escape I had had. The very gloves now upon my hands were, in all probability, poisoned.

Turning again to the table, I reread the directions given as far as the missing folio, carefully comparing it with the transcript I had made, and finding no error. Then, closing the precious book and packing it away in the stout paper, I took it to the hotel manager to be placed in his safe.

Certainly the story therein written was a remarkable and interesting one. Treasures were apparently concealed both at Crowland Abbey and at Treyf—of the whereabouts of which I was at present in the dark, and it seemed to me more than likely that the two plans would show the places where they were hidden. Yet the missing folio was tantalising. Just as the minute directions for the recovery of the Borgia emeralds were commenced, they broke off, leaving me utterly confounded!

Could it be possible that those who had formed this remarkable plot to obtain the book actually knew of its contents? To me it seemed very much as though they did, and, further, that the man Selby had abstracted the missing folio. If he had, then he was in possession of the actual secret of where the casket was concealed!

What I had read of the great treasures of the once magnificent Abbey of Crowland and of the emeralds of the notorious Lucrezia Borgia whetted my curiosity and aroused my eagerness to commence a real treasure hunt in earnest. Stories of buried treasure have always interested me, and I knew that in the troublous times in England, during the dissolution of the monasteries and the civil wars, everyone hid his wealth for fear of seizure. A glance at the correspondence from the King Henry VIII's commissioners to Thomas Cromwell, now preserved in the British Museum, and reporting the dissolution of the various monasteries, shows quite plainly that the abbots and monks hid the greater part of their treasures before the arrival of the king's men, and that the search made for them was usually in vain, so ingeniously did they contrive their places of concealment. It must also be recollected that the monasteries were the richest institutions in England, and that the altars and images of the abbeys were for the most part adorned with gold and gems. Many of the images of Our Lady are known to have been of solid silver and life-size. Little of this enormous wealth of hidden treasure has yet been discovered. Where, therefore, is it, unless buried in the earth? The treasure of the abbot of Crowland was, according to old Godfrey's chronicle, hidden in the fish pond or in that vicinity, a treasure the very list of which caused one to marvel, including as it did the great altar of silver which dated from the thirteenth century; the great chalice of gold, the gift of Thomas of Barnack; four chalices of silver; five patens, an alms basin, eight cups, and an image of Our Lady—all of silver; with two candlesticks, three cups, and five crucifixes in gold, as well as two silver boxes filled with precious stones. Surely, even with the law of treasure-trove as bogey before us, such a valuable collection was worth searching for!

But somehow, as I strolled along the small promenade towards the old village where the bronzed fishermen were just landing their crab-pots and packing their catch for the London market, I could not help being more attracted by the treasure at Treyf. The crafty old Godfrey had written that record so that the treasure he had concealed in Scotland should not become altogether lost. The Borgia emeralds were historic, and the Borgia poison also.

I felt impelled to write to Walter Wyman, explaining what I had discovered, and urge him to aid me in my search. Now that I had discovered the secret contained in The Closed Book I could remain in uncertainty no longer.

That afternoon I took train to Cromer, and in a Gazetteer which I found in the library there I discovered that the place called Treyf was really Threave Castle, a very historic pile of ruins situated on an island in the river Dee in the vicinity of the town of Castle-Douglas, district of Galloway, in the south-west of Scotland, on the line from Carlisle to Stranraer. This information was most gratifying, for it so happened that my old friend Major Fenwicke and his wife had a fine shoot with a splendid old mansion called Crailloch only fifteen miles or so away, and I knew that I should be warmly welcomed in that merriest of circles if I wished to make it my headquarters, for Fred Fenwicke kept open house, and his place was full of visitors year in and year out. A trifle older than myself, he was one of my very best and most trusted friends, therefore I was eager to pay him the visit I had so long promised, and, by reason of living abroad, had been compelled to postpone.

Then, on my return to Sheringham, I wrote a letter to Wyman, telling him briefly of the interesting discovery I had made, and by the same post wrote to Fred Fenwicke, announcing that I was eager to pay him a visit as soon as he could put up both of us. I explained nothing of my object, for if one starts to search for buried treasure one is apt to be met with considerable sarcasm and ridicule.

Here, however, I had in my possession facts that could not be disputed — facts which had resulted in a curious and apparently well-organised conspiracy.

Those poisoned pages held me terrified, now that I knew how fatal was their contact.

Chapter Eighteen
Lady Judith Speaks

The *table-d'hôte* that evening differed little from that at any other seaside hotel. The majority of the guests were holiday-makers from London in smart city-built "lounge-suits," the womenfolk being dressed by the providers of Westbourne Grove or Kensington High Street—some of the men in evening clothes and others not; the majority of women affecting that most handy makeshift, the blouse. A few were sturdy middle-aged men of means, who had come there for golf and not for lounging in beach-tents or promenading on the asphalt: these formed a clique apart.

There was a time, when I was a homeless wanderer, when hotel life appealed to me by reason of its gaiety, its chatter, and its continual change; but after years of it, drifting hither and thither over two continents, I hated it all, from the gold-braided hall porter who turns up his nose at a half-crown tip, to the frock-coated, hand-chafing manager who, for some reason unaccountable, often affects to be thought a foreigner. You may be fond of the airy, changeful existence of food and friends which you obtain in hotels; but I am confident that your opinion would coincide with mine if you had had such a long and varied experience of gilded discomfort combined with elastic bills as had been my lot. Try a modern hotel "of the first order" in Cairo, on the Riviera, or at any other place that is the mode today, in England or out of it, and I think you will agree with my contention.

Many a time for the purposes of my books I had studied the phantasmagoria of life as seen at the *table-d'hôte*, especially in the gambling centres of Aix, Ostend, and the patchouli-perfumed Monte Carlo, where one often meets strange types and with strange stories; but the crowd of the seaside resorts, whether at aristocratic Arcachon or popular Margate, are never any more interesting than the bustle of the London streets.

Therefore, on this night, I left the table quickly, refusing to be drawn into a long scientific discussion by my neighbour on my right, who was probably a very worthy lawyer's clerk on holiday, and evidently knew but a smattering of his subject, and went forth to stroll up over the golf links in the direction of Weybourne.

I wondered what Wyman had discovered regarding the disappearance of the Earl of Glenelg and his connection with The Closed Book. Those strange words of the terrified, white-faced girl, his daughter, still rang in my ears—her face still haunted me. Student of human character that I was, I had never seen terror and despair in a woman's face before. But one is a student always.

Noyes, too, had continued a careful watch upon the house in Harpur Street, where, I had no doubt, the book had been regained by some professional thief. Selby evidently believed that a burglary had been committed, yet feared to inform the police because the only thing taken chanced to be a piece of stolen property. Hence he could only sit down and abuse his ill-luck. Noyes had certainly very neatly checkmated the conspirators, whoever they were or whatever their object—the latter apparently being the recovery of the hidden gold.

For the present, eager as I was to commence investigations, I could only wait.

The sun had set away across the sea facing me, and as I walked over the cliffs a welcome breeze sprang up, refreshing after the heat of the hotel dining-room. The way was lonely and well suited to my train of thought. It led over a place known by the gruesome designation of Dead Man's Hill, and then straight across to the Weybourne coastguard station, standing as it does high and alone on that wind-swept coast. From the coastguard on duty I inquired my way to Kelling Hard, whence I had been told there was a road inland to Kelling Street, which led on over Muckleburgh Hill through Weybourne village and back to Sheringham. The bearded old sailor standing before the row of low whitewashed cottages pointed out a path down the hill, telling me that I should find the road a mile farther on, at a place called the Quag; then, as it was already growing dark, I wished him good-night and swung along the footpath he had indicated.

I am a good walker, and wanted exercise after that long transcription I had made earlier in the day.

Having gone about three-quarters of a mile on that unfrequented path I ascended again to the top of the cliff, where a hedgerow with a gate separated one pasture from another; yet so occupied was I with my own thoughts that I did not notice this gate until I was close upon it.

When, however, I raised my head suddenly I was close upon it, and saw, standing beyond, a woman's figure darkly outlined against the clear afterglow.

I looked again as I came quickly along the path in her direction, and my heart for a moment stood still. The woman was looking straight at me, as though hesitating to come through the gate until after I had passed; and beside her, also regarding my approach with suspicion, stood a big black collie dog.

I drew nearer, and had placed my hand upon the latch when our eyes met again.

No. I was not mistaken! She was the white-faced girl I had seen pass along Harpur Street that night, the woman from whose lips had come that exclamation of blank despair, the woman to whom the sign of the bear was the sign of death.

For a few seconds I believed that my constant thoughts of her had caused my vision to play some sorry trick; but, fumbling clumsily with the gate while she stood aside modestly to allow me to pass, I again reassured myself that it was actually Lord Glenelg's daughter.

Why had she followed me there? That was the first question that arose to my mind, for all these strange occurrences connected with The Closed Book had aroused my suspicion.

She glanced at me once, then dropped her eyes, and held the collie by his collar for want of something else to do. Her face was still pale and slightly drawn, and her eyes betrayed a deep, all-consuming anxiety; but her countenance was, I saw, really more beautiful than it had appeared to me on that wet night in the dismal London streets.

All these details I took in at a single glance. The all-important question was whether it were wisdom to speak to her?

We were strangers. Perhaps she had not noticed me on that night in London—in all probability she had not. Yet, if she were unaware of my existence, why should she follow me to Norfolk?

To speak might not be a very diplomatic move; but I suddenly recollected her despair at seeing the mysterious sign of the bear, and her father's apparent disregard of her future. Such being the case, ought we not to be acquainted?

This argument decided me, and with some hesitation I raised my hat after I had passed through the gate to where she stood, and in faltering tones begged to be allowed to introduce myself.

She frowned with displeasure, and next moment I saw I had made a false move. The golf-playing girl of today, with red coat and masculine manners, will treat a stranger just as a man may treat one. Modesty is, I fear, a virtue that in the modern girl is growing annually rarer, because nowadays if a girl blushes at her introduction to a stranger she is at once pronounced a "gawk," even by her own mother.

But there was nothing masculine about Lady Judith Gordon, only sweetness and a charming simplicity.

"I really have not the pleasure of your acquaintance, sir," she answered in a musical voice, but with a natural chilly hauteur. "I am not in the habit of accepting self-introductions from strangers," she added.

Her reply, if a trifle superior in tone, was nevertheless the only one that could be expected of a modest, high-minded woman.

"I have the honour of knowing you only by sight, I admit," I went on quickly, eager to remove her false impression, my hat still in my hand. "My name is Allan Kennedy, by profession a novelist—"

"You!" she gasped, interrupting me. "You are Mr Kennedy?" And her face blanched in an instant.

"That is my name," I answered, much surprised at its effect upon her. But taking up the cue quickly, I said, "Perhaps I need say nothing further, save that your interests and my own are identical."

She looked puzzled, and declared that she did not understand.

"Then forgive me if I mention a matter that must be distasteful to you, for I only do so in order to show how desirous I am of becoming your friend, if, after inquiries about me, you will allow me."

I said. "Do you recollect the other night dressing in clothes that were not your own, and, accompanied by your father the Earl, paying a secret visit to a certain street in Bloomsbury?"

Her face fell. She held her breath, wondering how much I knew.

"Do you recollect, too, how heavily the rain fell, and how you turned from Theobald's Road into Harpur Street in search of something? You saw the sign—the stuffed bear cub in the window, the fatal sign. Do you deny it?"

She was silent. Her lips twitched, but for a few moments no sound came from them. She was dumbfounded, and unable to speak. At last she stammered:

"I know, I know! But why do you torture me like this," she cried, "you who evidently know the truth?"

"Unfortunately I do not know the truth," I declared. "I may as well tell you, however, that I overheard your exclamation when your eyes fell upon the sign in that dingy upper room, and I followed you both home to Grosvenor Street, determined that if you would allow me I would stand your friend. Because of that I have ventured to introduce myself to you this evening."

"My friend?" she echoed. "Ah! it is all very well to offer me your assistance, Mr Kennedy; but I fear it can be of no avail. My enemies are stronger than you are. They have crushed all my life out of me. My future is hopeless—utterly hopeless," she sighed.

The collie, escaping from her hand, sniffed me suspiciously, and then settled near his mistress.

"Ah, no! there is always hope. Besides, I am utterly in the dark as to the meaning of your words. My surmise, based simply upon logical conclusions, is that our interests are, as I have already suggested, identical. You have heard of me, have you not?"

"I have read your books," was her answer, "and my father has spoken of you."

"He has spoken of me in connection with the sign placed in that window in Bloomsbury?" I suggested.

She nodded. Her splendid eyes met mine mysteriously.

"He is a friend of Mr Selby's?" I ventured.

"I believe so."

"Do you not, then, admit the truth of my suggestion that, our interests being in common, we should establish friendly relations whereby we may defeat our enemies?" I asked.

"I admit the truth of the argument entirely," was her response after a few moments' consideration; "and, although I recognise your kindness in offering to stand my friend, I cannot see how either of us can benefit. I must suffer—till my death."

"Your death?" I cried reproachfully. "Don't speak like that. I know how utterly helpless you are, how completely you have fallen into the hands of these mysterious enemies of yours. Yet I would urge you not to despair. Trust in me to assist you in every way in my power, for I assure you of my honesty of purpose. Be frank with me, and tell me everything; then we will form some plan to combat this plot—for plot it seems to be."

"Be frank with you?" she cried in a tone of dismay, but quickly recovered herself. "With *you*—of all men?"

"Why not with me?" I asked in great surprise at her manner. "Surely I am not your enemy?"

"If you are not at this moment, you have been in the past."

"How so?" I asked, amazed.

"You would have brought death upon me if you could," she cried huskily. "I was only saved by the protection of Providence."

"I really don't know what you mean?" I cried. "I have only seen you once before, on that wet night in London. Yet you actually accuse me of being your enemy?"

"No," she said in a hard voice. "My words are not an accusation. The fault, I feel certain, was not your own; but you might easily have encompassed my death without ever knowing it."

"I really don't understand!" I exclaimed. "Will you not speak more plainly? To think that I have ever been your enemy, consciously or unconsciously, for a single moment, pains me, for such a thing is farthest from my thoughts. I am only desirous of being your good and devoted friend. We both have enemies—you and I. Therefore, if we join forces in perfect confidence, we may succeed in combating them."

"Then I can only presume you have followed me here in order to put this proposal to me?" she said in a tone of indignation.

"I have certainly not followed you," was my quick response. "Indeed, I believed that it was you who had followed me! I am staying at Sheringham, and had not the least idea you were in the neighbourhood."

"The same with me," she replied. "My father and I are staying at my uncle's, Lord Aldoborough's, at Saxlingham, and I strolled over here this evening as far as the sea. Then our meeting must have been quite accidental."

"When did you arrive?"

"Yesterday."

"And your father may have come down here in order to be able to watch me?" I suggested.

She did not reply, although her troubled breast heaved and fell quickly in agitation.

"I know that you hesitate to accept me as your friend," I went on earnestly. "But before your final decision I would urge you to seek some information about me, for I can only repeat what I have already said, that our interests are in common, and that we should defend ourselves."

"From what?"

"From the evil which you fear may fall upon you," I answered, recollecting her words in Harpur Street.

"Ah, no!" she cried bitterly, as her fine eyes filled with tears. "It is useless for you to tell me this—perfectly useless! I, alas! know the truth. Before tomorrow," she added in a hoarse voice, "I shall have ceased to trouble you."

Chapter Nineteen
The Hand and the Glove

Do you believe in love at first sight? I did not until the moment when, in my brief conversation with the Earl's daughter, I detected the beauty of her character. I had often heard it said that only fools love a woman at first meeting her. Yet within that woman's heart was a fathomless well of purest affection, although its waters slept in silence and obscurity—never failing in their depth, and never overflowing in their fullness. Everything in her seemed somehow to lie beyond my view, affecting me in a manner which I felt rather than perceived. At first I did not know that it was love for her. Amid the strange atmosphere of mystery and conspiracy into which I had so suddenly been plunged, amid convulsions of doubt and fear which had during those past few days harrowed my soul, the tender influence of this woman came like that of a celestial visitant, making itself felt and acknowledged, although I could not understand it. Like a soft star that shines for a moment from behind a stormy cloud, and the next is swallowed up in tempest and darkness, the impression it left was beautiful and deep, but vague.

Perhaps you may blame me. Most probably you will. But man is ever the jetsam of the wind of destiny.

I glanced at her, and took in every detail of her countenance and dress. She was no longer in shabby black, but in a pretty costume of dove-grey cashmere, with silken trimmings of a somewhat darker shade; she looked daintily bewitching, supple and slim, grey lending relief to the delicate roundness, the gentle curves of a figure in which early womanhood was blooming with all its sweet and adorable charm. Her fair hair, streaked here and there with gold, was covered with a hat that suited her exquisitely, whether the eye sought harmony of colour or unity of lines. She wore no veil, and thus I could freely feast my eyes upon her beauty.

"I really don't understand you," I exclaimed, after a pause. "You do not trouble me, for until I saw you by chance passing into the street we were entire strangers."

"No benefit can be obtained by discussing the matter," she answered blankly. "Why were you watching in Harpur Street if not to witness my despair?"

"I had a motive in watching," I answered.

"Of course you had. You cannot deny that. My father has already spoken of you, and told me everything."

"And he is still triumphant?" I queried, recollecting his expression of satisfaction on seeing the fatal sign.

She was silent, her lips set closely, her fair face turned towards the open expanse of grey sea.

"Am I not right in suggesting that your enemy is a person named Selby, and that he—"

"Who told you that?" she cried. "How did you know?"

"By my own observations," I replied, as calmly as I could, yet secretly gratified that she should have thus betrayed the truth.

"Ah?" she sighed. "I see! I was not mistaken. You are not my friend, Mr Kennedy."

"But I am," I declared. "Give me an opportunity of proving my friendship. You apparently believe that I am implicated in some plot against you, but I swear I am innocent of it all. I myself am a victim of some extraordinary conspiracy—just as you are."

She looked me straight in the face as though hesitating whether she dared speak the truth. Next instant, however, her natural caution asserted itself, and, with tactful ingenuity, she turned the conversation into a different channel. She seemed uneasy, and eager to escape from my cross-examination; while I, on my part, became determined to obtain from her the truth and to convince her of my good intentions.

I was in a difficulty, because to reveal my connection with The Closed Book might upset all my plans. For aught I knew, she might inform the man Selby, who, gaining knowledge of my presence in England, would suspect that the precious volume had come again into my possession. Therefore I was compelled to retain my secret, and by so doing was, of course, unable to convince her of my intention to be her friend.

Mine was a painful position—just as painful as hers. For some reason quite unaccountable she held me in terror, and now that dusk was darkening to night, was in haste to return to Saxlingham, about three miles distant. It was apparent that my admission of having watched her and her father in Harpur Street had aroused her suspicion of me, a suspicion which no amount of argument or assertion would remove.

She was disinclined to discuss the matter further; and, after some desultory conversation regarding the beauties of Norfolk, she called her dog Rover, preparatory to taking leave of me.

"You must excuse me, Mr Kennedy," she said, with a smile, the first I had seen on that sad, sweet face. "But it is growing late, and it will be dark before I get back."

"May I not walk with you half the distance?" I urged.

"No," she responded. "It would be taking you right out of your way for Sheringham. I have known the roads about here ever since I was a child, and therefore have no fear."

"Well," I said, putting forth my hand and lifting my hat to her, "I can only hope, Lady Judith, that when next we meet you will have learned that, instead of being your enemy, I am your friend."

She placed her hand in mine rather timidly, and I held it there while she replied, with a sigh, "Ah, if I could only believe that you speak the truth!"

"It is the truth!" I cried, still holding her tiny hand in my grip. "You are in distress, and although you decline to allow me to assist you, I will show you that I have not lied to you tonight. Recollect, Lady Judith," I went on fervently, for I saw that some nameless terror had driven her to despair, "recollect that I am your friend, ready to render you any assistance or perform any service at any moment; only, on your part, I want you to give me a promise."

"And what is that?" she faltered.

"That you will tell no one that you met me. Remember that, although you are not aware of it, your enemies are mine."

For a moment she was silent, with eyes downcast; then she answered in a low voice, "Very well, Mr Kennedy. If you wish it, I will say nothing. Good-night."

"Good-night," I answered, and having released her hand she turned from me with a sad smile of farewell, and with her collie bounding by her side made her way over the brow of the hill along the straight white road, while I, after watching until she had disappeared from view, turned and walked in the opposite direction.

Anything like mystery, anything withheld or withdrawn from our notice, seizes on our fancy by awakening our curiosity. Then we are won more by what we half-perceive and half-create than by what is openly expressed and freely bestowed. But this feeling is part of our life; when time and years have chilled us, when we can no longer afford to send our souls abroad, nor from our own superfluity of life and sensibility spare the materials out of which we build a shrine for our idol, then do we seek, we ask, we thirst, for that warmth of frank, confiding tenderness which revives in us the withered affections and feelings buried, but not dead. Then the excess of love is welcome, not repelled; it is gracious to us as the sun and dew to the seared and riven trunk with its few green leaves.

Like every other man I had had my own affairs of the heart. I had loved unwisely more than once, but the sweetness, sensibility, magnanimity, and fortitude of the unhappy Judith's character appealed to me in all the freshness and perfection of what a true woman should be.

I cared nothing for the repugnance she felt towards myself, because I knew that it must be the outcome of some vile calumny or some vague suspicion.

As I passed back along the narrow path over the cliffs, my face set towards the gathering night, I calmly examined my life, and saw now that seven years had gone since the great domestic blow had fallen upon me and caused me to ramble aimlessly across the Continent; that I still stood yet in the morning of life, and that it was not too late to win the glorious prize I had asked of life—love incarnate in sovereign beauty, endowed with all nobility and fervour and tenderness and truth.

In any case, whether she became mine or not, I loved her with my whole heart; and to know that I could love again, in spite of all the torture of the past, was in itself both comfort and delight.

Chapter Twenty
Walter Wyman Rejoins me

That night I slept little, my mind being full of thoughts of the evening's adventure. Before my eyes I had constantly that pale, tragic face, just as, previously, visions of the countenance of the woman I had seen in the prior's dim study in Florence seemed ever before me. Was it by intuition that I knew that these two women were destined to influence my life to a far greater degree than any woman had done before? I think it must have been; for while I loved the one, I held the other in a constant, indefinable terror. Why, I know not until this day—not even now that I am sitting here calmly chronicling all that occurred to me in those wild days of ardent love, reckless adventure, and impenetrable mystery.

At noon Walter Wyman unexpectedly walked into my room with a cheery greeting, and, throwing himself down upon the couch in the window that looked over the sea, exclaimed, "Well, old chap, what does this extraordinary book contain, after all?"

I took the transcript from the place where I had hidden it, and, seating myself on the edge of the table, read it through to him.

"Oh, hang it!" he exclaimed excitedly, when I had finished, "then we may, if we are persevering and careful, actually discover this great treasure!"

"Exactly," I answered. "My suggestion is that we lose no time in making preliminary observations at the two spots mentioned by the man who hid it from his enemies."

"And supposing we found it, would it benefit us, having in view the law of treasure-trove?" was Walters very practical inquiry.

"Not very much perhaps," I admitted. "But we should at least clear up a mystery that has puzzled the world for ages—the actual existence of the Borgia poison and its antidote, besides rescuing Lucrezia Borgia's emeralds, and at the same time discovering the real motive of the strange conspiracy surrounding the book."

"I quite agree with that," exclaimed my friend; "but does it not strike you that we are considerably handicapped by that folio being missing—the very page of all others most important for the success of our search? Besides, this man Selby has, in all probability, read the chronicle, and therefore knows just as much, and probably more, than we do."

"That I grant you," I said. "But, nevertheless, I somehow feel that we ought to search both at Crowland, which is within easy reach of this place, and at Threave, in Scotland." And I explained how I had written to my old friend Fred Fenwicke, asking that we might both be allowed to come up and visit him.

"You certainly haven't let the grass grow under your feet, old fellow—you never do," he said, taking a cigarette from the box I handed to him and lighting it. "I think with you that we ought to try Threave, seeing that the plan is evidently of the spot. But we are unable to do anything till the sixth of September, when we ought to be there at three o'clock in the afternoon, according to the directions given."

"We have still three weeks, then," I remarked. "In that case we might go over to Crowland first and look around there. In all probability the other plan is meant to indicate where the treasure of the abbey is concealed."

"By Jove!" he exclaimed, taking the transcript from my hand. "This list of things, the silver altar, gold chalices, and boxes of gems are sufficient to make one's mouth water—aren't they?"

"Yes," I laughed. "We ought, if we act in a circumspect manner and arouse no attention on the part of the villagers, to be able to make a secret search. The one thing to avoid is public interest. The instant anybody suspects what we are after, the whole affair will get into the papers, and not only will our chance of success be gone, but our enemies, whoever they are, will know that The Closed Book is again in our possession."

"I quite follow you, Allan," he said with sudden seriousness. "We'll go to Crowland tonight, if you are agreeable, and set carefully to work in order to see if the plan tallies with any landmark now existing. It's a pity the old chap who wrote the record didn't label it, as he did the other."

"He may have wanted to give the plan but hold back the secret from anyone who casually opened the book," I suggested. "You see, the volume has evidently been preserved for centuries in the library of the Certosa Monastery at Florence—the house in which the monk Godfrey Lovel died—and, being written in early English, could not, of course, be translated by the Italian monks."

"I wonder how many people have died through handling those poisoned pages?" my friend observed. The deadliness of that secret Borgia venom appealed to him as it has appealed to the world through ages.

"Ah!" I said, "it is impossible to tell."

But my mind was on other things, and as soon as the opportunity offered I related to Walter my strange rencontre with Lady Judith Gordon.

"What?" he cried, jumping up from the couch; "you've actually seen her and spoken to her?"

"Certainly. She is charming, and I admit, my dear Walter, that I've fallen most desperately in love with her."

"Love! You actually love her?" he demanded.

"Indeed I do. She is the perfect incarnation of what a good, sweet woman should be. Is there any reason why I should not admire her?"

"None that I know of," he returned; "but I'm afraid of these people and their connection with this mysterious affair. Remember, all we know about them is that they have led very peculiar lives for years. But time will show whether you are wise. Certainly these people appear to have found the secret just as we have—the secret of the existence of a valuable treasure."

Chapter Twenty One
We Make Preliminary Investigation

"I thought buried treasure existed only in books!" I remarked, recollecting "Treasure Island" and other such romances. "Certainly I never anticipated that I should be actually engaged in a real treasure hunt."

"Nor did I, until I saw the gravity of the whole thing, and how deeply in earnest are these people."

"They have no idea that The Closed Book is again in my possession?" I asked.

"None whatever. The volume was stolen from Harpur Street, of course, and they are puzzled to know into whose hands it has fallen. All the chief dealers in manuscripts in London—Quaritch, Maggs, Tregaskis, Dobell, and the others—have been warned that if the Arnoldus is offered them it is stolen property."

"Well, it is not very likely that any of them will have the offer," I laughed. "It will be kept in a safe place now I have it in my possession again, you may depend upon that."

Walter Wyman had turned over the many folios of my transcript, and was reading the portion concerning the hidden treasure of the Abbey of Crowland. I think the list of gold and silver objects so plainly set out appealed to him.

"We'll go back to Peterborough tonight," he said, "sleep at the 'Angel,' and visit Crowland, as it is now spelt, tomorrow. I've heard that the ruins of the abbey are very fine. It will be an interesting outing, if nothing else."

"Before we go we had better take a tracing of the unnamed plan," I suggested. "It may assist us, and yet it may, on the other hand, be a plan of an entirely different place. One thing, however, is certain—namely, that it had been drawn there with some distinct object, just as the plan marked 'Treyf.'"

To this he agreed, and going downstairs I obtained the packet containing the book from the hotel manager's safe, and together we carefully traced the rough plan in question. It was merely an arrangement of lines and numerals, which told us absolutely nothing. Still, we both felt half-convinced that it must somehow concern the Crowland treasure which was hidden from the king's men at the time the abbey was dissolved and destroyed.

At seven-thirty, after an early dinner, we left by the London express for Peterborough, arriving back at the old-fashioned "Angel" just before eleven. In travelling I carried the precious Arnoldus myself, fearing to lose it; but at our hotel I again transferred it to the landlord's safe, with injunctions to the hotel keeper to be careful of it, as its value was considerable.

Next morning was bright and sunny, and taking a carriage from the hotel we drove out to Crowland, a fen village distant some seven miles.

Perhaps you may have visited it, an old-world straggling place clustering about the time-worn, blackened ruins of the ancient abbey, a venerable pile which even in its present gaunt decay displays mute evidence of a long-past glory.

As we stood before its restored tower and great ruined, roofless aisles, where arches still remain that are the wonder of the modern builder, we could not help reflecting on the vicissitudes through which the grand old place had passed from its foundation, A.D. 713, as a memorial to the Saxon Saint Guthlac, down to its complete dissolution and overthrow by Henry VIII. Because of its isolation in that great marsh, it was for centuries a place of refuge, where the monks were engaged in a noble and great work, employed in prayer, writing manuscripts, building bridges, making roads, or constructing by degrees that noble monument to the glory of God, the great abbey, the nursing mother of Cambridge University, and the very centre of Christian life in the fens of Lincolnshire. Though those venerable aisles are roofless, and the wonderful Early English life-sized statues in the western front of the nave are blackened by age and crumbling to decay; though all traces of the original dimensions of the place are lost in the ill-kept and weedy churchyard surrounding it, the old pile is still one of the noblest buildings in England, wonderful in its station, unique in its beauty, and a valuable relic of Christian devotion, interesting alike to the architect, the historian, and the antiquary.

The guide to the place, which we purchased of the sacristan, told us that the vast structure, consisting of the porch, western tower, and the north aisle, with the ruins of the nave, did not represent one-fourth of the original abbey church. Indeed, the grey, time-stained building which we stood before was little more than the north aisle of the church attached to the abbey, and therefore conveyed no more adequate idea of the extent of the monastic building than the ruins of a domestic chapel will of the castle or mansion to which it was attached. At the time of the dissolution it was standing in all its glory, with the wooden roof of the now ruined nave richly gilt, the great windows full of fine stained glass, two grand organs, and altar blazing with gold, silver, and gems.

The north aisle still remains roofed over,—but uninteresting—to do duty as the parish church; but the magnificent nave is stripped, mutilated, and open to the four winds of heaven, for what sacrilege the commissioners of Henry VIII did not commit in old Godfrey Lovel's day, Oliver Cromwell's soldiers completed when they stormed the place and shattered the remaining walls and windows in 1643.

Together we strolled into the space enclosed by the nave, wandering among the grey old ruins, where the quiet was broken only by the twittering of a bird. The morning was bright, with a warm sun and cloudless sky; but its very light seemed to render the venerable pile, rich with deeds long since forgot, the more bare, solemn, and imposing.

We were alone, for the sacristan, having received the sixpence for the guide, had returned to her cottage, allowing us to roam there at our own sweet will. Therefore, when in a spot where we thought we should be unobserved, I drew forth the transcript I had made of the old monk's record, and reread it aloud to my companion in order that my memory might be refreshed, and that he should know the exact wording of what was written.

We smiled at the simplicity of the old Abbot John sending Thomas Cromwell a present of his fen fish in the hope he would be appeased and pass by the abbey without seizing it; yet, as I afterwards discovered, the original of that very letter is still preserved in the British Museum, and I have had it in my own hand, thus showing that old Godfrey must have possessed the entire confidence of his abbot.

In front of where I stood, let into the ruined wall and beaten by the weather, was a grey slate which I knew to be of fifteenth-century workmanship. The incised marginal inscription, in Lombardic characters, read as follows:

"PETRE: PRECES: P: .ME: PETRO: PASTOR: PIE: P: ME."

This, being translated, reads:

> Peter (offer) prayers for me. Peter,
> Pious Shepherd (pray) for me.

In the centre of the slab was a floriated cross, and the words, "Orate p. aia Johanis Tomson." In 1423 John Tomson gave ten marks for the building of the abbey tower, and it appeared that the marginal inscription was a prayer addressed either to the Apostle St. Peter or to John Tomson's father confessor, named Peter.

Those great bare walls and high pointed arches, grey and frowning, rudely broken, yet perfect in grace and symmetry, surely furnished a striking instance of the uncertainty of all human labours. In the day when the soldier-monk Godfrey lived there it was the seat of devotion and learning, the abode of luxury and ease, possessing riches in abundance, and vessels for its use of the most costly description; now, except in that portion fitted as a church, it scarcely afforded shelter to a rook or daw, and the last remains of its once almost unparalleled magnificence were smouldering silently and mingling with the soil on which they stood:

"Whilst in the progress of long decay,
Thrones sink to dust, and nations pass away."

We turned again to the old chronicle of the monk who had lived there and actually seen those massive walls torn down by Southwell's men; the monk who, with the abbot himself and his friend the Scotch monk Maxwell, had at midnight on the first of December, 1538, concealed the greater part of the abbey treasures.

According to Godfrey's statement, Malcolm had kept watch at the south door while the abbot and himself had carried the three chests out and sunk them in the centre and at the deepest part of the fish pond. It was hidden in the same pond in which he had previously concealed the Borgia jewels—namely, in the lake at a spot indicated, being one hundred and thirty-one paces south of the grand altar. The pond was never dry, it appeared, even in the hottest summer, and like all other monastery waters contained carp for Fridays. The Borgia treasure he managed to secure before leaving Crowland with his friend Malcolm Maxwell, but the abbey plate and jewels and the silver altar he had been compelled to leave, the two others who alone knew the secret, in addition to himself, having died. He had recorded the existence of the treasure from a sense of religious duty, feeling that the Catholic Church should not suffer by entire loss of such a magnificent property.

His directions were by no means explicit, but in our eagerness we resolved to investigate as far as possible.

Passing up what was once the nave, where great trees now flourished and bushes grew in tangled profusion, we came to the high round-toothed arch and two massive piers which were all that remained of the central tower. Beyond, although the abbey church extended just as far eastward as the ruins ran westward, all had disappeared.

There was no sign of the whereabouts of the grand altar from which to take our bearings. The whole of the eastern side of the church had been swept away and converted into a modern churchyard.

"Perhaps the guide will tell us something," Wyman suggested, and at once began to scan its pages, while we stood in the rank grass beneath the shadow of that magnificent arch which is the admiration of all modern builders.

Presently he pointed out to me the original measurements, showing that the nave had been one hundred and forty-four feet long by twenty-eight feet wide and seventy-five feet high, which after careful comparison with other calculations, made it clear that the grand altar must have stood eighty-six feet from the broken pier of the central tower where we stood.

We had fortunately purchased a measuring-tape in Peterborough; therefore, without delay, we marked out eighty-six feet in a direct easterly direction towards the open fen pastures straight before us, and, looking round, discovered to our satisfaction some broken stone foundations hidden in the grass and weeds—evidently the lower stones of the grand altar mentioned by the monk Godfrey.

Some twelve feet farther on there were some similar moss-grown stones, which struck me as being the remains of the rear of the demolished altar; therefore from this latter point we determined to take our bearings, and begin our operations.

We stood and glanced around to find the monastery fish pond. Southward in the direction indicated, in the centre of a grass field, which, filled with mounds where old foundations had been overgrown, was a deep dip in the ground, a small pond quite unlike the deep lake full of old carp that we had imagined.

"That's it?" I exclaimed, much disappointed. "There certainly isn't much water there. I suppose we had better measure the hundred and thirty-one paces, so as to be quite certain that it really is the spot."

"Come along," cried my friend. "Let's do it separately;" and, turning our faces to the south, we paced on, each counting silently, and being compelled to scale the churchyard wall in our progress.

At one hundred and nine paces, however, I arrived at the edge of what had, no doubt, once been a big pond, for the grassy hollow was some thirty feet wide and sixty long, divided into two, and in each remained a few feet of muddy water from which the cattle drank.

The discrepancy in the distance puzzled us. Was it possible that the celebrated silver altar of Crowland and the three chestfuls of treasure lay buried in the centre of the slime of that half-dried pond?

Surely the lake must have been of much larger dimensions in Godfrey's day; and, if it were, then the distance between its edge and the grand altar would not be so great.

I produced the tracing of the mysterious plan contained in The Closed Book, but failed to comprehend it in any detail. The shaky lines, intended to be straight, were mostly numbered, as though denoting paces distant. But there was no number 131, or 109, as I had found it, hence we were utterly mystified, and both inclined to believe that in imagining the plan to concern Crowland we had been mistaken.

We both stood at the edge of the muddy pond and glanced into its green, stagnant water.

Was it possible that the great treasures of that half-demolished abbey, whose high ruined walls and buttresses cast their shadows behind, had been hidden deep in the mud below by the same hand that had written The Closed Book, the hand that had envenomed its pages and thus preserved the great secret from age to age?

It seemed almost incredible in these matter-of-fact times, and yet we both felt confident that the treasure enumerated in that list lay cunningly concealed somewhere in that vicinity.

Chapter Twenty Two
What Happened at Crowland

The long hollow in the field, with a small quantity of muddy water in the bottom, was by no means the kind of place where one would expect to find a treasure concealed. The fields around that neglected churchyard were uneven, where the foundations of the monastic buildings were now overgrown with rank grass and nettles, and in the centre was this hollow where undoubtedly the pond had once been.

Facing us there ran across the eastern boundary of the field a line of beeches, and then, beyond, the broad, bare, misty fenland, without a tree almost as far as the eye could reach, flat, inhospitable, and uninteresting. Like the Maremma, with which I was so familiar in Tuscany, there lay over everything a light mist—that miasma which in Italy is so deadly to the peasantry; and yet even more barren and more cheerless was it than the wide marshes on the road to Rome. The old windmill, with broken sails and roofless outbuildings, stood forth, the most prominent object in that flat, unbroken landscape, without hedgerow, a pitiful relic of the days when it paid to grind corn, before the advent of steam machinery; while clustered on the north side of the abbey were rows of old-fashioned cottages, mostly built of the stones of the monks' houses thrown down by Cromwell. The quiet old village of Crowland is still far from the railway, and modern progress has therefore been slow in reaching it.

As I stood beside that weedy hollow with my companion, I was bound to admit that although old Godfrey Lovel might have inhabited the monastery for eighteen years or so, and his chronicle might be proved to be correct on comparison with contemporary history, yet his statement regarding the distance of the fish pond from the grand altar was incorrect.

Walter pointed out that we had measured from a spot where we merely surmised the altar to have been, and therefore we might have mistaken the distance. Nevertheless, we gazed about us in uncertainty. We alone knew the existence of treasure there, being in possession of a secret lost to the world ever since the year of grace 1538.

Was not that in itself sufficient incentive to cause us to make a search?

"This is evidently where Godfrey Lovel hid the Borgia jewels," remarked Walter Wyman, referring to my transcript of the secret record which he held in his hand. "But he apparently dragged the casket out of the pond on the night before his departure for Scotland."

"Leaving the abbey treasure still hidden," I added.

"Certainly," he said. Then rapidly referring to my transcript, he added: "As far as I can make out, the silver altar and the three chests full of treasure hidden from Cromwell's men were not placed in the same lake as the Borgia jewels. Old Godfrey was clever enough not to suggest that, fearing that the casket he himself had secreted might be discovered by some prying person. You see he says that the abbey plate and jewels were buried 'at the opposite end to where, through many years, my own treasure lay well concealed.' Again he says: 'Once I heard rumour that Southwell intended to pump out the lakes.' He speaks in the plural, thus showing that there was more than one fish pond at this place. Of course, they've since been filled in, and this ground made comparatively level over the old foundations."

I glanced at the passages he referred to, and saw that his surmise was correct. There was certainly more than one pond there in Godfrey's day, and although the Borgia jewels were hidden in the water one hundred and thirty-one paces south-east of the grand altar, yet it did not actually allege that the abbey plate was submerged in the same lake, but at the opposite end. That would be south-west of the grand altar.

I pointed this out to my friend, and, both turning at the same moment, we saw the glint of sunshine upon water at the opposite corner of the rough and broken ground, level with the clock tower, and abutting upon the road which skirted the village itself.

Together we eagerly approached it, first, however, returning to the spot where we had fixed the whereabouts of the main altar, and counting the paces towards it. I counted them as one hundred and twenty-nine, while Walter made them one hundred and thirty-two.

The pond was big, full of dark water, and weedless, showing it to be of considerable depth. It had escaped our notice on entering the abbey grounds, and we both saw that although it was now bounded on one side by the high, black-tarred fence of a cottage garden, and at the end by some red-brick farm outbuildings and hayricks, it had nevertheless once been of considerable dimensions—unquestionably the fish pond of the monks from which they caught their Friday fare.

Once it had undoubtedly been well kept and cared for, but today the cattle grazing on that weedy ground drank from it, for round the mud showed prints of hoofs.

"This is it, no doubt," exclaimed Wyman, again referring to the record. "You see it says 'the pond was deep and dried not in summer, being fed by several springs.' This one is of fresh water, while the other is stagnant. If the treasure has not already been found, it is most likely sunk deep in the mud here."

We both gazed upon the unruffled surface of the water glittering beneath the sun, wondering in which part had been the centre of the original pond. At present it was not more than twenty feet across and perhaps fifty feet long. Its previous dimensions had, of course, been much greater, for it must have extended nearly the whole length of the abbey if, as seemed so probable, the depression on the east side of the field had been in connection with it.

Of course, we had at once seen that the abbey and monastic buildings had originally spread over all the fields southward, eastward, and northward; but we had here sufficient evidence of the existence of the ponds, the hiding-place of the treasure.

A flock of rooks were lazily circling around the tower, and as we stood there in silence at the edge of the pond the deep-toned abbey bell rang out the hour.

"I cannot see how we can search here without its being known," Wyman remarked at last. "How are we to pump out this pond and dig out the mud secretly? Why, the whole village would be here in half an hour if we attempted it."

"I am quite of your opinion," I answered. "And I would point out further that until we are aware of where the *centre* of the pond was it is no use searching at all. My idea is that the spot where the treasure lies is not beneath the water at all, but in another place, midway between here and the other pond—a place that has since been filled up with the débris when the abbey was destroyed. As you see, the ground has practically been levelled, yet at one time nearly the whole of this field was a deep pond. Recollect that there were sometimes as many as seven hundred monks here; therefore they required good-sized fish ponds. No; I feel confident that if we ever do discover the treasure we shall find it somewhere about the centre of this field."

"Which means that we've a lot of excavation to do, and that we must disclose our secret to the whole countryside—even if we were successful in obtaining permission from the lord of the manor, the Ecclesiastical Commissioners, or whoever owns the land."

"It means all that," I said, "and more. It means that if we do go to work without knowing the exact spot where old Godfrey and the abbot concealed the silver altar and the three chestsful of plate we might continue our investigations until doomsday and achieve nothing except the inevitable reputation of having made arrant fools of ourselves."

"But how can we know the exact spot?" inquired Wyman, who was nothing if not entirely practical.

"By this plan most probably. The other plan undoubtedly refers to Threave Castle, in Scotland; therefore, what more likely than this should record the exact spot where the chests were submerged," and I glanced at the tracing of the roughly drawn diagram with its crooked lines and puzzling numerals. "If we could only discover the key!" I added wistfully.

"I think it would be wise, seeing that we can carry our investigations here no farther at this point, to ascertain who is the proprietor of this land and other facts for our future guidance. I notice that the writer of this guide is the rector, the Reverend Henry Mason. Why not call on him and make some antiquarian inquiries?"

To this I at once consented, and a quarter of an hour later we were seated in the rector's cozy study under the shadow of the abbey walls. He was a short, elderly, spectacled gentleman of very affable manner, and full of information upon the subject which interested us.

Finding us interested in the history of the abbey, he produced from his bookshelves several rare volumes, including Felix's "Life of St. Guthlac," Histories of Crowland by Gough, Nicholls, and Canon Moore, and a volume of Cole's collection of manuscripts which contained many notable extracts from the abbey registers. These interested me most of all; and while Wyman chatted with the rector I scanned through the pages, finding references to the silver altar and the golden cups and chalices of which we were now in search.

My friend made some casual inquiries regarding the field which we had just been over, whereupon the rector said:

"The old fish ponds were originally there, but have since been filled in with rubbish and fallen stones. Traces of the ponds, however, still remain. You may, perhaps, have noticed them. In that field, too, at the beginning of the century, a fine silver cup was dug up by a workman while getting out some of the old stones with which to build a cottage. It was claimed by the lord of the manor, and is now in the possession of the Marquis of Exeter at Burghley."

"There may be some more," I suggested, laughing.

"More than likely," replied the clergyman. "According to a popular legend, a great treasure is buried somewhere hereabouts, but no one has yet been able to find it."

"Have they tried?" I asked.

"Oh, of course, the place must have been searched and dug over many times without success," was his response. "Not, of course, of late. I have known Crowland for the past sixty years, and no search has been made in my time."

"Whose permission would have to be obtained if operations were commenced on a serious scale?" I inquired, as though suddenly interested in this popular legend.

"My own," was his response. "The paddocks outside the churchyard wall are my private property. The last time search was made appears to have been in 1721, for in the register there is an entry of nine shillings having been paid to four men for digging in search of the supposed treasure. A note is added that nothing was discovered of any great value."

"Well," I said, "the legend is certainly interesting, and I, for one, would like to make investigations some day, if you would allow me."

"You are quite welcome, providing you replace all that you excavate," he answered. "Of course, it will require time, money, and a good deal of patience. Besides, it will not do for the villagers to know your object, otherwise you'll have a constant crowd of onlookers. When would you suggest making a start?"

"Ah! I must consult with my friend, Captain Wyman, here," I said. "At present I have a good many engagements. A little later—perhaps. But, of course, this is in strictest confidence."

"Very well, Mr Kennedy," he said. "If you really intend to investigate in earnest, I shall be most happy to render you assistance."

We remained with him a short time longer, and then walked back to the George Hotel, a small, old-fashioned place, where our driver had put up the horse, and took luncheon together in a cozy old-fashioned room overlooking East Street, the narrow thoroughfare roadway leading from the curious triangular bridge to the abbey.

This hotel was, we found, one of the very few in England which had not been spoiled by modern progress. The dishes were excellent country fare; but the one fact that impressed itself upon us was that the plate on the table was all early Georgian silver.

As far as we had gone everything had turned out well. The local legend appeared to bear out what was written in The Closed Book, and the fact that we had made a friend of Mr Mason, the rector, was also highly gratifying.

We had been consuming cigarettes with our glasses of old port—served in the old-fashioned style on the bare polished table—and I had risen to glance out through the wire blind into the sunny street prior to going forth into the ruins again, when of a sudden I heard the voice of someone approaching, and next instant two persons passed the window, and were lost to view almost before I was aware of their presence.

But in that moment, as they passed, I recognised in one—tall, thin, and grey-haired—the Earl of Glenelg, and in his companion—short, ugly, and hobbling—none other than Francesco Graniani, the hunchback of Leghorn, the man whose strange connection with The Closed Book was such a profound mystery.

"Look?" I cried to my companion. "Lord Glenelg has passed with the old hunchback antique-dealer who first told me of the existence of the Book. Why are they here—why has Graniani travelled all the way from Italy if not to seek the abbey treasure?"

"If you're not mistaken, Allan," answered my friend, jumping up and joining me at the window, "then you may be certain that the missing page in the book contains directions for the recovery, not only of the casket up in Scotland, but of the hidden gold here. They have no idea we are here, that's evident. But that they know more than we do is equally clear."

"But why is Graniani over here?" I queried.

"He's been brought over, no doubt, because he possesses some key to the hiding-place. The whole affair seems to grow more and more bewildering."

Chapter Twenty Three
Tactics of the Enemy

Walter Wyman, a thorough-going man of the world, was quick of resource. Indeed, it was his shrewdness and clever ingenuity that had extricated him from many a tight corner during his long journeys of exploration. More than once had he carried his life in his hand on that perilous trip from the Albert Nyanza up to Darfur and Kordofan, which he boldly undertook for the intelligence department of the war office prior to Kitchener's march to Omdurman; and more than once it was his quick foresight and promptness of action that had saved him.

The picture of health, he was an ideal British officer, well set-up, well-groomed, and well-clad; and as he stood there in a suit of grey tweed and Panama hat, a thoughtful frown crossed his merry countenance reddened by African suns.

"I'll tell you what it is, Allan, old chap. We ought to ascertain how the enemy intend to start their campaign. There's something decidedly funny about your old Italian hunchback being over here. Are you quite certain you've made no mistake?"

"Absolutely. Graniani has gone past with the Earl."

"But the latter is believed by everyone in town to be still in India. His own servants must, of course, be in the know, but the whole circumstances are suspicious. Now, the hunchback doesn't know me, therefore I shall have a much better chance of following them than if you came. They mustn't know that you are here."

"No. Go and see what their game is. I'll remain here and wait for you. They've evidently gone through into the abbey, and will be poking about there. Keep a sharp eye on them, and we may learn something from their movements."

"All right," he answered, and without another word went out, closing the door after him.

The maid came in and cleared the table. Then I was left alone standing at the window, the wire blind of which fortunately prevented me from being seen from the street.

An hour passed, tolled out by the musical bells in the tower, but my friend did not return. Something important was transpiring, no doubt.

To pass the time, I took from my pocket the transcript of the old record, and reread it from beginning to end. I made a note of various books to obtain in the reading-room of the British Museum, in order to verify the statements both regarding the doings of the Borgias and the events in Galloway in the middle of the sixteenth century, as recorded by the old chronicles. My own antiquarian tastes told me that, in order to properly pursue this investigation, we must be armed with historical facts and data; and that in all probability this might be obtained either at the British Museum or at the record office. In the history of the Borgias I had been interested for years, and had read many works dealing with that celebrated family of prelates and poisoners; but of the history of Galloway I confess that I was in almost total ignorance.

True, I had been in Galloway, shooting with my old friend Fred Fenwicke of Crailloch, when my eyesight was better than it now is, and had admired the wild beauties of the country—a land of hills, streams, and lochs, and full of charming spots as beautiful as any in Scotland. I had crossed the purple heather of Lochenbreck, had traversed the giant solitudes of Carsphairn and the boulder-strewn plains of Dromore; and had shot grouse at Shirmer's—the locale of my friend Mr Crockett's charming story, "The Lilac Sunbonnet,"—and fished the Dee for salmon at Tongland Bridge and in the murmuring Garpal where it runs over its grey rocks through the deep wooded glen in front of Fred Fenwicke's fine old mansion of Crailloch; yet with its historic associations I had never before had occasion to trouble myself.

I knew the titles of several books which, however, I thought might assist me, and put these down for reference.

But through it all—indeed, through all the day—thoughts of Judith Gordon, that beautiful yet tragic figure that had stood beside me on that cliff beside the summer sea, haunted me continually.

Sitting there, impatiently awaiting Walter's return, I reflected upon her attitude towards me, and saw that she held me more in terror than in abhorrence.

You may dub me a fool for this piece of folly of the heart. Nevertheless, I tell you that this was no mere idle fancy based upon a sudden admiration, but a deep and genuine attraction, such as men experience only once in their lives.

I had never lived before that hour. Though she had shown no sign of tenderness to me, she was woman in all that could render woman adorable to man. All my days, those long weary youthful days of work and worry in London, and those years of lazy, idle lotus-eating by the Mediterranean, had been passed in striving and in longing, and my ideal had ever fled from my grasp, leaving me tantalised, athirst, unblessed. But everything had now altered. Here, in the midst of this storm and stress of mystery, one woman had suddenly come to me, and I had stood by her side enchanted. I was not sorry now that the plenitude of happiness had so long been denied me; I was glad that fate had kept me unsated.

But these pages are simply pages of record, not of argument.

When Walter re-entered the room, his clothes dusty and his face perspiring, I saw from his countenance that something curious had occurred.

"I've watched them the whole time," he said breathlessly, as he closed the door behind him. "They've put up at the 'White Hart,' opposite the old bridge, and have been over the fields round about the ruins with a plan drawn on tracing-paper. They evidently know what they are about, for they haven't been in the ruins proper at all, fortunately perhaps for me, for I concealed myself there and watched all their movements. The old hunchback speaks English quite well."

"Speaks English?" I cried, surprised. "Why, in Leghorn he always feigned ignorance of any single word of English."

"For his own purposes, no doubt," laughed my friend. "Ten minutes ago I overheard him talking English with his lordship quite fluently. It seems as though this old Italian has a plan,—a tracing, no doubt,—and from it they are locating the whereabouts of the treasure. They have a measuring-tape with them, and have taken a lot of measurements, all from the southern buttress of the central tower. Their measurements, however, extended much farther than ours, indeed right away into the field beyond the one where are the remains of the fish ponds. You recollect where a footpath crosses, which, it appears, leads to a place called Anchor Church House, whatever that may be. Well, they measured, took angles by the buttress of the tower, and here and there stuck into the grass little pieces of whitewashed wood like labels gardeners use. They've evidently been marking out the ground in a long oblong patch, and both were exceedingly careful that their measurements should tally exactly with what was given upon the plan. Lord Glenelg went about sounding various spots by tapping the earth with his cane. The latter I discovered was a bar of iron painted dark-brown, and hooked to represent a walking stick—a clever contrivance to escape attention. He evidently expected to find some hollow spot."

"But that is not borne out by the record left by old Godfrey, is it? Why should they expect to discover a hollow?"

"Ah! that's a mystery," he responded. "I merely tell you what I've just seen—namely, that they have some plan from which they are working in a slow, scientific, and methodical manner, not in our field, but in the one beyond, in what I've ascertained is called the Great Postland. They have a compass with them, and have taken proper bearings."

"Well, they'll have to get the permission of the owner of the land before they can dig, that's certain. I wonder to whom it belongs?"

"To the Church, no doubt. If we warn our friend, the rector, we'll no doubt be able to stop their little game, at least for the present," remarked Walter. "Unless, of course, the magic of an earl's name carries more weight than ours. Recollect that Lord Glenelg is a Fellow of the Society of Antiquaries and a well-known archaeologist."

"But why is he investigating a spot that is not mentioned in The Closed Book?" I queried. "This seems to me an independent search altogether."

"Perhaps; but it is directed towards the same end—namely, the discovery of the abbey treasure. Yet, where the hunchback obtained his plan is certainly a mystery. They marked out an oblong on the grass about twenty feet long by ten feet, and then gauged the center of it. At the exact spot the old Italian placed a piece of newspaper under a big flint which he found on the footpath, and then took up the whitened pieces of wood with which he marked the ground."

"And then?"

"They went back to the inn together, and as soon as they were out of sight I cut down a big bunch of nettles at the spot with my stick, and then moved the stone and bit of newspaper about fifty feet westward." He laughed.

"So, if they make any attempt at investigation they'll be entirely out of it," I remarked with satisfaction.

"Of course. We don't intend that they shall make any find, even if they possess the missing leaf from The Closed Book, which seems more than possible."

What possible connection there could be between old Graniani and the Earl of Glenelg was to me an entire enigma. Everyone knew the Earl to be a man who had made archaeology a profound study, for he was author of the standard work upon medieval domestic architecture, and possessed at his seat, Twycross Hall, in Staffordshire, a very fine library of early printed books, including a splendid example of Caxton's "The Mirrour of the World," and "The Boke of the Hoole Lyf of Jasan,"—purchased at the Ashburnham sale for two thousand one hundred pounds,—besides such treasures as "The Boke named Corydale," "The Proffytable Boke for Manne's Soule," — 1490, — and the Perkins copy of the first book printed in England; truly a magnificent collection, unique, as every bibliophile is aware.

I listened to my friend's description of how, concealed behind the crumbling ruins, he had watched intently every movement on the part of these two men so widely different in social standing and even in nationality. His opinion coincided with mine that they had returned to the inn to await the darkness before setting to work to excavate; whereupon the question arose as to whether it were best to warn the rector of their intentions, or to allow them to proceed and watch the result.

To me it seemed probable that his lordship, patron of twenty odd livings as he was, would not deign to ask permission to make the search, but just make it in secret as he felt inclined. Certainly, neither of the pair had any idea of my presence there, or they would never have gone openly to work to take these measurements. As matters now stood, we had the spot marked, while the scene of their investigations had been transferred some distance away. Even if the treasure were concealed in that farther field, they certainly would not secure it.

"Well, is it worth while seeing Mr Mason and making an explanation to him?" I asked. "For my own part, I think not. We have only to watch their failure."

"And if they have retained the missing leaf they may post up to Scotland and forestall us there," My companion remarked dubiously. "Without doubt the search about to be made here is the outcome of the curious conspiracy which is puzzling us."

"But why did the prior and his accomplices sell me the Arnoldus if they wished to retain it in their possession?" I asked. "Why did Graniani follow me to Florence, and watch me through the church window; why did my servant Nello warn me against possessing the forbidden volume, and why did that dark-eyed woman, the confidante of the prior, steal it and carry it post-haste across Europe, transferring it in Paris to a second woman, who carried it to London? To me the whole thing is an enigma."

"And to me," Wyman admitted. "This is certainly no ordinary affair. We have, however, at present to remain in patience and watch in secret the development of events — a development which I feel confident will bring with it some almost unheard-of revelations."

Chapter Twenty Four
Forestalled

Walter went out again, and returned after an absence of about three-quarters of an hour. They had telegraphed to Peterborough, he said, but of the nature of the message he knew nothing. After he had left me it appeared that he watched the pair ascend the curious old triangular bridge which now stands in the centre of the village at the juncture of crossroads, and once, no doubt, spanned two narrow rivers long since dried up. On the top of this old Saxon bridge, approached by three flights of much-worn steps, Lord Glenelg and the hunchback halted, and stood gazing around. Then again Graniani drew another plan from his pocket, took bearings of the northern angle of the one remaining tower of the abbey, and, his compass in hand, pointed away to a comfortable old-fashioned stone house in East Street, between the abbey and bridge, the brass plate on which showed it to be occupied by a Mr Wyche, a solicitor.

Openly, and watched by the idlers at the bridge, the lounging place of the villagers, they made a measurement to the corner of the house in question, going over the ground twice in order to make no miscalculation, Walter watching them from the bar window of a small beer-house. The villagers evidently supposed the pair to be surveyors, and took but little notice; nevertheless Wyman kept careful observation upon their every movement.

"What they intend doing at the corner of that house in East Street I can't for the life of me imagine. They made a small mark in charcoal on the wall about two feet from the ground; then again returning to the top of the bridge and referring to the plan, took their bearings a second time and marked a spot right out of the village to the north-east of the abbey, in the centre of the field about ten yards behind the old windmill."

"And then?" I asked, much interested.

"Then, having done this, they went to the telegraph office and wired to someone in Peterborough—afterwards returning to the 'White Hart,' and engaging beds for the night, saying that they had decided not to return until the morrow."

"Why, surely they intend to make a search for the treasure?" I gasped.

"Without doubt," was his reply. "My theory is that they've telegraphed to some of their friends who are awaiting them in Peterborough, and that they mean to make a secret search tonight when all the villagers have gone to sleep and everything is quiet."

When dusk fell we again called upon the rector, explained how we had discovered the presence of our rivals and their intentions, and arranged to return to him at ten o'clock. The feature of the case that aroused the rector's indignation—and most justly, too—was the intention of the others to search without permission. To me, their mode of facing matters boldly showed that they were in possession of positive information, and relied upon securing the treasure and getting away before anyone knew of their intentions.

When Walter once took up an inquiry, or set out upon a journey, he never rested until his object was accomplished. He was one of those men who seem continually active, and unable to rest in idleness for ten consecutive minutes, and, happy possessor of such a fine physique, was never tired. We watched the pair away from the "White Hart" again, for they were both smoking and wandering about, apparently enjoying the rural quiet, but in reality awaiting darkness. Then, when they had gone away—in the direction of the old South Eau, we learned—we both lounged into their inn, and called for ale, and chatted with the rosy-cheeked servant who brought it. A judicious sixpence released her tongue, and by careful questions we soon learned all we wished about the two guests. They were staying till morning, but did not expect any visitors. One, the tall gentleman, was a doctor, and might be recalled; therefore their coachman from Peterborough, who would remain there also, might be called up during the night, and they would be compelled to leave. His lordship had recourse to a clever fiction then. He was a doctor who might be called in the middle of the night! I suppose it never occurred to the rustic mind that, if a doctor, his practice was not in Crowland, and therefore he was scarcely likely to receive an urgent call.

The other man, she told us, was a foreigner. They had brought a bag full of papers and plans, but kept it locked. Both took a great interest in old ruins, and for that reason they had taken some measurements.

One fact she forgot she remarked before going out. The tall gentleman had said that a young lady might arrive during the evening and inquire for him. If she did, she was to be asked to wait.

A young lady! Was it possible that Judith was about to follow her father there?

As ten o'clock chimed from the abbey bells we took our candles, and, wishing the worthy landlord good-night, went to our rooms and there waited until all was still. Crowlanders retire early to bed, and presumably the policeman, like all others, has to meet another guardian of the peace, perhaps, at the end of that long, straight old road called Kennulph's Drove, that runs towards Peterborough, for we saw nothing of him when we carefully crept down, drew the bolts, unlocked the door, and, closing it noiselessly after us, made our way to the rectory.

Mr Mason, ready attired in hat and overcoat, opened his door noiselessly ere we had approached it, and we slipped into his study to tell him all that we had witnessed. Then, feeling that we ought to go forth at once and take up our position to watch, we all went out, skirting the churchyard and passing down behind the high hawthorn hedge which formed the boundary of the field wherein were traces of the fish ponds.

The night was dark and starless, with that oppressive stillness that foretokened a storm. Behind us lay the black ruins of the abbey, rearing high and gloomy; and as we passed along, led by the rector, who knew every nook and corner, a silence fell upon us.

The rector's object was to approach the spot marked with the paper and stone as near as possible, yet having good cover to conceal us. In this he was eminently successful; for, having traversed the field on two sides, he suddenly suggested that we should crouch down in a low hedge only thirty yards from the scene of operations.

We conversed together in low, expectant whispers for almost an hour, until, indeed, the rector began to fear that our vigilance was in vain, when of a sudden we heard on the hard road far distant the sound of wheels approaching, on the road skirting the village on the Welland side, Mr Mason declared.

They approached until they had gained the point where we ourselves had left the road, then stopped. The vehicle bore no lights, but from where we lay concealed we heard men's voices in greeting, as though his lordship and the hunchback had met them there by appointment, and then we heard the jingle of spades and the clatter of iron as some implements were apparently taken from the cart.

Without loss of time the party approached us; and a lantern being turned on by one of them, search was made for the piece of paper held down by the stone. This was quickly found, whereupon more lights were turned upon the spot, and then we saw that the treasure seekers numbered four; two of them were newcomers, apparently well equipped for the undertaking.

So close were we that we could overhear nearly all their conversation, for in that still night all sound travelled a great distance. But their words were few. Lord Glenelg assumed direction of the work, and before long the whole four, his lordship included, were busy with pick and spade, making a large square excavation. Their lamps showed an excellent light upon the work, and were additionally useful to us, for we lay back in the dark shadow, impossible of discovery.

Suddenly, as one of the men bent down to examine the ground, the light fell upon his big, clean-shaven countenance, Walter gripped my arm, whispering "See! That's the fellow Selby! Can you see his face? He's the man who probably holds the missing page of The Closed Book."

I looked, and obtained a fairly good sight of his dark, sinister-looking visage—a hard, clean-shaven, furrowed face that had the miscreant stamped upon it. He seemed to be wearing a rough suit of dark serge, with a soft felt hat, which he had pushed to the back of his head. Seen under such auspices by the uncertain light of the lamp, he was not the kind of man one would care to associate with: loosely built, gross in manner, and deep of voice.

I watched him narrowly for a few moments, but he soon continued digging with the others, and when he stood upright his face was not within the zone of light. All worked with a will, knowing, of course, that the undertaking must be finished before the dawn, and from all four the perspiration soon poured, and their quick, deep breaths reached us even where we crouched, content within ourselves that their labour must be in vain.

Through nearly two hours they toiled on, removing the earth around a line of huge stones which appeared to be the foundations of one or other of the monastic buildings long since swept away. Time after time the abbey chimes sent out their solemn music far over the wide, misty fenlands; but with pick and spade and crowbar they slaved away in their efforts to recover the gold and jewels, the great treasure of what was one of the wealthiest abbeys in England.

The hole they had made was so deep that two of the conspirators were down working out of our sight. The other two were Selby and the hunchback.

Suddenly, above the sharp ring of the picks, we heard a heavy thud, and then another.

"Look?" broke from Selby excitedly. "At last! Here's the first of the chests—bound with iron. Hark!"

And again he struck it heavily with his pick, while his companions were around him instantly, dropping on their knees and examining the find.

"That's one of them, without a doubt!" cried Lord Glenelg, as excited as any of the others. "Come! Let's get it out. How very fortunate that we fixed the exact spot!"

The hearts of all three of us sank within us. How unfortunate for us, after all, that Walter had moved their paper-mark from its original position!

Chapter Twenty Five
What the Buried Chest Contained

From our hiding-place in the bushes we all three watched intently, wondering what was the nature of their find.

That they had discovered something of interest seemed certain, but from our position we could not see its nature. The whole four were in the deep hole, working eagerly and digging around what was apparently a strong chest buried in the earth.

The moments seemed hours, until at last, with loud gasps, they drew the object to the surface, and their lamps revealed it to be an old chest about five feet long, narrow, and looking in that uncertain light very much like a coffin. But it was, we saw, strongly protected by great bands of iron bolted upon it, and locked by three ancient locks along one side.

"By Jove!" we heard Selby cry excitedly, "it's heavy, isn't it? Let's get these locks off," and, taking aim, he struck at one with his crowbar, using all his might. But the stout iron resisted all his efforts, although he repeated them from time to time.

Then the four turned their immediate attention to the locks, carefully examining them by the aid of their lamps.

"They're still very strong," we heard his lordship say. "The only way will be to file the hasps, and then force them."

Thereupon two files were produced from the tool-bag, and Graniani and Selby set to work upon the hasps, while the other two stood by impatiently.

The work was more difficult than they anticipated; but at last the whole of the three fastenings were wrenched off, and, with a cry of expectation, Lord Glenelg raised the lid, and, holding his lantern above his head, peered within.

His companions, in their haste to investigate the contents of the chest, bent and delved with their hands; but their exclamations were those of bitter disappointment, for instead of gold chalices and silver cups, they withdrew only a quantity of damp and bulky leather-bound volumes, evidently ancient religious manuscripts which had formed part of the treasure of the old abbey at the time of its dissolution. Perhaps, indeed, they had been hidden for some reason long before those fateful days of Southwell's visit, for the monk Godfrey did not mention them in his detailed list of secreted treasure.

The disappointment of the investigators was very great. Above the low chatter we could hear the old hunchback grumbling to himself in Italian, while Selby expressed his dissatisfaction pretty strongly in English, declaring that they were not in search of old books, but something of more intrinsic value.

"These are evidently a rare find," remarked his lordship, opening several of the big musty volumes and glancing at them. "But the damp, unfortunately, seems to have spoilt most of the miniatures."

"The finding of that box makes one thing plain," Walter whispered to me. "The abbot would never have buried a box of manuscripts in water, therefore this discovery shows that the treasure itself does not lie concealed in the same spot. Let them go on, for they must fail. In a couple of hours it will be five o'clock, and the village people will be astir. They dare not work very much longer, and they certainly will not attempt to come here again."

"But those books," I said, with the envy of a keen collector; "are they to secure them? They may, perhaps, contain something of interest to us."

"I think not," my friend responded. "Let them take the lot. We are playing for bigger stakes."

"Quite right, Captain Wyman," added the rector. "They must not discover us at this point."

After a cursory glance at the big volumes, some of them fastened with heavy bronze clasps, like The Closed Book itself, they ascertained that there was nothing else in the chest, and then three of them returned to their work of excavation, while his lordship commenced to carry the books, in small piles, across the field to the high road where the horse was tied up.

I confess that I would have liked to jump up and secure one of those fine old tomes. I was only restrained by my friends, who were determined, as a matter of policy, to let him cart them away, Mr Mason declaring that in due course he should claim their return, as an outrageous theft had been committed.

Lord Glenelg had made several journeys, backwards and forwards across the fields, when, just as he returned, a stir among the treasure seekers showed us that they had made another discovery, which, a few minutes later, we saw was a fine image of the Virgin, about four feet in height, dark and covered with the clay in which it had been embedded.

As it lay there upon the grass they placed their lanterns beside it, and with their pocket-knives scraped away the clay until it shone bright beneath.

"There was a celebrated image of Our Lady, in silver, here," remarked Selby, as he scraped diligently. "Perhaps this is it."

A few seconds later the thick-set man who was assisting, and who was a stranger to me, cried:

"It certainly isn't silver. Look! It's only one of those gilded wood things."

And again there arose a chorus of dissatisfaction and disappointment.

The statue was evidently a very antique one; but so well had it been preserved in the clay that the gilt still flashed upon it where they had scraped away the dirt, and in the early grey of dawn that was now spreading we could just distinguish the bright silver stars upon the blue robes.

Again they all returned to their work with pick, spade, and "grubbers," toiling on in the hole they had made, their heads only being visible above the surface, until the abbey bells chimed out, and then solemnly struck five o'clock.

Day had broken, and the warning notes of the bell caused his lordship to order a cessation of the labour. All four regarded the surface and looked with regret upon their rather fruitless efforts, well knowing that the damage they had done would, in an hour, be discovered, and that to continue their secret search of the spot would be entirely impossible.

"We can't return; that's very evident," remarked Selby. "The village constable will be put on to watch, I expect. Therefore, we shall have to wait a month or so before we come back."

"Couldn't we perhaps square the constable?" the fourth man suggested.

"I doubt it. These country policemen are so much more straight than the men in town. As like as not, they'd split upon you, so as to get their promotion. You see, the work we've done tonight is a bit ugly, for a magistrate would probably call it stealing."

"Rubbish!" snapped his lordship. "Don't stay gossiping here. Let's pack up and get away. There are a lot of labourers already on the move. Don't you see the smoke from the cottage chimneys over there? We shall have someone across this footpath to the fields in a minute if we don't get clear away."

Scarcely, indeed, had he finished speaking when the dark figure of a man, with a fork over his shoulder, whistling to himself on his way to work, appeared at the stile at the opposite corner of the field, and took the footpath in their direction.

They noticed him, and, hastily snatching up their picks and spades and other tools, all four made off in the direction where the cart stood, and, ascending into it, drove rapidly off down the long highway across the fen, in the mists of which they were quickly lost to sight.

As soon as they had gone we emerged from the spot where we had remained cramped for so long, and rushed to the big hole they had made.

My first investigation was the old chest, and in it I discovered several manuscripts which his lordship, not having finished transferring them to the cart, had been compelled, in his haste, to leave. Of these we took possession, and the labourer, on passing, discovered the hole with considerable surprise, especially on recognising Mr Mason.

In reply to the man's inquiry we told him that thieves had been trying to discover something hidden and had found some old books, for we wished the whole village to know of the secret attempt that had been made, in order that the people should keep a watchful eye upon the abbey precincts for further depredators.

Presently, when the man went on to his work, and it had grown lighter, we were able to see the extent of their investigations, which was certainly far greater than we imagined; while Walter, after making some measurements, showed us the spot which they had at first marked out, and from which he had removed their landmark.

The chest and books were, of course, the property of the abbey, so we carried them to the small room in the restored portion of the fabric that the rector kept as a kind of museum, and there investigated them.

They were of little interest, all being works of theological writers, copied in the thirteenth and fourteenth centuries, save one (Cambridge University Library MSS., Dd. XI. 78, ff. 61, 92.), a small quarto manuscript, beautifully illustrated, written by William, a monk in Ramsey Abbey, in Huntingdonshire, in 1191, which commenced "*Incipit Vita beati Guthlaci metrice composita*," a poem on the life of St. Guthlac, dedicated to Henry de Longo Campo, the contemporary Abbot of Crowland.

It was Mr Mason's opinion, as well as my own, that the chest had been buried there fully a century before the dissolution, at some time when the abbey feared attack, and the worthy rector was already eager to demand of Lord Glenelg the return of the whole of the other volumes that had been surreptitiously carried away.

At present, however, it was agreed to make no sign. The manuscripts would, no doubt, be well preserved in his lordship's collection, and there was no fear of their going astray.

Then, having completed our examination, we returned to the rectory, where we had hot coffee to warm us after our night vigil. Mr Mason promised to set a night watch upon the field until such time as we should deem it advisable to make our search; for I pointed out to him that a journey to Scotland was imperative, in order to forestall our friends if they attempted to make a search there, and that we should be unable to excavate the site of the monastery fish ponds until our return from Galloway.

As a matter of fact, we all felt, from the conversation we had overheard, that it was not their intention to return at present, as they had no wish to fall into the hands of the police.

"Well," remarked Mr Mason, as we sat over our coffee in his study, "the whole affair is most mysterious and remarkable. Lord Glenelg evidently possesses certain information upon which he is working."

"We hope that ours is equally precise," I laughed. "That is why we intend to go north and take preliminary observations. We can only make our investigation at a certain hour on a certain day, the sixth of September."

I was not more definite as I did not intend, at present, to give the secret away. In a hunt for treasure success depends to a very great extent upon strict secrecy. To arouse undue interest is always to be avoided. The Crowland treasure concerned the rector to a great degree, but the Borgia jewels would, if we discovered them, surely be our own.

At half-past seven we returned to "The George," which had already been open an hour or so, and we went in as though we had returned from a morning walk. Neither servants nor landlord suspected anything until the villagers discovered the big hole near the abbey, and then, I believe, we were viewed with considerable suspicion. Indeed, I was much relieved when, at eleven o'clock, we drove out along Kennulph's Way and through the village of Eye back to "The Angel," at Peterborough.

Chapter Twenty Six
A Discovery in Harpur Street

At two o'clock that afternoon we were back in Dover Street, utterly fagged out by our long night watch among the rank grass and nettles of the damp fenland.

It seemed certain that the quartette had returned to London by the early train from Thorney or from Peterborough, and had carried back with them the manuscripts they had found; therefore, curiosity prompted Wyman to go forth about four o'clock, in order to try and discover something regarding Lord Glenelg's movements.

When we parted in Piccadilly I went on to the British Museum, for I had been wondering if anything might be preserved there that would give me an accurate ground plan of Crowland Abbey before its dissolution. If only I could get that I should be able to fix the exact spot where the carp ponds once existed.

Professor Dawson Fairbairn, assistant keeper of the manuscripts, had, in the days before my self-exile from London, been one of my personal friends. He was perhaps the first authority upon palaeography in Europe, one of the founders of the new Palaeographical Society, and an expert upon Latin and early English manuscripts. A man of middle-age, he was by no means the dry-as-dust professor one would readily associate with such an unattractive study as the deciphering of mouldy vellum rolls. On the contrary, he was a short, stout, round-faced man, of merry demeanour, whose eyes blinked at one good-humouredly through his pair of circular gold-rimmed spectacles.

I found him in his room, busy deciphering a half-effaced page of an illuminated manuscript, but he placed aside his work to greet me. While in Italy I had had a good deal of correspondence with him regarding several rare documents that I had succeeded in finding, and more than one of which I had sent for his inspection and opinion. Of these we commenced to chat.

I did not care to show him The Closed Book, for various reasons. The secret it contained was my own, and I wished to preserve it to myself, for I recollected that he was an expert himself and could read that difficult script at the end of the volume as easily as I could a printed page.

"I am just now taking an interest in the history of Crowland Abbey," I said presently. "Do you know of anything in the collections that would give me an adequate description of the monastery as it was in the early sixteenth century?"

"Crowland Abbey! How strange!" he ejaculated. "This codex I have been examining evidently came from there. It was sent to me for my opinion, along with several others, by Lord Glenelg, only a couple of hours ago. All the manuscripts undoubtedly once belonged to that abbey."

"Lord Glenelg has been here?" I exclaimed.

"No—not personally. He sent them by a queer little old Italian with a humpback. I've met the old fellow before somewhere, only I can't think where. Abroad, most probably, when I've been buying for the Museum. He's something of an expert."

"His name is Graniani," I said. "But did his face recall to you any particular incident?"

"No, only I felt that I disliked him."

"Lord Glenelg was, I thought, abroad."

"So did I," was the great expert's reply. "I was very surprised to receive these from him," and he pointed to a pile of heavily bound volumes on the table, those very manuscripts that we had watched unearthed a few hours before. "They've evidently been kept in a very damp place, for they're half ruined and effaced."

"You received no explanation concerning them?"

"None. Only it seems such a curious coincidence that you should come and inquire for references to Crowland just at a moment when we have this important discovery of the abbey's liturgical and other books."

"I found a reference to it by a monk named Godfrey in a manuscript I purchased in Italy recently, and it has aroused my interest," I explained.

"A reference to it by Godfrey?" he echoed, looking up at me quickly through his spectacles.

"Have you actually found the missing Arnoldus?"

"It is an Arnoldus," I responded; "but why do you ask? What do you know of it?"

"I know, my dear Mr Kennedy, that if you have really rediscovered the book I mean, you hold the secret of the hidden treasure at Crowland," was his reply.

"But what is known of the treasure?" I asked eagerly.

"All that is known is contained in an old pocket-book belonging to this monk Godfrey now in the Harley Collection. I'll send for it," and, turning up one of the huge bound catalogues, he noted its number upon a slip of paper and sent one of his assistants for it.

The young man returned with a small squat volume, much-worn, bound in a cutting from an ancient antiphonarium, and secured by a small bronze clasp.

"You will see that the book is full of useful recipes, domestic accounts, a calendar of saints' days, and memoranda of all kinds. Among the latter is the entry to which I refer." And he opened it at a page wherein a slip of paper had been inserted.

There, sure enough, was an entry in Latin, in the same well-known hand as that upon the envenomed pages of The Closed Book. Freely translated, the memorandum was as follows:

"I, Godfrey Lovel, now monk of the Certosa of Florence, and once a brother of the Order of St. Benedict, at Crowland, in England, am about to die, and have therefore written a full account of my life and adventures, and have also given full directions for the recovery of the abbey treasures, so that the secret shall not be altogether lost. I have plainly told also where the emeralds of my lady Lucrezia are concealed. All this will be found clearly written in my Arnoldus, which I have now concealed in a place of safety. Let him who seeks to know the secrets beware! He will grasp the hand of Death midway."

There was nothing else, so the professor informed me: only that single entry—a few rough, ill-written lines which told that the treasures of the abbey were actually concealed, and that the secret of their whereabouts was contained in the Arnoldus that had so curiously fallen into my hands.

Was it any wonder that his curiosity was at once aroused, or that he sought to know what I really had discovered?

"It is true that I am in possession of the missing manuscript," I said; "but, unfortunately, one folio of it is missing—the very folio which gives definite instructions for the recovery of the hidden treasure. At present I am unable to make investigations because I cannot find any plan of the abbey, the cloister court, and adjacent buildings. It is to ask your assistance in this matter that I've come to you today, although I would also ask you, as a favour, to regard the matter at present as entirely confidential, for I do not wish anyone to know that I'm engaged upon a treasure hunt."

"I shall, of course, respect your confidence entirely, Mr Kennedy," the professor said; "and if I can be of any assistance in the matter I shall be delighted. It would be a grand thing to recover the treasures of Crowland. There must be a good many valuable things among them, for the place was one of the wealthiest of the Benedictine houses."

"Well," I said, "do you happen to know of any existing plan or any written description of the monastic buildings?"

He reflected deeply, taking off his glasses and carefully wiping them.

"At the moment I really cannot think of anything," was his quiet rejoinder, "at least of nothing more than what has already been published in the various histories. You have, of course, seen them?"

I responded in the affirmative, whereupon he promised to make investigations and look through various catalogues, a work which I knew would mean considerable study and research.

I learned further from Professor Fairbairn that he knew nothing of the man Selby, although he was, of course, on friendly terms with Lord Glenelg, who, as a bibliophile, was frequently at the Museum when in London.

"It is evident from these manuscripts," I said, indicating them, "that his lordship is making some careful investigations; therefore I wish that my inquiries should be absolutely secret from him—you understand?"

"Perfectly," was his reply. "I am quite as much interested in the Crowland treasure as you must be, therefore I will commence tomorrow to search for the particulars you desire, and will write you. Are you only in London temporarily, or have you returned permanently?"

"I'm staying with my friend Captain Wyman the traveller, at 14A Dover Street. A letter directed there will find me."

"Has not the other portion of the entry here struck you as curious?" he said, pointing again to the open page of the old monk's note book. "This reference to 'my lady Lucrezia's emeralds.' Can 'Lucrezia' actually be Lucrezia Borgia, and the emeralds those historic ones which we know were in his possession about 1506?"

I affected ignorance. What could I do in the circumstance? I had asked the professor's assistance regarding the Crowland ruins, but the other matter I intended to keep entirely secret. In a few days I would go north to visit Fred Fenwicke, in Galloway, and make investigations for myself. Therefore I replied:

"I know nothing of the jewels. Yet it really seems probable that Godfrey, if he had lived in Florence, might have known the notorious Lucrezia Borgia of poison fame."

"And that warning about meeting death hand to hand—what can that mean?"

"Oh! the old fellow's way of trying to frighten the inquisitive, I suppose," was my response. Then, when I had thanked him for his promise, we took a turn down the long gallery where the English manuscript charters are exhibited in glass cases to the public, and at the door he bade me farewell, repeating his intention to assist me in every way possible, and expressing a hope that, as reward, he might have sight of the long-lost Arnoldus.

Until Professor Fairbairn could complete his search we could only wait, the good rector taking care that no further theft was committed.

To search at Crowland before being in possession of a plan of the fabric as it was originally, and the buildings surrounding it, appeared to be a useless proceeding. Though Wyman and myself were both convinced of the existence of the treasure there, we were not at all certain of our measurements from the grand altar, nor of the exact position of the filled-up fish ponds. Therefore, if we could obtain any plan showing the position and extent of the cloister court, the monk's parlour, the refectory, and the chapter house, all of which must have once existed, the position of the fish ponds would certainly also be shown, and thus assist us very materially.

Again, suppose that on the day and hour appointed for taking measurements at the castle of Threave the sun was hidden by the clouds? Should we be compelled to wait another year before our measurements could be taken with sufficient accuracy?

This fear haunted me as I wandered through Bloomsbury towards Harpur Street, a sudden desire having seized me to examine again the exterior of that mysterious house. It struck me that a watch should be kept upon that smooth-faced fellow Selby, by which means we might be enabled to foil any attempt to filch the treasure from us.

As I halted at last at the corner of Theobald's Road and looked down the short, sad street, I saw it was deserted; therefore I strolled along it on the opposite side to the house in question, just as I had done on that well-remembered night after my long chase across Europe.

As I lounged past, pretending to be utterly disinterested, I glanced up at those two dingy first-floor windows. What met my gaze there held me bewildered and speechless.

Chapter Twenty Seven
If you Knew the Truth

At first I could scarce believe my own eyes. In the window, just as I had seen it on that fateful night, was the stuffed bear cub, and behind the smoky panes was a pale, haggard face peering forth wistfully, yet cautiously, as though in expectation of the passing of some person to whom the signal would convey a meaning, a face upon which anxiety and terror were betrayed—the countenance of the woman I had so suddenly grown to love.

In an instant, at sight of me, she drew back and was lost to view, there remaining only that curious yet fatal sign that conveyed so much to the person or persons for whom it was exhibited.

The house presented the same dingy, neglected appearance as before, the steps uncleaned and covered with pieces of paper and wisps of straw, the jetsam of the street. The shutters of the basement were still closed, and upon the area gate was a stout chain and heavy padlock. It was a roomy yet depressing place, more depressing than any other in the whole of Bloomsbury, a strange air of mystery pervading it from basement to attic.

My first impulse was to ascend those neglected steps and inquire for Lady Judith; but, on reflection an instant later, the fact that she had withdrawn so quickly from the window made it evident that she did not wish me to discover here there—that, indeed, she was in Selby's house in secrecy.

She had evidently been watching long and vigilantly for some person she expected would pass for the purpose of receiving the sign. The intent, anxious look upon her countenance told me this. But instead of the person she was looking for, I, the least expected, had suddenly come upon the scene and detected her. Her mouth had opened as her eyes met mine, and I knew that a cry had escaped her as she had fallen back behind the dusty curtains.

She was still watching me most probably, therefore I did not glance up again, but merely walked on as leisurely as before, and turned the corner out of Harpur Street.

I stood for some minutes deliberating whether it were policy to go boldly to the house and inquire for her. What could I lose by so doing?

Little—very little. What could I gain? A few minutes' chat, perhaps, with the woman who, although she held herself so aloof from me, was nevertheless always in my thoughts.

I was determined to get at the bottom of the mystery of that secret sign; therefore, without hesitation, I drew a long breath, turned again into Harpur Street, and, ascending the steps, rapped loudly at the door.

The place sounded hollow, as a half-empty house always does. But there was no response.

I listened attentively at the door, but the roar of the traffic over the granite in Theobald's Road prevented my hearing anything distinctly. Nevertheless, my quick ear caught sounds of whispering within. A door somewhere in the hall was closed and locked, and then I heard a man's low, gruff voice exclaim, "Not yet—not yet, you fool!"

All was silent again, and I waited in patience for a couple of minutes longer. Then I gave another sounding *rat-tat-tat* that rang through the hollow house.

Again there was a movement in the hall, and softly footsteps crossed the linoleum, which was comparatively new, I felt sure, by its stickiness. Somebody was whispering; then a few seconds later the chain was withdrawn, and the door was opened half-way by Mrs Pickard, the little wizened old lady in black cap and dress, the same who had crossed the Channel bearing The Closed Book to England.

Fortunately she did not recognise me, so I inquired, "You have a lady named Gordon here? She has just recognised me from the window. Will you ask her whether she will see me for a few moments, as I wish to speak with her on a rather important matter?"

"She has noticed you," was the little old woman's reply, "and she's just putting on her hat. She'll be down to speak with you in a few moments, if you'll wait," and she admitted me to the hall, which was covered with a cheap black-and-white oilcloth, and showed me to the dining-room, which overlooked the street—a big, old-fashioned apartment, very dingy, with ceiling and walls smoke-grimed, and furnished in an inexpensive and tasteless style, which bore "hire system" marked upon it as plainly as though the chairs and tables were ticketed "easy payments taken." The carpet was one of those Kidderminster squares that always appear in hire-system furnishing, and the furniture was of veneered walnut, covered with dark-green plush. There was no overmantel, no sideboard, nothing, indeed, to give it the slightest air of comfort. The room somehow looked as though it had only just been furnished, and that with some motive, for it was evidently not the dining-room in use.

After making a tour of inspection, I stood before the empty old-fashioned grate, listening intently. There were footsteps in the room above—the drawing-room—but no other sound. The dismal outlook, the utter cheerlessness of the room, the sooty curtains waving slowly at the half-opened window, added to the atmosphere of gloom which pervaded the interior even to a greater extent than the exterior. It was certainly a house of mystery.

Once I thought I heard renewed whisperings in the hall; but only for a moment, then all was silent again.

At last the door opened, and there appeared my pale-faced love, neatly dressed in black, with a small toque that suited her admirably, and a bodice that showed off her figure to perfection. Her sombre attire heightened the pallor of her countenance, yet, as she approached me with a sweet smile and outstretched hand, I saw that she possessed a marvellous self-control.

"Only fancy your recognising me, Mr Kennedy!" she cried. "I'm so glad. You left Sheringham suddenly, and no one knew where you had gone."

"I, too, have been wanting to meet you again," I said, "and believed you to be still at Saxlingham."

"I returned to town yesterday," she answered. "But if we are to talk, had we not better go for a walk?" she suggested. Then she added, in a low, confidential whisper, "There are eager ears here."

Nothing loath to escape from that house of mystery, I agreed to her proposal, and she let me out, after considerable trouble with a very complicated lock, which I noted could not be undone by anyone unacquainted with its secret—another suspicious circumstance.

Outside, we turned towards Theobald's Road, and I walked beside her in the hazy glow of the London sunset, full of admiration of her beauty, her grace, and her sweetness of expression.

As we walked towards Oxford Street I told her of my desire to be, if not in public, then in secret, her friend.

"But why?" she asked, opening her splendid eyes widely.

"Because—well, because I believe we shall be good friends some day," I said lamely, for it was on the tip of my tongue there, in that crowded street, openly to declare myself.

"We are good friends now, otherwise I would not be out walking with you here," she remarked.

"Exactly; but there is still a stronger reason," I said. "You will recollect that when I met you on that path across the cliffs you confessed to me your unhappiness—that in your heart there lies concealed some terrible secret which has driven you to despair, and which—"

"My secret?" she gasped, looking at me suddenly with the same expression of terror I had seen upon her face on that wet night in Harpur Street. "Who told you of my secret?"

"No one," I said quietly. "But to me the truth is apparent, and it is for that reason that I desire to stand your friend. You recollect you spoke of your enemies, who were so strong that they had crushed you. Will you not let me render you assistance against them; may I not act on your behalf? You surely can trust me?"

I asked her the reason of her visit to that house of mystery and the meaning of the symbol of the bear cub, but she hesitated, just as she had done before. Ah! how blind is man to the beginning of any series of great consequences!

All our previous conversation passed through my mind like a flash, and I saw how utterly I had failed to convince her of my good intentions in her interest.

The curious breach between father and daughter was inexplicable, just as much as their secret presence in London or their association with that dingy house in Harpur Street.

"I know that in ordinary circumstances the small knowledge you have of me would cause you to hesitate to allow me to become your confidential friend," I went on in deep earnestness. "But these circumstances are surely extraordinary ones. You are in distress, threatened by enemies who terrorise you, and are driving you to despair; and I believe I am also right in suggesting that you possess no friends?"

She had grown paler, and I knew my words made an impression upon her. We were then walking in the crowd of Oxford Street, and I was compelled to bend and speak confidentially to her, lest others might overhear. Surely that great busy thoroughfare was a strange place in which to court a woman's love! But love is always one of life's ironies. Many are the world's wonders; but surely Honour, Conscience, and Love are the three greatest. They will never be explained, and never cease to be bewildering. Of such are the source and the end of what is wonderful in our life—the sea and the shower, the aggregate whereof is in God and the atom in man.

I saw from her countenance, and knew from the trembling of her hand, that she would confide in me if only she dared. The mystery of it all was maddening. My natural intuition told me that she was not averse to my companionship, yet the mention of her secret—whatever it was—caused the truth to arise before her in all its hideousness, holding her transfixed by the crisis that she knew must inevitably ensue.

"It is true," she sighed at last. "I am in sore need of a friend; but I fear your help is impossible. Indeed, if our friendship were known to certain persons it would place me in a position of even graver peril."

"Then your enemies would be mine," I remarked quietly. "This is as it should be. But why would my association with you place you in peril? I don't understand."

"Oh!" she cried, "I cannot explain. I would tell you everything if I could—everything. But I cannot, for your sake as well as for my own."

"For my sake?" I echoed. "Would knowledge of it affect me so gravely?"

"I fear it would," was her reply. "It is best that you should remain in ignorance."

"But believe me, I cannot bear to think of you utterly friendless as you seem to be," I went on earnestly. "Why do you not let me be your friend in secret?"

"Because if you were my friend it would be necessary for you to know the whole truth before you could help me. Yet, in my present position, I can explain nothing. If I did, it would be fatal to me—and perhaps to you also."

"You are so very mysterious, Lady Judith!" I said. "Cannot you be more explicit? What you tell me only excites my curiosity and interest."

"I can tell you nothing more—absolutely nothing," she said, quite calm again. "I am unfortunately a victim of certain strange and incredible circumstances; that is all."

"But why are you so averse to my friendship?" I demanded. "I assure you that I will do my utmost to serve you if you will accept me as your friend."

"I do not doubt it. I can only regret that our friendship is debarred," she answered.

"Why debarred?"

"Because of circumstances which, as I have already told you, I am unable to explain. Besides, I have long ago read in the newspapers that you reside abroad. I could not think of keeping you here in England on my account."

"I intend to live in England for the future," I hastened to assure her. "In fact, I'm on the lookout for a home at an easy distance from London, and in the meantime I am the guest of my old schoolfellow and friend, Captain Wyman, of whose recent explorations in Central Africa you may have heard."

She shook her head slowly, and in a low, mechanical voice, almost as though speaking to herself, said, "I cannot see why you should be so ready to sacrifice everything for my sake. It is far best if we part now, never to meet again. It will be best for both of us, Mr Kennedy, I assure you. Remember, once and for all, that our friendship is forbidden."

Chapter Twenty Eight
The Stranger in Black

"Forbidden!" I cried, taking her proffered hand and keeping possession of it. "Why is our friendship forbidden? I thought you had accepted my friendship! I do not know the truth about yourself—nor do I wish to know. I only know that I desire to serve you in every way a man is capable. I only ask you to allow me to love you, to let me think of you as my own."

"Ah, no!" she said, withdrawing her hand. "It is not just that I should allow you to thus go headlong into ruin. My duty is to warn you of the dire consequences of this reckless devotion to myself," she added with that sweet touch of her woman's nature that had all along held me charmed. "Hear me, Mr Kennedy, I beseech of you. Pause and reflect upon the consequences. You say you are my friend. That may be so, but when I tell you in reply that no friendship is permissible between us, will it not be best if we part at once—

(About five lines missing here.)

of my return to London—not by mere chance surely, but because I am destined to serve you."

A man's arguments in such circumstances are never very logical. What other words I uttered I do not recollect. I only know that her determination to tell me nothing about herself rendered her the more attractive.

But to all my persuasions, my pleadings, and my utterances she was still the same woman of honour, fearful lest I should come to harm through association with her, fearful lest the unknown fate she dreaded should fall upon us both at the hour of our supreme happiness.

At one moment I felt that I was acting foolishly in thus trying to persuade her into accepting me as her friend, and at others the fact that in social standing I was far beneath her, the daughter of a noble house and well-known in London, impressed itself upon me.

For half an hour we walked onward, heedless of where our footsteps led us. She told me of her recent travels in the East with her father, of their delightful time in the cold weather in India, and afterwards in Sydney and Melbourne.

"My father has been a wanderer ever since my poor mother's death," she exclaimed, with a touch of sadness. "He will never remain in England long, because life here always brings back recollections of her. They were a very devoted pair," she added.

"And so you have accompanied him?"

"Yes, ever since I left the convent school in France. My journeys already have included two trips round the world and a yachting voyage to Spitzbergen."

"Well," I laughed, "I thought I had some claim to be a traveller; but you entirely eclipse me."

"Ah, but I am tired of it—terribly tired, I can assure you."

I told her how I, too, had suffered from that nostalgia that comes sooner or later to most persons who live abroad, that curious indefinite malady of the heart which causes one to long for home and friends, and to waste in the flesh if the desire is ungratified. You who have lived abroad have experienced it.

I told her how I had lived for years beside that brilliant tideless sea until I had become sun-sick and tired of blue skies, whereupon she sighed and said:

"Italy!—ah, yes! I know Italy. I have, alas! cause to remember my visit there."

"Is the recollection of it so bitter?" I inquired, quickly on the alert.

"Yes," she answered in a hard voice. "It is years ago now; but I recollect every one of those incidents as vividly as though they only happened yesterday. Milan, Florence, Perugia, Rome—all cities whose very names are now hateful to me. Yet I suppose the past should be of the past." And she sighed again, her eyes fixed upon the pavement.

What could I say? What question could I put to her?

Could it be that her journey to Italy had had any connection with the strange conspiracy that seemed to be in progress, or was it possible that her travels in the South had been fraught with some youthful love episode of a tragic nature?

Her character, sweet and modest, was yet so utterly complex that I could not understand it. I was, therefore, uncertain of the security of my own position, and thus feared to explain to her that The Closed Book stolen from Harpur Street was in my hands, lest it might be against the interests of the investigations I had undertaken.

She made no mention of the old hunchback from Leghorn, who had no doubt visited at Harpur Street, perhaps even made the house his headquarters. Yet I felt sure that she was acquainted with Graniani just as she knew Selby.

Again and again I reverted to my affection for her, begging and imploring her to view my suit with favour, or if not, at least to allow me to stand her friend. But she was obdurate, although my words caused her much genuine emotion.

I saw that, although driven to desperation by reason of some unspeakable secret, she was nevertheless a woman of honour. If I sought to assist her, I should place myself in deadly peril of my life, she declared. This she would not allow me to do. Why? Was it because at heart she was really my friend?

I wonder if there are others who have experienced a similar feeling—a desire to commence life afresh, guided by a good woman? If they have, they will know the feelings which were mine. I was no mawkish youth, callow in his first affection, and carrying his heart upon his sleeve. On the contrary, I had known love, I had enjoyed my allotted share of it, and just as prosperity had come to me the great sorrow of my life had come also to me, and I had gone abroad to bury myself in an Italian village.

Dusk darkened into night, and the street-lamps commenced to glimmer as we strolled on and on westward, through that maze of highly respectable streets and squares which constitute Bayswater, until we suddenly found ourselves in the boarding-house region of Powis Square. Then, at her suggestion, we turned and retraced our steps to the Edgware Road, proceeding towards the Park. The cloud that had earlier fallen upon her seemed now removed, and she grew brighter.

Her father, she told me, had returned to London, and was at home; but she expected they would both leave again tomorrow for the North.

"To Scotland?" I suggested with some anxiety.

"Oh, I really don't know," was her reply. "My father is most erratic in his movements. I only know that he goes to the North, and that I go with him."

"But tell me," I asked very earnestly, "has your father ever mentioned his intention of going to Galloway?"

She looked up at me in some surprise.

"Yes, he did so the other day, while we were at Saxlingham," she responded. "But why do you wish to know?"

"Because I have a reason—a very strong one," I answered. "He goes with friends, doesn't he?"

"With me—I know of no one else who is going. We may be going to Castle-Douglas; but of course I am quite in the dark. Very often I have set out from Charing Cross with him and have not known our destination until we have been in Paris or Brussels. Again, we have, on several occasions, been living quietly at home in Grosvenor Street when all our friends have believed us to be on the other side of the equator. It is quite exciting, I assure you, to live in secret at home, see nobody, and only go out at night, and then always in fear of being recognised," she added.

"But why does your father do these things; he surely has some motive?"

I recollected that the town of Castle-Douglas was near the castle of Threave.

She gave her well-formed shoulders a shrug, and her countenance was overspread by a blank look of ignorance which I was compelled to admit was feigned.

Mystery crowded on mystery. I could make nothing out of it all. Put yourself for a moment in my place, and ask yourself whether you could solve the extraordinary problem surrounding this popular peer and his daughter who, while appearing frequently at the most exclusive functions in London, were sometimes living in absolute secrecy in their own house, or wandering over the face of the world without apparent motive, yet evidently with some fixed but secret object.

The more I reflected, the more utterly mystified I became.

"It is impossible—quite impossible?" she said when, at the Park Lane corner of Grosvenor Street I halted to take leave of her. "We must not meet again. I hope, Mr Kennedy, you will think no more of me," she added; "because it pains me quite as much as it does you. As I have already told you, I would explain the truth if I were allowed—but I cannot."

I saw that her eyelids trembled slightly, and I, folding her hand in farewell, pressed it with a deep meaning which she understood, and to which she responded.

"But we are friends, Lady Judith; we are friends, are we not?"

In response she drew a long sigh, and shook her head, saying, "Mr Kennedy, I know you are my friend, and one day, perhaps, I shall require to put your friendship to the test. Until then, let us remain apart, because it will be best so. You know the fears I have—the fear that evil may befall you."

"I am ready to serve you at any moment," I answered.

She withdrew her hand, sighing again, and, filled with emotion by my final declaration, hurried away through the hot, oppressive night.

For a moment, full of vague regret, I watched her departure, then turned on my heel and strolled down Park Lane into Piccadilly on my return to Dover Street, my mind full of that sweet-faced woman.

Those strange words of hers rang in my ears. At what did she hint? Tragedy, deep and mysterious, was underlying it all, I was confident, yet as a man of action I felt impelled towards that other spot mentioned in The Closed Book—the grim castle of Threave, that scene of foul deeds, that through the Middle Ages was the home of the Black Douglas. That her father intended to go there was evident, and it therefore behooved us to lose no time in going North and making preliminary investigations.

The advisability of going North without delay filled my mind until I had become oblivious to all about me, and indeed I was walking quite unconscious of the hurrying traffic in Piccadilly until I felt a slight touch on the arm and heard a woman's low voice exclaim in Italian, "Pardon, Signor Kennedy, but I believe we have met before?"

I started and turned quickly aside to recognise in the speaker the very last person whom I expected to meet in that busy London thoroughfare— the dark-eyed, well-dressed woman whom I had encountered in the prior's study at Florence, the woman in black who had made confession to Father Bernardo.

Chapter Twenty Nine
Some Explanations

My first thought, of course, was that the woman was a thief, for it was she who had so cleverly stolen The Closed Book from my study at Antignano and carried it to Paris, there transferring it to the hands of old Mrs Pickard, of Harpur Street.

My first impulse was to tax her with the theft; but fortunately I saw a necessity for careful tact, and therefore responded pleasantly in the same language, "Yes, signorina. It was one afternoon not long ago in Florence, if I remember aright."

"It was," she said quickly. "I wish to speak with you in private. Where can we go that we are not observed? I know so very little of London."

For a moment I reflected. If she really wished to give me any information I ought to secure it at all hazards. Her manner was that of one who feared recognition in that public thoroughfare, and wished to speak with me in private; therefore I hailed a passing hansom, and as we were getting in I recollected that, it being dinner-time, we might secure a quiet table in the upstairs room at Scott's at the top of the Haymarket. Therefore, to that famed restaurant I gave the cabman directions.

Her manner was as though haunted by a grave suspicion that she was being followed, and during our drive along to Piccadilly Circus she scarcely uttered a single word save to express satisfaction at finding me in a giant city like London, and to drop the remark that she had been following me for an hour past—the latter proving that she had seen me with Judith, and had undoubtedly noted my tenderness towards her.

My wooing in those crowded London streets that evening had certainly been strange, but really not extraordinary when one considers how many declarations of love are made among London's millions amid the roar of traffic and the hurry and scurry of outdoor life. There exist few places in the heart of London that are adapted for lovers' walks and lovers' talks, and those few spots are so well patronised that the majority of lovers carefully avoid them. Romance is enacted among the smoke-blackened bricks and mortar of London just as often as in the briar-scented country lane or on the shingly beach of the popular seaside resort. The quiet thoroughfares of London, where one knows not his neighbour, are always more private than any country lane, with its sneaking yokels and the local gossip of its nearest village.

Still, the mystery with which this handsome, dark-eyed woman had accosted me, and the rapidity with which we had driven away, caused me to reflect. She was either my enemy or my friend—which, I intended to discover.

In the upstairs room of the restaurant we found a quiet corner safe from intrusion or observation, and when I had ordered a light dinner I asked for her explanation.

"I arrived in London three days ago," she explained in Italian, "and have been in search of you ever since. I saw you leave that house in Bloomsbury together with the signorina, and have been following you ever since—oh! so far that I am very tired. But I kept on, because I desired to speak to you. The risk I have run is very great," and she glanced around apprehensively at the half-dozen diners scattered about the room. "If I am discovered then the worst must come."

"Why?"

"Because they do not know that I am in London, or that I am determined to warn you."

"Of what?" I asked eagerly.

"Of this plot against you."

"By whom?"

"By the persons you believe are your best friends," she answered, bending across the small table towards me, and speaking in a low half-whisper.

"And why do you wish to give me this warning?" I inquired suspiciously, recollecting that this fine, handsome woman had acted as a thief, and had evidently herself participated in the plot—whatever it might have been.

"Because I am ordered to do so by one who is your real friend."

"And what's his name, pray?"

"Padre Bernardo of Florence. It is at his orders that I have sought you tonight."

Her reply surprised me. The fat, good-humoured prior of San Sisto had certainly been very friendly towards me; but I had never believed, after what had occurred, that he was actually my friend. Had he not, by means of a ruse, endeavoured to induce me to withdraw from my bargain over my precious Arnoldus? Was he not an exceedingly clever and ingenious person, this Bernardo Landini? His actions had been puzzling from first to last, rendered, indeed, doubly mysterious when viewed in the light of my discovery at the end of that rare volume, and by recent events in London and at Crowland.

It was surely curious that he should send this woman to me, of all other persons. Yet somehow she seemed to be in his confidence. If not, why had they talked in his study with closed doors?

Suspicious that this woman had approached me with evil object, I nevertheless allowed her to explain. She was attired very much in the same manner as when I had first encountered her—namely, in plain black, a gown of apparent Parisian make, and a stylish hat that suited her dark beauty admirably, yet not at all loud in design.

She leaned her elbows on the table, and bending forward, with her gloved hands held together, thus explained her object in seeking me:

"I have been sent to warn you," she said with a strange look in her dark eyes—those eyes that had once haunted me in that sun-blanched city by the sea.

"But you called at my house at Antignano and obtained possession of the manuscript which I had bought of Father Bernardo," I said. "Why?"

"Because its possession constituted a danger to you," was her answer, still speaking in Italian.

And I wondered whether she were aware that its vellum leaves were impregnated with a deadly venom that had not yet lost its potency.

"But that was no reason why you should steal the manuscript," I said, in Italian, rather bluntly.

She raised her wine-glass to her lips and drank slowly in order to reflect. Then, setting her claret down, exclaimed:

"Ah! my action was under compulsion. You should have been warned by the prior of the evil that possession of the book would bring upon you."

"Well, now tell me, signorina—for I haven't the pleasure of your real name—"

"Anita Bardi," she interrupted.

"Well," I said. "I wish to inquire one thing—namely, whether our friend the prior has any idea of what the Arnoldus contains?"

"No. He is entirely in ignorance of it. If he had, he certainly would never have been a party to this dastardly plot against you."

"But what is the motive of this conspiracy?" I inquired, much puzzled.

"Your death," she answered without hesitation. "Your enemies intend that you shall die."

"Very charming of them," I laughed, pretending not to take her words seriously. "But why, I wonder, are they so anxious for my decease?"

"Because you have gained their secret—you are believed to have read and understood what is contained in that newly discovered manuscript."

"And if I have, I surely purchased the book at the price asked for it?"

"Ah! you see the prior had no right to sell it to you. A mistake was committed from the very first. How did you first know of its existence?"

"Through a dealer in antiques in Leghorn, named Francesco Graniani, an old hunchback."

"I thought so!" she exclaimed. "I hear that he is in London. All this goes to show that you should be warned."

"Of Graniani?"

"And of others also. I saw you with Lady Judith Gordon, and—if you will pardon me—you seemed attracted towards her."

She spoke frankly and looked me steadily in the face with those great dark eyes of hers.

"And if I am?"

"I presume you have not been long acquainted with her?"

"Not very long."

"Then, before you allow yourself to fall beneath her spell, as you seem to be doing, just make a few inquiries. It will not be difficult, and may be the means of saving you from dire misfortune—perhaps even saving your life."

"How? I don't understand."

"Possibly not. I only ask you to heed my warning. I am not here to explain the motives of others."

"But you can surely tell me why I should hold aloof from Lady Judith?" I demanded.

"No, I cannot," she responded, speaking in broken English for the first time, and apparently forgetting herself in her excitement. "If you are not warned it is your own fault."

"You say you know her," I observed. "Where did you meet her?"

"In Italy—under strange circumstances."

"With her father?"

"Yes," she answered after a moment's hesitation, and across her countenance there spread a strange look of mystery. "But we need not discuss that subject further," she added, lapsing again into Italian, which she spoke with a Florentine accent. "I wish to ask your forgiveness for stealing your book. I can only urge leniency on the ground that I acted at the instigation and under compulsion of others."

"I forgive you if you will tell me who instigated you to commit the theft," I said.

"No, I cannot do that. I ask your forgiveness, and in order to atone for what I have done I came here to warn you of the great peril which threatens you. Beware of your association with Judith Gordon!"

"What?" I cried. "Do you mean to insinuate that she is my bitter enemy?"

"Beware of her is all I say."

"And how do you suggest I should act?" I demanded, much surprised at this strange woman's allegations against my love.

"You should again obtain possession of the Arnoldus. It may help you," was her curious recommendation.

It was on the point of my tongue to say that it was already in my possession; but my natural caution again asserted itself. The woman was one whom I should deal with diplomatically in order to learn her motive.

"Perhaps you can tell me where it is?" I suggested.

"In the hands of an Englishman named Selby, who lives in that house in Harpur Street which you quitted this evening."

Then she was evidently unaware that Selby had suffered its loss, and as far as I could judge she seemed dealing honestly with me. This fact puzzled me more than ever. Suddenly I recollected that mysterious sign in the window, and I asked her the meaning of the bear cub.

"Yes," she answered with a sudden gravity that had not hitherto fallen upon her. "I saw it there today," she added slowly. "It has a signification, as you suspect."

"An evil one?"

"Yes, an evil one—stranger than you could ever guess."

"Will you not tell me?"

But again she shook her head, and declared that a silence was imposed upon her regarding it, as upon other matters. She had merely sought me in order to warn me, an innocent and unsuspecting man, against falling into the cunningly prepared trap laid for me.

She was quite calm, determined, unemotional. Once or twice, as newcomers entered the dining-room, she betrayed fear of recognition, but beyond that seemed absolutely cool and unruffled.

From her I had gathered two facts—namely, that Graniani was somehow at the bottom of the whole of the strange affair, as I had all along suspected, and that the woman I had grown to love was carefully plotting my ruin. This I refused to believe, and frankly told her so.

She allowed me to go on without a word of contradiction. Her manner was that of a well-bred woman, about thirty I judged her to be, her gesture and speech betraying refinement, and her eyes large, expressive, and sparkling. Indeed, she was a woman who might attract any man, and I daresay I should have found myself lost in admiration had it not been for my passionate love for Judith.

"I have only told you the truth, Signor Kennedy," she answered quietly in Italian. "I would, however, ask you to promise me to tell no one of our meeting. Remember that if you wish for advice in the future you have only to write to me *poste restante* at Charing Cross, and I shall duly receive your letter."

The Charing Cross post office is the usual address of foreigners when travelling in England, therefore I knew not whether she suggested that place because of secrecy or convenience. She made no mention of Lord Glenelg or of his search after the treasure; and, thinking that discretion were best, I did not refer to it, for I intended to keep my own counsel even though her allegations and the fact that she had so boldly accosted me formed in themselves an additional mystery.

So we finished our meal, and after some further desultory conversation which showed that she, on her part, was somewhat disappointed at the manner in which I had treated her confidences, I gave her my club address, saw her into a cab, and then we parted.

Chapter Thirty
Humours of a House Party

In the calm, mystic sundown of the August evening, after nine hours in the express from Euston, I was driving with Wyman in Fred Fenwick's Perth-cart up the side of Loch Ken, that long romantic stretch of water hemmed in by the high, heather-clad hills of Galloway. We were covering that seven miles of winding road that lies between New Galloway station and New Galloway burgh.

Southern Scotland surely possesses no wilder or more charming and picturesque district than the Glenkens, and here in the heart of them, the drive was refreshing, for the air was keen after stifling London; and the many burns and cascades we passed fell with soft rippling music over the mossy, bracken-covered roadsides.

The magnificent scenery, the sunset glow upon the unruffled surface of the loch, the dark purple of the distant hills, and the marvellous shades of the heather, did not, however, attract us, for we were both too full of the warm welcome which we knew was awaiting us at Crailloch, beyond Balmaclellan village. Through the long, white High Street of New Galloway we rattled in the dusk, up the steep hill, over the Ken Bridge, and then, following the broad river bed, turned in at last through the lodge gates and pulled up before the great square Elizabethan mansion, with its ornate exterior and high, twisted chimneys.

Fred Fenwicke, still in shooting-kit, came forth ere we could bring the cart to a standstill, and from the lighted hall came a chorus of hurrahs, expressing pleasure at our arrival.

"Well, Allan, old fellow!" cried Fred, grasping my hand warmly, "this is a real pleasure, to see you in Scotland again! Connie's in there somewhere, and there's a whole crowd of boys you know." And then he turned to give a similarly cordial greeting to Walter, and left me to enter the fine hall, where the majority of the house party had, in the idle hours before dinner, assembled to greet us.

The instant I entered a merry voice shouted, "What, ho, there! Allan the Author!" It was Sammy Waldron, or, to give him his correct name, Captain

Samuel Waldron, of the Bengal Police, home on two years' leave, and one of the best of good fellows.

Then Mrs Fenwicke, one of the smartest of women and the best of hostesses, whom everyone called Connie, shook me warmly by the hand, expressed her pleasure at our coming, and next moment we found ourselves in the centre of perhaps one of the merriest house parties in the whole of Scotland. Many of the people I had met before in that same big, well-furnished hall, with its splendid trophies of the chase and of Indian frontier wars. Fred Fenwicke and his wife, the merriest and most easy-going pair of any I knew, usually had the same party for the shooting, many of them being Anglo-Indians. In addition to Sammy Waldron, a well set up, fair-haired officer, tough as nails, who for over twenty years had been engaged on and off fighting the Indian frontier tribes, and who was usually the life and soul of the party, there was Jack Handsworth, or Major John Handsworth, C.I.E., owner of wide estates within sight of the Himalayas, who was never seen without a cigar except at meals; his son Godfrey, a smartly groomed fellow of whom everyone held golden opinions; Miss Handsworth, Jack's sister; Mrs Payling, an exceedingly pleasant and very good-looking widow of middle-age, who lived in summer in England and in winter in India, whose manner of speech was very deliberate, who was possessed of a keen sense of humour, and who always wore exquisite gowns, and wore them well. She was, indeed, one of those few women whose clothes seem part of them. In addition, there were two brothers named Sale, well-known solicitors in London, a merry pair, full of humour; and several other men and women whom I knew more or less intimately.

Certainly Fred Fenwicke never made a mistake in the arrangement of his house parties. His guests were never ill-assorted. Sometimes he had a quiet set of visitors, but this was seldom. Indeed, the fun and merriment at Crailloch was always a continuous round, for everyone did just as he liked; shot, cycled, fished for salmon or trout, went excursions, or wandered over the heather-clad hills. There was no restraint, and everyone came there for thorough enjoyment.

"Well," exclaimed Fred, as we stood with him in the dining-room having a "peg" before dressing, "nice lot of boys I've got this time, aren't they?"

"Too keen a crowd for me, I fear!" I laughed, for I knew from experience that when the shooters who were my fellow-guests foregathered, the fun was fast and furious.

For answer, my old friend only raised his glass in welcome and laughed across it merrily.

About thirty-eight, tall and dark, with a distinctly military bearing, and dressed in a smart tweed and gaiters, he looked the very pink of condition.

Living that healthy, open-air life on the Scotch estate had tanned his face and neck, and had brought him to a perfection of "fitness" seldom seen in a man. His vitality was marvellous. From the moment he came down in the morning to open the letter-bag until the small hours when the last billiard players drained their final "pegs," he was constantly active. He loved the country, he loved Scotland, he loved shooting, of which he had plenty, and above all loved the companionship of the few men who were his intimate friends—the men who now formed the house party.

Connie Fenwicke was just as happy, just as fond of country life, and just as generous in her hospitality as her husband. Wife and husband thoroughly understood each other, and such was their independent position that, when tired of life at Crailloch, they took a voyage to Australia, where Fred Fenwicke was interested in certain companies. Though fond of Scotland, and living there even through the town season, they were nevertheless essentially cosmopolitan, well-known in Monte Carlo, in Florence, and in Rome. More, indeed, need not be said save that they were a pair such as one seldom met, whose house was hospitality itself.

Walter was not so intimate a friend as myself; but before that night was out Fred Fenwicke had admitted him to that charmed circle of close acquaintances, and he declared himself absolutely at home.

Dinner was always the solemn function at Crailloch, as it is in most country houses, for the shooters were then clean, the ladies in pretty frocks, and amusing, and Fred's *chef* was acknowledged to be one of the best in Scotland. After the ladies had left the table and coffee had been served in the big, old dining-room, with its splendid family portraits, I took Fred aside, for I had detected in him an anxiety to know the reason I had so suddenly come up to visit him. He knew that it was not on account of sport, for near-sightedness prevented my shooting, and I had heard him pass a remark *sotto voce* at table with Sammy Waldron that it must be on account of some love affair.

In order to set my old friend's mind at rest I took him along to his study, the only sanctum private from guests, and told him that the reason of the suddenness of my visit was because I wanted to study on the spot the history of Threave Castle.

"Oh! that's it!" he cried, removing his cigar from his lips. "Well, I suppose you've got some book or other in view, eh?"

"H'm, yes," I answered after a moment's hesitation. "I'm studying the history of the place. Perhaps I may write a book about it. I want you to help me. Have you any books dealing with the subject?"

"I fear I haven't," was his response. "Threave is about fourteen miles from here, on a solitary and un-get-at-able island in the Dee. I've never been there myself; but I know a man, Mr Batten, the archaeologist, who lives in Castle-Douglas, who has the finest collection of works dealing with Galloway and the neighbourhood, and who has written a book regarding those parts. I'll write to him. He'll lend you a lot of books, no doubt, and perhaps he'll go over to Threave with you. He's an excellent fellow, and a great friend of mine. But," he added, "Walter is helping you, I suppose?"

"Yes. We are making certain investigations," was my cautious reply. "At present we can't say anything definite, except that I may possibly lay the scene of my new book there."

"Well, I'll assist you, Allan, old chap, if you'll promise to be silent upon Crailloch and all the boys here." And he laughed merrily. "When I told them you were coming they all wanted to know if you were going to write a book. They haven't forgotten those articles last season about Nice and Monte."

"I'll let them down lightly, I promise you," was my reply. "Only I tell you my object in confidence. I don't wish the whole crowd to know."

"Of course not, my dear fellow," he responded. "I'll help you. I'll write to Batten, and we'll arrange a little picnic over to Threave. You needn't tell anyone your real reason for going there."

And so I left the arrangements in his hands. After three days of merriment and nights of music, billiard playing, and practical joking, Fred received a note from Mr Batten saying that he had obtained permission from the laird for us to visit Threave, and that he would be pleased not only to accompany us, but also to lend me the several rare and out-of-print works in his collection that dealt with the history of the famous stronghold.

To us this was good news indeed, and two mornings later, in a party of ten, including several others on cycles, we drove in a pair-horse brake away along the bank of Loch Ken, through the long, whitewashed villages of Parton and Crossmichael, down to a spot beside the winding Dee, where at a lonely farmhouse we were met by Mr Batten, who proved a most affable and valuable guide.

The party was an extremely merry one, and being compelled to leave the brake some half-mile from the river, each of us carried part of the provisions off which we were to lunch on arrival on the island.

The day was superb for August, one of those brilliant mornings seldom experienced in Scotland so late in the season, and much good-humoured banter was exchanged as the whole party trudged through the wide fields of corn just falling to the sickle.

Presently, on coming up the brae-face, we suddenly obtained a view of the broad, winding river sparkling in the sunshine below; and beyond, upon its solitary island, given over to the rooks and waterfowl, rose the stern, grim keep of what was once the home of the Black Douglas, which even today stands out grey and forbidding in the autumn sunlight.

Wyman was walking beside me, carrying a basketful of bottles of soda water, and as the view burst upon me I turned to him and said:

"Can it be possible that the casket of which old Godfrey speaks is hidden upon that island?"

"Maybe," was his reply. "It certainly looks just the sort of outlandish place to hold a mystery. But we must say nothing to anyone. Let's take our observation in silence. They'll enjoy their picnic while we will refer to that memorandum you made of the parchment record."

At that moment Sammy Waldron, ruddy and sun-tanned, in a rough cycling suit, came up and began to chaff Walter regarding the soda—he himself being the bearer of a quantity of that spirit very precious with men on such occasions, being assisted in its transport by the ever humorous Mrs Payling, well turned-out as usual, and brimming over with good humour. Being a widow, with a son in the Indian service, she was essentially a man's companion as well as being a *chic* woman. She was chatting with Mr Batten, while Fred Fenwicke was walking with Connie and two ladies of the party a little in advance.

At last we all gained the water's edge, and, depositing our loads, proceeded to examine the laird's boat, a key of which Mr Batten had obtained. It was half-full of water, and there were no oars.

After some search a labourer was discovered who knew the spot where the oars were concealed, and he having pointed them out under a hedge, we discovered that they were so badly rotted by the weather that there was scarcely any blade left, and, further, that there were no rowlocks.

Sammy, Godfrey Handsworth, and the two Sales commenced to bale out the water with drinking-glasses, while the rest of the party, now being very hungry and thirsty, sat impatiently on the bark watching, and passing sarcastic remarks upon the slow progress of the work.

At length, however, it was concluded, and some of the provisions were taken aboard: Sammy being elected coxswain, with the two Sales as rowers. Then they took in a male volunteer on the trial trip

"The husbands' boat for Margate!"

"Nice day for a sail!" and "Man the lifeboat!" were among the derisive shouts and jeers amid which the venturous party put off into the stormy and rather dangerous waters of the Dee. The course of the boat with such oars and without rowlocks was necessarily erratic, and the absurd antics of the rowers and of Sammy as coxswain convulsed us on shore. Amidstream the rowers, affecting fatigue, commenced to refresh themselves upon the provisions which we had sent across, and calmly lunched, leaving us hungry and empty.

After a long and tempestuous voyage they landed their first freight; then returned and took a second and a third. In the fourth Wyman and myself were included, and after running on a mud bank and having a very exciting and ludicrous time of it, we at last, laughing merrily, sprang ashore on that wild, unvisited island, where, according to The Closed Book, the wonderful emeralds of Lucrezia Borgia had, through centuries, lain hidden.

Mr Batten assured us that no one had landed there for at least a year or more; but the instant we gained the shore we turned our first attention to discovering any traces of those whom we knew were aware of the old monk's secret in common with ourselves.

Chapter Thirty One
Under the Gallows Knob

The low-lying island upon which we found ourselves was certainly a dismal, out-of-the-world place, covered by rank grass and nettles, and yellow with St. John's wort. Ruined walls were scattered around the castle of Threave itself, a square, roofless tower, which in the bleakness of its gaunt and terrible majesty suggested the idea of an armed skeleton, in the facial apertures of which lay the darkness of death and decay.

This was the monument of the Douglases' pride and the engine of their oppression during their galling ascendancy, when Archibald rode with his retinue of two thousand armed retainers, many of them the most noted desperadoes, and ravaged the Border. The huge fourteenth-century fortress, once the pride of kings, was still a massive pile, with walls nearly seventy feet high, built of common grey moor stone.

As we wandered through it, the wind howling through the narrow slits where archers had sent forth their shafts, our friend Mr Batten pointed out in the lowest story the dungeon, arsenal, and larder; the barracks on the first floor; and, above, the apartments of state, where the Black Douglas lodged his friends or feasted his vassals, the walls of all massive, but now crumbling to decay.

Around the castle were the remains of a strong barbican, flanked at each angle by a circular tower, which had been secured in front by a deep fosse and vallum, both water and walls of the latter having long since disappeared.

Then, standing outside—while the rest of the party, seated on the grass, were eating their luncheon, laughing merrily and thoroughly enjoying the novelty of reaching such a place—Mr Batten pointed to a large granite bracket projecting from the front of the castle, high up near the roof: the far-famed "Gallows Knob" or "Hanging Stone," which the Black Douglas was wont to boast was never without a "tassel," either in the shape of a malefactor, or, if none such were in custody, some unoffending vassal!

When the Douglases maintained their power in Galloway the deeds committed within that grim, grey fortress were such as invest it with fearful interest. I recollected having read of its sinister memories, and some of them were now recalled to me by Mr Batten, who made a deep study of the subject. Indeed, as I stood there with Walter Wyman, apart from the gay Crailloch house party, gazing up at the high grey walls that had once sheltered the old soldier-monk and chronicler, Godfrey Lovel, I recollected how well the weirdlike halo that, to the present day, surrounds the place is expressed in those plaintive lines of the unfortunate Inglis of Torsonce:

> Threave's Castle looms as dark by day,
> With its walls of moorland grey,
> And the sad and sullen stream
> Which, like some dank, unwholesome dream,
> Creeps on its stagnant way,
> In mossy pool and quagmire pent
> Around the island battlement.
> Dismal is the granite pile
> With barbican and flanking tower,
> That frown beneath the merry smile
> Of laughing noontide hour.
> Dismal is the island when,
> With herbage rank and stunted thorn
> That clothe the blood-besprinkled fen
> In leaf and bough forlorn,
> Some evil spirit haunts it yet.
> The dreary annals of the past
> Athwart the meadow wan and wet
> Their spectral shadows cast;
> No feathered minstrel tunes his throat
> On lowly bush or lofty spray;
> No skylark pipes his dulcet note
> In the sun's yellow ray;
> And still the prisoned oxen low
> To reach the farther shore,
> Like captives of the spear and bow
> In Douglas raids of yore;
> No rural lover comes to hide
> The stolen tryst at eventide;
> And the otter seeks his prey,
> And the wild duck leads her brood,
> And desolation and decay
> Sleep in the ghastly solitude.

Mr Batten was called over to the luncheon party by Connie Fenwicke, who cried, "I say, Mr Batten, leave the author to meditate, and come and have something to eat. And you also, Captain Wyman. Allan will come when he's hungry; he's feasting on ruins at present."

Wyman excused himself for a moment, but Mr Batten succumbed to the temptation of cold partridge and claret.

With Walter, I walked behind one of the round flanking towers, scrambling over the fallen masonry, and when out of sight of the others we commenced to search carefully for any traces of previous visitors there. The rank grass and weeds were trodden down here and there by recent footsteps; but we concluded that it had been done by some of our party who had wandered about the place prior to our own landing. We wondered whether Lord Glenelg or his companions had already been there; but the absence of any evidence that the laird's boat had been used for months convinced us that they had not.

"Our first direction is to follow the shadow of the keep to its easterly angle when the sun shines, at 3:30, on the sixth of September," I began, when Walter interrupted me with: .

"But has it occurred to you that since that record was written the calendar has been altered? What was the sixth of September in the sixteenth century is not the sixth of September in the present day."

"By Jove?" I gasped. "I never thought of that. But what is the precise difference?"

"I happened to be looking that very point up not long ago," said Walter, "which is what brought it to my mind now. About 1582 Pope Gregory XIII decreed that ten days should be omitted, and October fifth was reckoned as the fifteenth. But this was not universal till 1751, when a bill was passed for regulating the commencement of the year, and for correcting the calendar. By that bill eleven days were omitted after the second of September, so that the ensuing day was the fourteenth."

"In that case, then, September sixth of Godfrey Lovel's day is really our September seventeenth. That gives us nearly two weeks more time than we had counted on," I remarked. "Yet it will be half-past three before we leave today, and we shall then, at any rate, be able to see the vicinity of the spot, although we cannot fix it exactly until the day and hour indicated."

"I wonder whether we shall really find the casket?" Walter said, eagerly. "To me this is just the sort of place where some treasure lies buried. The day before we left town I went to the British Museum and looked up the history of the place. Our record in The Closed Book is certainly borne out by history. Maxwell of Terregles was keeper of the Threave in Godfrey's day, the dawn of the Reformation, and seems to have had rather a rough time of it, just as the old monk has written. John Gordon of Lochinvar, Dean Vaus of Soulseat, the Macdowalls of Freuch and of Mindork, who burned Brodick Castle and invaded Arran, and James Earl of Bothwell, of Earlston, as mentioned by Godfrey Lovel, were all his prominent contemporaries. Therefore it is certainly likely that the ex-favourite of Lucrezia Borgia did actually conceal the casket intrusted to him somewhere on this island, which in his day was, of course, impregnable."

"I quite agree," I answered, looking wonderingly around. "Of course, the directions are complicated, purposely no doubt; and today it seems quite useless to attempt to follow them. We must arouse no suspicion of our intentions."

"We shall require assistance when we really do investigate," my companion remarked.

"Then we'll take Fred into our confidence. He would thoroughly enter into the spirit of the thing—that I know."

We walked back to where the others were still seated on the grass, in the shadow of the high grey wall, with its grim "hanging knob," and a chorus of jeers at my studious nature greeted me.

"Going to write a book, I suppose, Allan?" cried Sammy Waldron, his mouth full of sandwich. "Put me in it, old fellow. I'm good-looking enough to be a hero, aren't I?"

Bertie Sale opened a bottle of soda clumsily, and squirted it in a lady's face, and Mrs Payling, to whom Walter turned his attention, was discovered actually talking frocks with Connie, and was allowed to continue, for both men and women admired her for being so well turned-out on every occasion. Godfrey Handsworth had been heard to remark that it was a pity that she was not twenty years younger; but, as it was, she was still very handsome, with a figure that many a younger woman envied.

Fred Fenwicke and Connie looked after everyone's comfort. On such occasions they never took servants. Everyone helped himself and looked after a lady, and, as such *al fresco* luncheons were weekly in the shooting season, this kind of entertainment had been brought to a fine art.

The men smoked and idled, some of them lying stretched upon the grass, while others escorted the ladies around the ruins, the chief excitement being the loss of Connie's Aberdeen "Jack," a one-eyed dog of Satanic expression and cunning, the terror of Campbell, the sturdy, good-humoured gamekeeper of Crailloch.

I sat on the grass, smoking, chatting, and drinking whisky and soda with Fred,—Walter, Sammy, and Mr Batten, while the others wandered about the island. The afternoon was absolutely perfect, with as blue a sky as ever seen in Italy, and across the wide sweep of river, towards Greenlaw, rose the long, low heathery hills.

From where we idled Mr Batten pointed out to us the peaks Bengairn and Cairntosh and the highlands of Balmaghie, and related several archaeological facts that in view of our forthcoming explorations, were of intense interest to us.

"You see that great rugged hole in the wall, half-way up the front of the castle?" he said, pointing to it. "The hole looks almost like a window, but it is a breach made by the cannon known as Mons Meg, now to be seen at Edinburgh Castle. The piece of artillery was made by a blacksmith and his sons at Buchan, and was used by the king in his operations against Threave. The charge consisted of a peck of gunpowder and a granite ball the weight of a Carsphairn cow. The first discharge produced a panic among the inmates of the castle, and the second shot went through the walls and carried away the right hand of the Countess, the celebrated Fair Maid of Galloway, as she sat at table in the banqueting hall about to raise a wine cup to her lips. The garrison quickly surrendered, and the blacksmith was granted the forfeited lands of Mollance and Barncrosh."

"Curious?" I remarked. "Only a legend, I suppose?"

"Not at all—a historical fact. As late as 1841 Mr Gordon of Greenlaw, tenant of this island, discovered an immense granite ball which, on examination, was found to be a bullet, in all respects the same as those belonging to Mons Meg, while a massive gold ring inscribed 'Margaret de Douglas' was discovered by a workman employed to clear out some rubbish when the castle was repaired as a barrack for French prisoners. This was the actual ring supposed to have been on the hand of the Fair Maid of Galloway when it was blown away at the siege."

Such discovery caused hope to arise within us. I exchanged glances with Wyman, and saw that he considered this additional evidence that treasure might be hidden beneath that turf on which we were lounging.

Presently we all rose to rejoin the party, and again Walter and I managed to separate ourselves from the rest and strolled around the small marshy island.

It was ten minutes past three, and the sun, still shining brightly, cast a long, straight, sharply defined shadow in the direction of the broad river and the high land of Greenlaw. The great square tower was higher on the eastern angle than the western, therefore from its position to the sun the eastern angle threw a longer shadow, which, together, we followed through the grass-grown ditch which was once the fosse and up the bank, then, counting forty-three paces, we halted at a spot covered with nettles or grass.

"The starting point for measurements must be somewhere here. Fifty-six paces with the face toward Bengairn," I remarked. "I'm no astronomer; but I suppose that, on the date mentioned, the shadow will be more to eastward or to westward. We will, at any rate, mark this spot," and, finding a piece of broken hurdle, used some time or other to pen in cattle which had grazed on the island, I stuck it deeply in the ground just at the farthermost point of the great oblong shadow across the grass.

Chapter Thirty Two
The Major Makes a Statement

While the rest of the party examined the dungeon, I clambered over the ruins, and ascended by the winding, broken stairway to the summit. I walked with Wyman across the weedy, neglected ground beyond the dried-up fosse, reconstructing the stronghold in imagination by the position of the broken barbican.

Over the self-same ground the unfrocked monk of Crowland had wandered with his companion in misfortune, the monk Malcolm. We looked back at the gateway of the castle, so high up that it was on a level with the second floor. Through that, the only exit from the castle, old Godfrey had fled with his fair charge across the drawbridge, over the island to the river, and across the narrow temporary bridge, then existing, to the shore — away back to safety in England, leaving Lucrezia's casket, with its precious contents, safely hidden.

The long, straight shadow veered round slowly; and by four o'clock, when the party carrying the empty baskets and picnic accessories strolled back to the spot of embarkation, it had shifted a considerable distance from the spot where I had driven in the stake.

Everyone pronounced the picnic a distinct success. It was an entire novelty to go to that historic spot, unvisited from one year's end to another, and certainly to us it had been a very interesting experience. We had taken certain observations which would, later on, be of the greatest use to us.

The ferrying back of the party, in twos, by Sammy Waldron and Bertie Sale, was fraught with just as much hilarity as the arrival. The old boat was declared to be leaky, for it now had a quantity of water in it, compelling the ladies to hold their skirts high and place their feet out of the way of the wash. On the first trip Bertie "caught a crab," owing to the absence of blade to his oar, and the remainder of the rowing was done Indian fashion, the craft, being rudderless, always taking an erratic course. Time after time they crossed and recrossed, until there remained only Fred Fenwicke, Walter, and myself. All of us embarked at last, and, with triumphant shouts, set a course toward the opposite shore; but ere we had gone far we ran deep into a submerged mud bank, and notwithstanding our combined efforts for nearly half an hour, beneath the derisive cheers of the rest of the party, we remained there.

One desperate effort, in which Sammy broke his oar in half, resulted in our getting clear at last, and slowly we continued across to the opposite bank, being greeted with mock welcome on our return from that perilous voyage, during which the vessel had been so long overdue.

Together we walked in a straggling line back to our brake, which we left at the farmhouse of Kelton Mains, and at the invitation of Mr Batten we drove back into the clean, prosperous little town of Castle-Douglas and took tea with him, after inspecting his pictures; for, in addition to being a well-known archaeologist, he was an amateur artist of no small merit. True to his promise, he lent me a collection of valuable books dealing with Threave, and then, in the glorious sunset, we set out on our long drive back through the Glenkens to Crailloch, the cyclist contingent going on ahead. Fred Fenwicke was of the latter party, and both he and a friend named Gough, curiously enough, had punctures within a hundred yards of each other, and had to be picked up by us.

Ten days of merriment went by. One night, dinner was as usual a merry function, but the ladies being tired, retired early, while the men idled, gossiped, and played billiards. Connie's boudoir adjoined the billiard-room, and I was sitting there alone with Fred, about half-past one, preliminary to turning in, when, looking me straight in the face, he said:

"Look here, Allan! What's your game over at Threave? I watched you that afternoon, and saw you poking about and counting your paces. I was on the top of the castle wall and looked down on both of you when you thought yourselves unobserved."

For the moment I was somewhat taken aback, for I had no idea we had been watched, nor that we had aroused his suspicions. When a man is in search of hidden treasure he does not usually tell it to the world, for fear of derision being cast upon him, therefore I again naturally hesitated to explain our real object.

But he continued to press me; and, being one of my oldest and most intimate friends, I called in Walter, and, closing the door again, explained briefly the explorations we intended to make, and how I had gained the knowledge of the hidden casket.

He listened to me open-mouthed, in amazement, especially when I described the deadly contact of those forbidden pages, and the attempt made by Lord Glenelg and his companions to find the treasure of Crowland Abbey.

"Lord Glenelg, did you say?" Fred remarked when I mentioned the name. "I know both him and his daughter Lady Judith Gordon. We first met them in Wellington, New Zealand, three years ago. He has a shoot up at Callart, in Inverness, and curiously enough they're both coming here to stay with us on Saturday."

"Coming here?" I gasped. "Lady Judith coming here?"

"Yes. Pretty girl, isn't she? I'd be gone on her myself if I were a bachelor. Perhaps you are, old chap."

I did not respond, except to extract a strict promise from my host to preserve my secret.

"Of course I shall say nothing," he assured me. "Father and daughter are, however, a strange pair. It's very remarkable—this story you've just told me. I don't half like the idea of that bear cub being shown in the window in Bloomsbury. There's something uncanny about it."

I agreed; but all my thoughts were of his lordship's motive for coming there. Like myself, he had shot with Fred before, it seemed, and my host and Connie had, last season, been his guests for a week up at Callart. In Scotland, hospitality seems always more open, more genuine, and more spontaneous than in England.

"Of course, Glenelg is something of an archaeologist, like yourself," Fred said; "but if what you say is true, there seems to be some extraordinary conspiracy afoot to obtain possession of certain treasure, which, by right, should be yours, as the purchaser of this remarkable book. I must admit that Glenelg and his daughter have been both to Connie and myself something of mysteries. When we were in town last Christmas, Connie swore she saw Lady Judith dressed in a very shabby kit coming out of an aerated bread shop in the Fulham Road. My wife stopped to speak, but the girl pretended not to know her. Connie knew her by that small piece of gold-stopping in one of her front teeth."

"But why should she go about like that?" I asked.

"How can I tell? They were supposed to be away in Canada, or somewhere, at the time; they're nearly always travelling, you know. We came home with them on the *Caledonia* the first season we met them."

"They're mysteries!" declared Wyman bluntly. "The girl is, at any rate."

"What do you know of her?" inquired Fred eagerly.

But Walter would not satisfy us. He merely said:

"I've heard one or two strange rumours—that's all."

I was torn by conflicting desires: the desire not to meet his lordship beneath that roof, and the all-impelling desire to be afforded an opportunity of more intimate friendship with that sweet, sad-hearted woman whom I adored.

Fred Fenwicke was just as interested in the strange circumstances as we were, and promised at once to do all in his power to assist us. I knew him to be a man of sterling worth, whose word was his bond, and whose friendship was true and continuous. Equally with Walter Wyman, he was my best friend, and, with the exception of keeping back the fact that I loved Lady Judith, I was perfectly frank with him, telling him the suggestion that had crossed my mind—namely, that it would perhaps be as well if I left Crailloch before his lordship's arrival.

"Why?" asked the Major at once. "Does he know that you are making this search?"

"I suppose he does," Wyman replied. "He evidently knows that The Closed Book has been in Allan's hands, and that he has deciphered it."

Fred remained thoughtful for a moment, then said:

"But it may be that he's coming here with the same object as yourself—to see Threave and make investigations. If that's so, I'd go over to Castle-Douglas, and stay at the 'Douglas Arms'—a very comfortable hotel. You'd then be right on the spot."

"Yes," I said; "that's what we will do. And, meanwhile, you will watch his lordship's movements for us, won't you?"

"Of course," laughed Fred, now entering thoroughly into the spirit of the thing, for the excitement of a treasure hunt appealed to his vigorous nature.

Our plans were, however, quickly doomed to failure; for next morning, at breakfast, Fred announced to us that Lord Glenelg had written from Edinburgh to say that urgent family affairs called him to Paris, and that, consequently, neither he nor his daughter could come to Crailloch just at present.

The very wording of the letter, which he read to those at his end of the table, was to us suspicious, that his lordship had learned that we were Fred Fenwicke's guests, and on that account feared to come. This idea I put later to Fred himself, and he entirely coincided with my opinion.

"They're mysterious, very mysterious, old fellow," he said. "I don't half like the idea of those people you told me about—the hunchback and the other fellow—who are behind them. Yet, on the other hand, Lord Glenelg is a man well-known, with a very high reputation when he was in Parliament, ten years ago. He was an Under-Secretary, if I recollect aright."

"But what is their game, do you think?"

"Their game at Crowland was to find the hidden treasure of the abbey," he answered, "and they may probably try the same thing at Threave."

"That's exactly what we've feared," chimed in Walter. "I believe they are in possession of some further fact, of which we know nothing. There's a conspiracy against Allan, too, the nature of which we are at present in ignorance."

"But why?" I asked, recollecting all the curious events of the past, and remembering my conversation with that strange woman in black who had so ingeniously stolen the Arnoldus.

Wyman shrugged his shoulders, saying:

"It is never any good inquiring into the motives of either man or woman. The cleverest man can never gauge them accurately."

"Well," remarked Fred Fenwicke, "the move in this case is undoubtedly the recovery of the treasure."

"But the treasure, if it exists, is mine!" I said. "I purchased the book and deciphered the secret. Therefore I may surely make investigations with profit to myself?"

"You may make investigations, but without profit, I fear, so far as Threave is concerned," was Fred's calm reply.

"I don't understand you," I said. "The book was offered to me at a fair price, and I purchased it. Whatever I found within I may surely use to my own advantage?"

"Observing, of course, the law of treasure-trove," was my host's remark.

"Of course."

"Then whatever you find must either go to the Crown or to the lord of the manor."

"You mean Colonel Maitland?"

"No, I mean Lord Glenelg," my friend said.

"Why Lord Glenelg?" I demanded quickly.

"Because, according to the *Glasgow Herald* this morning, he has purchased both the island and castle from Colonel Maitland, so, whatever is found on that property undoubtedly belongs to him."

Chapter Thirty Three
Will the Sun Shine?

Fred took from his study table the *Glasgow Herald* of that morning, and there, sure enough, was a paragraph stating that the Earl of Glenelg had purchased the historic castle of Threave, together with the islands, from the laird, Colonel Maitland. The Gordons had been connected with the property since the seventeenth century, it was stated, hence the purchase by the Earl.

"Curiously enough," observed Fred Fenwicke, "Maitland's solicitors are my own: Burton, Brooks, and Co, of Union Street, Glasgow. From them I could get to hear the actual situation."

"Wire them in the morning, and ask if the property is really sold. The papers often get hold of news of that sort prematurely," I said, clutching eagerly at the last straw, for our enemies had certainly forestalled us by this purchase, which, if actually effected, upset all our plans. If Lord Glenelg had paid for the property then the Borgia emeralds could never be ours.

Fred proposed to wire, and at noon that day Wyman and I were in the express travelling towards Euston.

For some days yet it was impossible to follow the old monk's directions for the discovery of the spot at Threave; therefore, with the prospect of the Crowland treasure being revealed, we eagerly went on the following day to the British Museum and were closeted with the professor.

"I had no idea that this most interesting document existed," he said, as he sat at his table and unfolded to our gaze a dark old parchment, whereon was a large but rather roughly drawn plan, very similar in style to those in The Closed Book.

"You will see here," he said, pointing to an inscription in a small Gothic hand underneath, "that it was prepared by Richard Fosdyke, the celebrated architect, by the order of John Welles, the last abbot. From the difference in the drawing on the north side, it was apparently intended to make certain additions to the monastery buildings; but having compared it with the ground plan of the present ruins, it is proved that the abbey was dissolved before the work was carried out."

"It is the exact positions of the fish ponds that we are very desirous of ascertaining," I said. "What is your opinion?"

"There can be but one. They are here," and he pointed to two squares drawn at some distance at the north-east of the abbey church, and in an exactly opposite direction to the written record of old Godfrey. "This square of buildings enclosed the cloister court," the expert went on, "and here you see is the chapter house, the refectory, and the mausoleum, all of which have now disappeared."

Then he took out a plan of the present ruins, and we compared the two carefully, being surprised at the wide ramifications of the original abbey and the extent of the outbuildings.

I inquired if it were possible to have a tracing of it, when our friend the professor took from a drawer a large sheet of tracing-paper upon which he had already had a copy made. This he gave to me, expressing pleasure that he had been of any service to us in our investigations.

"I am myself intensely interested in the work you have undertaken," he said. "If you really hold Godfrey Lovel's Arncldus then you may, after all, be successful in discovering both the abbey treasures and the Borgia emeralds."

"That is exactly what we are trying to do, but unfortunately we are not alone in it."

"You mean that the Italian hunchback has discovered something?"

"Why, has he been here since my last visit?"

"He was here all day yesterday. He has in his possession some curious plan or other."

My companion suggested that we should go that very evening to Crowland, place the plan before our good friend Mr Mason, and commence investigations in an open and straightforward manner. This course we adopted, and arranged to leave for Peterborough by the Leeds express.

At five o'clock, however, the Captain returned to tell me that he had received an imperative call from Paris, and must be away for several days. As there was nothing to be done until the seventeenth, his absence made no difference with our plans, though I found my patience sorely tried by the long wait. I employed the time in searching the British Museum for more detailed accounts of Threave, but without success. Within less than a fortnight Wyman had rejoined me, and we were making plans for a leisurely trip back to Scotland when I received a telegram from Fred Fenwicke that accelerated our plans. It ran:

"Come back tonight without fail. Go on to Castle-Douglas, and put up at 'Douglas Arms.' Will meet you there tomorrow morning."

At ten o'clock on the following morning we were back again in Scotland, breakfasting in a cozy room in that old-fashioned hotel, the "Douglas Arms," at Castle-Douglas, and anxiously awaiting Fred Fenwicke.

We had spent a comfortable if rather warm night in the sleeping-car from Euston, and both of us being constant travellers, neither felt the fatigue of the long railway journey. The urgency of Fred's message caused us the greatest anxiety, and as we sat there together our eyes were watching the window for his arrival.

Outside, the long, broad street, the principal thoroughfare of the town, was already filled with the August sunshine, the roadway almost as white as those glaring roads of Italy, the sky almost as blue as it was in my once-loved Tuscany.

We had engaged that room for ourselves, for there seemed to be a party of London holiday-makers staying in the hotel; at least so we judged them to be by the gorgeous tweeds of the men and the tourist kit of the women. Loud laughter rang in the corridors of the quiet, eminently respectable place, and before the door was a coach upon which the party were slowly settling themselves for a drive through the beautiful Glenkens.

At last, just as the coach drove away, and the old post-house settled down to its normal quiet, Fred Fenwicke opened the door and closed it quickly after him.

"I'm glad you fellows have come," he said in quick excitement. "There's something strange going on here. Yesterday I was cycling through here, and while passing down the road along Carlingwark Loch, the same road by which you drove the other day, I overtook Lady Judith. She was walking slowly, talking with an old hunchback."

"A hunchback?" I cried. "Then it must be Graniani."

"He was Italian, that's all I know. I didn't wait to acknowledge her because the fact struck me as very curious, and I thought it would be best if she were unaware that I had discovered her. So I ran on here, and on inquiry found that the lady, who had given the name of Miss Fletcher, had arrived on the previous day, and that the old Italian, who had signed his name in the visitors' book so badly that it could not be read, had arrived that morning."

"And they are both here! I wonder why?" I asked, amazed.

"Well, I suppose their visit has some connection with the search they intend to make over at Threave," Fred said. "At any rate, I thought it best that you should be on the spot, and watch what was happening."

"But the sale of the island?"

"Brooks wired me yesterday that the contract is signed, but the money is not yet paid over. The sale is to be completed on the sixteenth of September."

"Ah, Lord Glenelg, too, evidently thought of the change in the calendar. Well, we must take our chances of a clash with him. Today is the fifteenth. On the day after tomorrow, at three-thirty, we ought to be at Threave and take our observations by the sun."

"But suppose it's a wet day?" suggested Fred, always practical.

"Ah! suppose it is?" I echoed. "Then all our chance may melt away from us."

Half an hour later, while the Major and the Captain strolled along to have a chat with Mr Batten, at the office of the British Linen Company, of which he was manager, I excused myself and remained behind.

Scarcely had they gone when Graniani passed the window with Selby, both well-dressed and presenting a prosperous appearance. They were speaking in Italian, in order, I suppose, that those who overheard should not understand their conversation. But I knew from the hunchback's gesticulations that he was excited by some untoward event.

Judith was undoubtedly alone; therefore I rang for the waiter and sent him with my card to "Miss Fletcher."

Five minutes later she entered the room half-timidly, as though fearful of detection. Her hand trembled, her face was pale, and I saw that she was in a highly nervous condition.

"I had no idea you were here, Mr Kennedy," she gasped. "What brings you here?"

"I am here to be near you, Lady Judith." I answered, holding her small white hand. "You are still in distress. How may I help you?"

"How can you help me?" she echoed. "By leaving here at once. If you remain you will imperil your life. Ah! you don't know the terrible risk you are running."

"But why are you here?" I demanded. "I believed you were in Edinburgh."

"I am not here of my own free will," she said slowly. "It is because I am compelled."

"Compelled! By whom?"

"By your enemies, Allan. Ah! heed me — do heed me, and get away from here at once."

"Why may I not remain as your protector?" I demurred.

"Because I need none; for me there is no protection," and she trembled as she stood before me.

"Where is your father?"

"I don't know," she responded. "Some strange events have happened since we met last."

"But you still trust me, dearest?" I cried passionately, bending until my lips touched hers lightly. They were cold, and her features seemed like marble.

"Yes," she murmured. "I still trust you, Allan. My only fear is for your safety, not for mine. Recollect that we are dealing with people who are desperate—who will stick at nothing in order to gain their own sinister ends."

The thought of that weird sign in Bloomsbury crossed my mind, and I fell to wondering.

"If you reciprocate my love, dearest, it is all that I desire in life," I said quietly, in deepest earnestness. "You are in peril, you have told me, and I am your protector. You tell me nothing, because a silence is imposed upon you."

"Ah, Allan! I dare not tell you. If I did, you—even you—would hate me; in years to come even you would detest my memory. With me life is now short; but even though surrounded by a thousand perils and pitfalls, I am nevertheless happy because I know that I shall die loved by one upright and honest man."

"Die?" I echoed. "Why do you always speak of death being imminent? This is a mere morbid foreboding. You should rid yourself of it, for it surely isn't good for you."

"Ah?" she sighed bitterly, "you do not know, Allan, or you would not think so." Then, a moment later, she turned to me and implored me to leave Castle-Douglas and return to London.

This I refused to do, though I said nothing of the presence of Graniani or Selby, for even now I was not quite convinced whether she were playing me false. If Judith were really my friend, if she really loved me as I hoped, why was she not a little more plain and straightforward? It was this fact that still held me in a turmoil of suspicion. My passion for her increased, but my position seemed somehow very insecure.

That a deep and impenetrable mystery surrounded her was apparent; but she seemed determined upon increasing it instead of giving me some clue to its elucidation, however slight.

I suggested that we should walk out of the town and talk, but at first she refused. She evidently feared that those two men might encounter her in my company, although to me she pleaded a headache. The whole affair was so queer and unconventional that I myself became more bewildered.

At length, however, I induced her to go for a stroll, allowing her to chose the way. She evidently knew the direction in which the hunchback and his companion had gone, for she took the road that led across the town and around the end of the beautiful loch towards Whitepark, where we presently struck a quiet, unfrequented path, whereon we strolled slowly in the shadow of the trees.

Since we had last met she and her father had been in Aberdeen, Glasgow, and Edinburgh, and she had left him two days ago at the County Hotel, in Carlisle. He had told her that he was leaving for London that night, and had instructed her to go on to Castle-Douglas and await a letter from him. She was still waiting for it. That was the reason she was there.

She made no mention of the two men also there, beyond her remark about my enemies being desperate ones.

For fully a couple of hours we wandered, heedless of where our footsteps led us, for she seemed thoroughly to erjoy that bright, fresh land of hills, streams, and lochs. In those sweet moments of peaceful bliss beside my love I forgot all my suspicion, all the mystery, all the desperate efforts that I was making to combat those who intended to filch from me the secret that was mine.

Many were our exchanges of affection as we lingered in that leafy glen, where deep below a rippling burn fell in small cascades with sweet, refreshing music. I saw that she wished to tell me everything, but was compelled to silence. I knew only that she loved me, she trusted me, but that she feared for my personal safety.

At last she expressed a wish to return, and with lingering footsteps we went towards the pointed spires of the town that lay beside the loch beneath our feet. Sweet were her words; sweet indeed was her personality, and sweet her almost childlike affection.

We parted at the entrance to the town, so as not to be seen together; and although I groaned beneath that weight of anxiety and uncertainty, I verily trod on air on my way back to the "Douglas Arms."

Wyman and Fred had not returned, therefore I went along to Mr Batten's, where I found them entertained to luncheon, and took my seat in the vacant place at the table. Our host was, I fear, puzzled at the reason of our sudden decision to spend a few days in his town, yet we told him nothing, fearing to arouse local interest in our search.

At three o'clock we went back to the "Douglas Arms"; but judge our dismay when the "boots" informed us that "Miss Fletcher" had left the hotel hurriedly, in company with "the hunchback and another gentleman," and had departed by the half-past two o'clock train—the express for Carlisle and the south.

"Well, that's a strange move," remarked Walter, when he heard of it. "I suppose Lady Judith got to know we were here, and cleared out rather than run the risk of meeting us."

"Yes," said Fred reflectively. "Very curious. I wonder what their game really is? You've forestalled them over the investigations at Crowland without a doubt; but I fear they are just a trifle too ingenious for us at Threave. I've ascertained that at Grierson's, the ironmonger, the hunchback and another man gave orders for several new picks and spades to be sent to Kelton Mains, that farmhouse through which we pass to get to Threave. They were sent there today."

"Well," I laughed, "they may be useful to us the day after tomorrow if they are not claimed. My belief is that those men never anticipated that we should follow them so closely."

"But will the sun shine?" queried Walter Wyman, gazing moodily out into the empty street. "That's the question."

Chapter Thirty Four
The Red Bull of the Borgias

The seventeenth day of September—the day upon which the sun would lead us to the discovery of the buried casket—dawned grey and overcast.

The instant I awoke I rushed to my window and looked out upon a sunless scene. Dark rain-clouds were everywhere, and my heart sank within me at the prospect of a wet and dismal day. The previous day we had spent in making careful inquiries in the neighbourhood regarding the reappearance of our enemies, whom we expected might try and take us by surprise. The only fact we could fathom was that Grierson, the ironmonger, had sent the tools to Kelton Mains, and been paid for them by a money order posted at Dumfries; but the farmer at Kelton knew nothing of them, it seemed, but had received them expecting someone sent by the laird to call for them. We had written a line to Sammy Waldron, at Crailloch, overnight, and expected him to cycle over during the morning. He would, of course, be excited over what was occurring, for he knew nothing except that Fred, his host, was away on some mysterious errand.

When I came down, rain was falling, and the greyness of the morning was certainly mirrored in the faces of all three of us.

"'Rain before seven, shine before eleven,'" remarked Walter, trying to cheer us; but we ate our meal almost in silence, until Sammy, hot and covered with mud, burst in upon us.

"What in the name of fortune does all this mean?" he cried, surprised to find Walter and myself. "I thought you two fellows had returned to town. The whole house is on tenter-hooks regarding Fred's whereabouts. I got your note at seven-thirty, and slipped away without any breakfast and without a word to anyone except Connie."

"Look here, Sammy!" exclaimed Fred, "we're going this afternoon to do a bit of secret digging—after a buried treasure."

"Buried treasure!" he echoed, and he burst out laughing. "Sounds well, at any rate. I'm always open to receive a bit of treasure from any source."

"Well, we want you to help us to dig. It is believed to be over at Threave."

"What! the old ruin we went to the other day?" Sammy exclaimed. "Better buy a new pair of oars, old chap, if you don't want the whole crowd of us shipwrecked."

The suggestion was a good one; and, although the weather was so much against it, Sammy presently went forth, purchased a pair of heavy second-hand oars, and stowed them away in the bottom of a light wagonette which we had hired at the hotel to take us to Kelton later in the day.

Sammy was just as excited as we were, and entered as keenly into the spirit of the thing. Like Fred, he never did anything by halves. He was a man with muscles like iron, and possessed the courage of a lion, as proved by the many tight corners he had been in during the Indian frontier wars of the past fifteen years or so. As a shot, Sammy Waldron was only equalled by his host, Fred Fenwicke; but, while the latter's form showed best among the grouse, Sammy was pre-eminently a hunter of big game, who sent presents of bears and tigers to his friends, instead of pheasants and grouse.

The morning wore on. A long council of war was held, but the rain did not abate.

Not indeed until we sat down to luncheon at twelve did the weather clear, and with it our spirits rose again. At half-past one the clouds broke and the sun came forth fitfully. Then all four of us, eager to investigate, and not knowing what difficulties were before us, mounted into the wagonette and drove out along the winding road to Kelton Mains.

On descending, a surprise awaited us, for when we asked for the tools sent there from Grierson's the farmer told us that three gentlemen, one a deformed man, had arrived there the day before, claimed the picks and spades, and had crossed to the island and been occupied in digging until it was dark.

The trio of investigators might still be on the island for aught we knew.

This was certainly disconcerting, and we walked through the fields to the water's edge full of expectancy. We, however, found the old boat moored in its usual place, which showed that the party had returned to shore. Therefore we embarked, eager to take observations and follow the directions laid down, even if we were not that day able to make investigation.

Sammy took one oar and I the other, and very soon the keel ran into the mud bank of the island, and the grey, dismal old castle, with its "hanging stone," towered above us. In an instant all four of us sprang ashore, the boat was moored, and we started off in the direction of the great ruin. Fortunately the sun was now shining brightly, and there, sure enough, lay the long, straight shadow across the wet grass in our direction.

I looked at my watch and found it a quarter-past three. In fifteen minutes we should be able to follow accurately the directions.

Suddenly, to our dismay, we saw, as we approached the point where the shadow ended, that a great hole had been dug in the immediate vicinity. We rushed forward with one accord, and in an instant the truth was plain— investigations had already been made!

The hole was a deep one, disclosing a flight of spiral stone steps which led to a subterranean chamber, the dungeon, perhaps, of some building long since effaced. At any rate, it showed that the excavators had hit upon some underground construction, the nature of which we knew not. The tools had been left there unheeded, as though the trio had departed hurriedly.

"That's curious!" Wyman cried to me. "Read old Godfrey's instructions aloud to us."

I took out of my pocket a book in which I had made a note of the exact wording, and read to my companions as follows:

"DIRECTIONS FOR RECOVERING THE CASKET.

"Go unto the castle at 3:30, when the sun shines, on September 6th, and follow the shadow of the east angle of the keep, forty-three paces from the inner edge of the moat."

Sammy then measured the paces, and found they were, as specified, forty-three.

I again glanced at my watch. It was just half-past three.

"Then, with the face turned straight towards Bengairn, walk fifty-six paces," I said, reading from the record.

Sammy took his bearings, and was starting off when I heard a footstep on the grass behind me, and, turning suddenly, found myself face to face with the man Selby, who, until that moment, had evidently been hiding in the ruins, watching us.

"By what right are you here?" he demanded.

"By the same right as yourself?" was my response. "What right have you to challenge us?"

By the man's dark, smooth face I saw he meant mischief.

"I have been left in charge of this property by its owner," the man declared. "You have no right to land here without his permission, therefore I order you to return to the shore."

"Ho! ho!" cried Sammy, in quick defiance, "those are fine words, to be sure. I fancy you'd better remain quiet, or we shall have to be very unkind to you."

"What do you mean?" the big fellow cried in a bullying tone.

"I mean that we aren't going to be interrupted by you," was Sammy's cool rejoinder. "If your friends have gone away and left you alone, like Robinson Crusoe, on this island, it isn't our concern. The laird of this place is still Colonel Maitland, and you have no authority here whatever."

"I forbid you to take any observations," Selby shouted, his fists clenched as though he would attack us. "And as for that man there," he cried, pointing to me, "he'd best get away before my friends return."

"Now that's enough," cried Sammy. "We don't want any threats;" and, before Selby was aware of his intention, the other had seized him by the wrists and was calling to us to secure him with the cord I had carried from the boat. He cursed and struggled violently, but in the hands of the four of us he was quickly bound and rendered powerless, much to his chagrin. He commenced shouting, whereupon I took out my handkerchief and gagged him tightly with it. Then, on his refusal to walk, we all four carried him into the roofless castle and there bound him to a big iron ring that we found in one of the walls, and thus made him our prisoner.

It was the only way. The fellow intended mischief, for we found in his pocket a loaded revolver. Having relieved him of that, we left him there, secured in a spot where he could not observe our movements.

Without loss of time we returned to the place we had marked, and the athletic Sammy, laughing over Selby's utter defeat, set his face towards the distant mountain of Bengairn and walked fifty-six paces, all three of us walking beside him to check is measurements.

"Seek there," I read from my notes, "for my lady Lucrezia's treasure is hidden at a place no man knoweth." Then, omitting several sentences, I came to the words: "Item: How to discover the place at Threave: First find a piece of ruined wall of great stones, one bearing a circle cut upon it as large as a man's hand. Then, measuring five paces towards the barbican, find—" And there the record broke off.

"Look?" cried Fred, pointing to a small piece of ruined wall about a foot high cropping up out of the tangled weeds and nettles. "Those are evidently the stones, and yet you'd never notice it unless it were pointed out."

We all four rushed to the spot he indicated, and, on tearing the weeds away, there, sure enough, we discovered that one of the large moss-grown moor-stones bore a circle cut upon it about the size of one's palm.

"Five paces towards the barbican!" cried Walter. "One—two—three—four—five! Here you are?" and he stamped heavily upon the grass. "Why," he exclaimed, "it's hollow!"

We all stamped, and sure enough there was a cavity beneath.

With Fred, I rushed off to the hole dug by our enemies, and, obtaining their tools, brought them back. Although the record in The Closed Book was carried no farther, it was evident that some opening lay underneath where we stood.

As the excavation made by our enemies was three hundred yards away, in an opposite direction, we concluded that they had only deciphered the first portion of the directions and not that final or unfinished sentence in the record, a page of which was missing.

Without further ado, however, we seized pick and spade, and commenced to open the ground at the spot where it sounded hollow. At a depth of about two and a half feet, through stone and rubbish, we came upon a big flat slab, like a paving-stone.

Was it possible that the historic emeralds of Lucrezia Borgia were actually hidden beneath? Our excitement knew no bounds, especially so as Selby had loosened his gag, and we could hear him shouting and cursing in the distance. We had, however, no fear of his shouts attracting attention, for the spot was far too lonely, and his voice would not reach the river bank, so broad was the stream.

With a keen will we all worked, digging out the earth from around the slab until at last I drove the end of a pick beneath it, and, using it as a lever, succeeded in raising the huge flat stone sufficiently to allow the insertion of a crowbar. Then, all bending together, we raised it up, disclosing a deep, dark, cavernous hole which emitted the damp, earthy smell of the grave.

"Who'll go down with me?" asked Fred.

"I'll go presently," volunteered Sammy, "when the place has had a bit of airing. There's foul air there, I expect. Perhaps it's a well."

Fortunately we had provided ourselves with two hurricane lanterns, and one of these I lit and lowered into the hole by a string. It remained alight, showing us, first, that the air was not foul; and, secondly, that the place was not a well, but a small stone chamber, the floor of which was covered with broken rubbish, and that the walls were black with damp and slime—not at all an inviting place in which to descend.

Fred was the first to let himself down, and, taking the lantern, he disappeared.

"I say," he cried a minute later, "it isn't a chamber. It's a kind of low tunnel—a subterranean passage!"

The announcement caused us even increased excitement; and, while Sammy and I let ourselves down to join Fred, we arranged that Walter, armed with Selby's revolver, should remain on the surface and so guard against any trickery on the part of the man who was our prisoner. It would, we knew, be easy enough to trap us like rats while we were down there.

"Wait till we come back, Walter!" I cried, and then, with my lamp, followed my two companions into the narrow burrow which ran down a steep incline in a southerly direction. Fred went first; but so dark was the way and so blocked in parts by fallen stones that our progress was very slow. We remembered that in such places of secret communication there were often pitfalls for the unwary; hence the caution we exercised.

We had pursued our way for, as far as we could judge, nearly a quarter of a mile, Sammy and Fred joking all the while, when the passage gave a sudden turn and commenced to ascend. This alteration in its direction struck me as curious, because, up to that moment we had walked in an absolutely straight line. But as I turned aside to follow my friends a small touch of colour on the wall attracted my attention; and, halting, I held up my lamp to examine it.

It was a crude drawing of a bull, outlined roughly in paint that had once been scarlet, but was now nearly brown, owing to the action of time and damp.

"Look?" I cried, almost beside myself with excitement. "Look! The red bull of the Borgias! The casket is concealed here!"

Chapter Thirty Five
What we Found at Threave

The bull *passant gules* of the Borgias was certainly a significant sign, deep there in the bowels of the earth, so far from the scene of the Borgias' forgotten triumphs.

My two companions were beside me in an instant, and both agreed that the bull placed there was a signal to the person who gained the secret of The Closed Book—an invitation to search at that spot.

All three of us closely examined the rough stones with which the low tunnel was arched; but none of them showed signs of having been disturbed. The passage had, without doubt, been constructed by the Black Douglas as a secret means of ingress and egress to his stronghold, and most probably all trace of it had been lost in the day of Godfrey Lovel. He and his friend Malcolm had perhaps rediscovered it, and old Godfrey had there ingeniously hidden the precious casket which he had brought from Italy, and which had for years previously been concealed in the fish pond at Croyland, or Crowland, as it is now spelt.

The position in which the bull had been drawn showed that it was placed there to attract the eye of the person possessing the secret. To any other it would convey nothing. Yet, although we searched hither and thither, high and low, we discovered no cavity nor any place where the casket was likely to be concealed.

Presently, after full half an hour's search, Fred discovered upon the flat surface of a stone some little distance further up the tunnel the numeral "15" marked in the same paint, and evidently put there by the same hand as that which had drawn the bull—only with one of those queer sixteenth-century fives like a capital N turned the wrong way about.

"Can this mean that the place is fifteen paces off?" I queried.

"Or it may be fifteen stones away," suggested Sammy, starting at once to count them. "Why, look!" he cried a few moments later; "here's a stone that's been removed at some time or other." It was a block about two feet long, and when I rushed forward and touched it, it moved beneath my hand.

Without a second's hesitation I grasped it, and with all my might tugged it out of me wall, allowing it to fall to the ground with a heavy thud, Sammy being compelled to step aside quickly.

Then, plunging my hand deep into the cavity behind, I felt something and pulled it out, with a loud cry of joy, which was echoed by my two companions.

It was the long-lost casket!

About a foot and a half long, ten inches in height, and six broad, it was covered with stout old untanned leather, the lid being curved and studded with nails. The lock was an antique, and therefore a complicated one, no doubt; but having no key, we at once set to work to force it open with the short crowbar which I had carried down there. So stoutly made was that ancient box that had seen so many vicissitudes and hid in the mud of the abbey fish pond at Crowland for many years, that for some time I could not manage to force it open; but after several trials, in the dim, uncertain light, I at length succeeded in wrenching up the lid, and there found within several old jewel cases which, on being opened, were found to contain those wonderful emeralds which were the most valued treasures of the Borgias.

We handled them gingerly, at my suggestion, not knowing whether those faded, velvet-lined old cases might not be envenomed with poison of the Borgias, like the vellum leaves of The Closed Book.

The jewels we examined were, however, magnificent in their antique gold settings. Three collars of wonderful green gems, each emerald the size of one's thumb nail, and each set separately to form drops, were the first ornaments we drew forth—emerald collars of which we knew the world had never seen the equal. Several bracelets, pairs of earrings, and pendants were also among the collection; one emerald, unset, and evidently the greatest treasure, being almost the size of a pigeon's egg—a truly marvellous set of gems, the like of which none of us had ever before set eyes upon.

There were eight small cases in all, seven of them as full of jewels as they could hold, while the eighth contained that which, in the day of Lucrezia Borgia, was more powerful and potent than the mere possession of wealth—a small sealed bottle of rock crystal and a larger phial of greenish Venetian glass, the latter containing a thick dark-brown fluid.

This latter discovery interested my companions, who were much puzzled by it. But I knew the truth, and told them so. That tiny crystal bottle contained the actual secret venom of the Borgias, given by Lucrezia to old Godfrey, and the dark-brown fluid was the antidote.

The secret poison of the Borgias was no longer a legend. We had it actually in our possession!

I put my hand again into the cavity, while Sammy raised a lamp to peer within. But there was nothing else.

With our precious find stowed in our pockets we at last moved up the incline, in order to explore the full extent of the subterranean passage. The casket itself interested me; and, handing my lantern to one of the others, I carried the heavy old box, which through those centuries had contained treasure worth a king's ransom. Then, delighted with our success, we pushed forward and upward, finding the air fresher nearly every foot we progressed, until at last, nearly three-quarters of a mile from the point we had descended, the tunnel went suddenly upwards, and we found farther progress barred by a huge oaken door strengthened by a kind of network of iron battens securely bolted on to it.

We tried it, but it would not budge. It was very strongly secured on the other side, and all our efforts to open it proved futile.

Having battered upon it and used our crowbar to little effect, we heard a frightened and muffled voice on the other side demanding who and what we were.

"Let us out, old chap?" I shouted. "Can't you open the door? Who are you?"

"My name's John Kirk," was the man's hoarse answer. "Where are you, and who are you?"

"There are three of us. We've been along an underground passage, and this is the end of it. Where are we?"

"This is the old dairy in Threave Mains. Wait a bit, and I'll get the master."

"Threave Mains?" cried Fred. "Then we've passed right under the Dee into Balmaghie! You can see the Mains from the castle—an old white house about three-quarters of a mile away. I hope the master, whoever he is, will let us out of this very soon."

We did not have to wait long; but the fact was that some old panelling in the ancient part of the building, now used as a dairy, had first to be taken down, and then the door was revealed and opened, letting us out once again to the light of day.

Truth to tell, we were nothing loath to breathe the fresh air once more; and the dirty and disreputable figures we cut as we emerged, I think, filled the good farmer with some suspicion. We told him of our explorations underground, not mentioning the treasure, of course, whereupon the old man said, in his broad Galloway dialect:

"I've heard talk of a passage under the river to the castle, but I thought it was only a fable. I had no idea it ended in this wall."

"Well," said Sammy, "you go down and have a smell round yourself. You'll find it interesting. You won't want a boat in the future to get over to the island."

Whereat we all laughed, and after examining the old oak panelling, and coming to the conclusion that the dairy was originally the most ancient part of the house, we gave the farmer a trifle to repay him for the removal of the woodwork, and departed, carrying the jewels, in their cases, secreted in our pockets, and leaving the unfortunate Selby still a prisoner on the island, with Walter guarding him. One thing was at least reassuring—namely, that the casket, having been discovered beneath the bed of the river, could be claimed by neither of the owners of the property on either side.

In the lightest of spirits we joined the high road at the Black Bride Burn, and hurried along for a mile to the Bridge of Dee, where we knew we could obtain a boat to fetch Walter off the island. This was done, and while Fred and Sammy rowed back upstream, I idled on the wayside railway station close to the river, the whole of the jewels being transferred to my care, while the old casket had been wrapped in a newspaper we had picked up by the roadside.

The farmer at Threave Mains had looked askance at the old box until, in order to satisfy him, I showed that it was empty. He had no use for empty boxes, he said, laughing; but he was not aware of its precious contents then in our pockets.

I had a long wait at the railway station; but about six o'clock my companions returned, bringing Walter with them. The latter had feared, as we did not return, that some accident had happened to us, and had been amazed to find Sammy and Fred, afloat, hailing him.

Selby was still at the place where we had secured him, bound hand and foot, shouting and cursing until he was hoarse, and uttering all kinds of threats against us. But we had secured the historic jewels of the notorious Lucrezia, and now intended to make the best of our way to Crailloch. With that intention, therefore, we tidied ourselves as well as we could, and walked on to Dildawn, the fine estate of our host's good friend, Charlie Phillips, and there borrowed a conveyance to take us home, a distance of about fourteen miles as the crow flies.

So disreputable our appearance, so mysterious our movements, not to mention the absence of guns or game bags, that our friend's curiosity was aroused; but we merely explained that we had been out for a day's excursion and got stranded, the railway being of no use to us. He gave us some whisky, smiled knowingly, but was much puzzled.

"My opinion is that you fellows have been up to some trick or other that you oughtn't to have been," was his remark as we drove away.

"All right, old chap," shouted Fred; "we'll tell you all about it some day." And the smart pair of bays swung away down the drive.

We agreed to say nothing to anyone, not even to the rest of the party at Crailloch. At present, in view of our forthcoming investigations at Crowland, it was not judicious to make any statement. We had forestalled our enemies at Threave, and for the present that was sufficient.

Our tardy and unexpected return gave rise to a good deal of comment, as may be imagined. The ladies of the party were soon around Sammy imploring him to tell them the reason of our mysterious movements, and many questions were put to Fred by the men. But to all we were dumb. We had been visiting friends was all we explained.

"Friends!" exclaimed Jack Handsworth, sucking at his cigar. "Been down a drain somewhere, by the look of your clothes," a remark that was greeted with considerable laughter.

That night, after the others had retired, the four of us held a secret sitting in Fred's study, where we examined our find, and discovered it to be more remarkable and important than we had believed it to be. The emerald collars were magnificent; but, besides what I have already enumerated, there was a magnificent Byzantine cross of diamonds, containing in the back the relic of St. Peter, which is known to have been the property of Lucrezia's father, the Borgia Pope. In the Vatican archives are several mentions of it; but on the death of Alexander VI it unaccountably disappeared, having been given, no doubt, to his golden-haired daughter. There was a heavy gold bracelet, too, in the form of a serpent, and several fine rings. One, in gold, was engraved with the sacred tau, believed in the Borgia era to guard the wearer against epilepsy; another, of agate, carved with an image of St. John the Divine, which was worn in those days as a protection from venom; and in a third was set a piece of toadstone or bufonite—the fossil palatal tooth of the ray fish *Pycnodus*—the most potent periapt against black magic.

The most interesting of all, however, was a beautiful ring of gold *niello*, of the fourteenth century, with a hollow bezel or sharp point pierced by two tiny holes, which had undoubtedly been used to contain poison. It was quite easy to see that this ring, if charged with the deadly liquid, could be used with fatal effect in a hand-grasp with an enemy—a curio of world-wide interest, the actual poison-ring of that veneficious bacchante Lucrezia

Borgia, which had caused the death of so many unsuspecting and innocent persons, from cavaliers in Ferrara to cardinals in Rome.

I turned it over in my hand and felt the sharpness of that fine needle-point. Surely the controversy regarding the venom of the Borgias would now be set at rest forever.

The crystal perfume bottle, with its few drops of that deadly cantarella poison, I held to the light and examined carefully, as well as the antidote—both presents given to Godfrey by Lucrezia herself, with instructions how to use them.

I was in the act of replacing both bottles in the old jewel case, with its faded lining of purple velvet, when I noticed the top of the lining was loose, and on touching it it fell away and a small folded piece of damp-stained parchment came into my hand.

There was faded writing upon it in Godfrey's erratic script, and the words I deciphered caused my heart to leap.

Chapter Thirty Six
Shows the Actual Spot at Crowland

The words, badly faded by the action of the water which had apparently got into the casket during its years of submersion, we made out as follows:

"Ye who hast dared to learn this secret may ye benefit greatly by it. Know ye now also that ye may discover the treasure of our good abbot John of Croylande by means only of this plan I have hereunto drawn.

"Godfrey Lovel, sometime monk at Croylande."

Below was a rough plan similar to those in The Closed Book, but which needed no second glance to show the exact spot where the abbey treasure lay hidden.

"See?" I cried excitedly. "The secret is at last revealed to us! What is written in The Closed Book was only in order to mislead any curious person who attempted to search. The truth was deposited in this casket by Godfrey before he left Scotland."

And my three companions bent eagerly, and for themselves slowly deciphered the words after I had repeated them aloud to make certain of no misreading.

"Well, our next step is undoubtedly to go down to Crowland," Fred remarked. "Let's get the treasure first, and clear up the mystery afterwards."

"Certainly," we agreed in chorus, and then, after placing the Borgia jewels in Fred's iron safe, we all smoked and discussed our future plans, finally deciding to go up to London again in the morning, as Crowland could be more easily reached from King's Cross than from Scotland.

Next night, therefore, we arrived in town, Fred and Sammy putting up at the Euston Hotel, and I going home with Walter as his guest. On the morning after our arrival I deemed it wise to pack up the Borgia treasures, all save the poison-ring, the tiny crystal bottle, and the antidote, and deposit them with my banker's manager, just as I had already placed The Closed Book in safe keeping.

The historic ring that had dealt death so frequently and had enabled the House of Borgia to become the most powerful in Europe, I put with the little bottle in the old velvet-lined jewel case and placed them aside in a drawer in Walter's writing-table, intending later to take them down to Professor Fairbairn at the British Museum.

Fred Fenwicke had some pressing affairs to attend to in London, therefore it had been arranged not to go to Crowland till the following day.

We were much puzzled regarding the whereabouts of Glenelg and the hunchback, and also wondered whether Selby still remained a prisoner at Threave. The loaded weapon upon him proved that he intended mischief, therefore neither of us expressed much regret at leaving him in such evil case. The silence of his companions was, however, ominous.

While I had been down at the bank Walter had strolled round to Harpur Street, only to find the house still closed. Of Judith's whereabouts I knew nothing. She had disappeared. Through those weeks I had been living in alarm and dread. Scarcely a day passed without some puzzling incident, and I longed to see my love again and hear a full and frank explanation from her.

I recollected how, when we had parted outside the town of Castle-Douglas, I lingered there speaking gently, making a thousand promises at which she smiled. At last it became imprudent for us to tarry there longer, and as we stood to bid each other farewell, face to face, I saw her eyelids quiver. And then I did not dare to seek her lips.

Yet it was all so strange, so mysterious, such an utter enigma, that I had become overwhelmed by fear and suspicion, bewildered, staggered, and aghast.

I idled away the morning, and about noon I received a note from the woman Bardi, in response to the letter I had sent her, making an appointment to meet me under the clock at Charing Cross Station at three o'clock. I was there to time, and found the dark, neatly dressed figure awaiting me, just as strange, just as mysterious as before.

We walked together down Whitehall and across St. James's Park, chatting affably in Italian. I put to her a number of questions, but gathered little in response. Her motive puzzled me, for she neither assisted me nor repeated her words of warning.

"I am returning to Italy soon," she told me. "I suppose you have made up your mind to live here in England in future?"

I responded in the affirmative; and then, halting in the quiet path beside the lake, I tried to obtain from her the identity of the person who induced her to steal my Arnoldus, but she steadily refused to tell me anything.

Just before five o'clock, after giving her tea at Blanchard's, I took my leave of her, more than ever puzzled. She had fenced with every question, and with the exception of giving me to understand that Judith Gordon was not my friend, she had really told me nothing. Therefore, I resolved to trouble myself no further about her in future. The woman had been proved to be a thief, and therefore unreliable. Yet my sole aim now was to get at the meaning of the bear cub in the window, and the actual motive of the remarkable conspiracy.

On entering the hall in Dover Street I ascended the stairs to the second floor and rang at the door of Walter's cozy flat. There was no response, and at first it struck me that the faithful Thompson had gone out upon some errand in the immediate neighbourhood. I pressed the electric bell again and again, but there was no sign of life within. Of a sudden, however, I recollected that Walter had that morning given me a latch-key, and taking it from my pocket I let myself in; but judge my dismay when in the small hall quite close to the door I found the white-haired old valet lying half doubled on the carpet, motionless as one dead.

My first idea was that he might be intoxicated; but on bending over him, and drawing his face into the light, I saw that its pallor was deathlike. He seemed to be in a sound sleep.

Then glancing into the sitting-room at the farther end of the passage, I noticed that the drawers of Walter's writing-table had been broken open and turned hurriedly out on to the floor. The truth next instant was apparent. The old valet had been rendered insensible by callers during our absence, and the place had been ransacked.

I dashed on into the room, and went to the drawer wherein I had placed the ancient jewel case with its strange contents, but found it empty. The ring and the poison had been taken; but what was infinitely worse was that I had left in the cover of the case, where it had been concealed all these years, the plan of the hiding-place of the treasure at Crowland!

I was beside myself with anger and chagrin. Our enemies had ingeniously outwitted us, after all, for that female accomplice had held me in conversation purposely while the search was made, thus showing that they were well acquainted with our success at Threave.

Yet when Walter had locked the box safely in his drawer with the key upon his chain. I had never dreamed that a bold attempt would thus be made to obtain it. Ingenious it was, for, as was afterwards proved, Wyman himself had been called by an urgent telegram to Richmond, which turned out to be fictitious.

At first I was so aghast that I knew not how to act; but, obtaining the assistance of the young valet in service in the flat below, I succeeded at last in getting Thompson round and hearing his story, which was to the effect that about half-past three o'clock two men called, one of them short and the other clean-shaven, tall, and powerful. They inquired for Captain Wyman, and entered the hall on pretext of writing a message on a card. The instant, however, that old Thompson turned his back a handkerchief was clapped over his face and held there tightly until in a few moments he lapsed into unconsciousness.

The description of one man tallied with that of Selby; but the other, who had thin, sandy whiskers, was unknown to me.

As soon, however, as Thompson felt a trifle better, and began to inspect the disorder caused by the intruders, I ran downstairs and telephoned to Fred at the Euston Hotel. The Major was not in; but Bailey, the hall porter, who answered me, promised to give my message to Major Fenwicke or to Captain Waldron, whichever of the two should be first to return.

Therefore I could do nothing but wait. Walter arrived in about half an hour, and was followed five minutes later by Fred and Sammy, all three standing dumbfounded when I explained what had occurred.

The secret venom of the Borgias and the ring were now in the possession of our enemies, and neither of us knew in what way it might be used against us. They had also secured the secret of the Crowland treasure, for they would undoubtedly find the piece of parchment behind the loose top of the case. It had fallen out in my hand, and would do so in theirs.

Selby's action was certainly a bold bid for fortune, and showed conclusively that he was aware of our success in Scotland, the theft being committed no doubt in the belief that the jewels discovered were in my friend's rooms. My intuition to place them in the bank only a few hours before was certainly a fortunate one.

The woman Bardi was still acting in concert with the conspirators, and the fact that Walter had been called to an appointment at Richmond by a telegram signed by a friend showed how ingeniously and swiftly it had all been worked.

"Well," exclaimed Fred, gazing around the disordered sitting-room, "our policy seems quite clear. First, we should go down to Crowland and prevent any investigations being made there; secondly, we will arrest Selby for assault and theft the next time we meet him; and, thirdly, we must at all hazards regain possession of the ring and poison, for we can't tell what atrocious assassinations these people will not commit now they have a poison so subtle, so deadly, and so impossible of detection."

"Yes," I cried. "Think of what possession of such a secret compound means! They might contrive to use it upon us at any moment by sending us an envenomed letter, by placing it on the knob of an umbrella or walking stick, by impregnating our gloves, our hats, or any object left about, just as the Borgias used it in the old days."

"It certainly isn't a very bright prospect," remarked Waldron. "I'd rather face a revolver than a secret poison. I've seen too much of poisoning in India. We in the police know something about it."

Old Thompson was thoroughly unnerved by the drug; therefore, it being decided that we should all four go down to Crowland by the last train, Walter gave him leave to shut up the flat and go over to see his married daughter at Hackney Wick.

A telegram to Frank, the ostler at "The Angel," at Peterborough, brought the carriage to meet us at the station by the ten-thirty train from London, and by midnight we were comfortably installed at "The George," at Crowland, the inn which to Walter and myself was already full of memories.

We had telegraphed to the rector, and he called upon us, notwithstanding the lateness of the hour. Sitting together in the private room, I briefly related to him our success in Scotland, and how we had discovered the actual plan of the spot where the treasure lay concealed.

My words at once filled Mr Mason with eager interest; but when I told him of our irreparable loss his spirits fell and he shook his head and sighed. I explained the dastardly manner in which the thieves had drugged my friend's valet, and our determination to give Selby into custody.

Then, while we were discussing the possibility of using the ground plan of the abbey given me by Professor Fairbairn, Fred suddenly interrupted us as he took something from his pocket-book, saying:

"It's true we've lost the plan we discovered at Threave; but on the night of our return to Crailloch I thought it would be advisable to take a copy of it, so I made a rough tracing. Here it is." And he opened a small piece of foreign notepaper to our view, disclosing an accurate copy of the stolen plan.

He received a chorus of praises for his foresight, and Mr Mason expressed his eagerness to commence excavations at once, in order to forestall the others. He had not yet demanded back the books found by Lord Glenelg, having waited to confer with us as to the present advisability.

Upon the table we compared the tracing given us by Fairbairn with the copy of old Godfrey's plan made by Fred, and Mr Mason recognising the points where we were of course in ignorance, we came, after a long and careful examination and comparison, to the conclusion that the wealth of the abbey as enumerated in The Closed Book was concealed at a spot nearly a mile from the abbey, in the centre or the Great Postland Fen, in a field which was on his own property—for he was squire of the place, as well as rector—about midway between Thornbury Hall and the Decoy Farm. The position of St. James' Bridge and the ancient stone cross at Brotherhouse were both shown, as well as the old Asen Dike and the Wash-bank at Cloot. The plan showed that the old abbot was crafty enough to carry the treasure sufficiently far into what must at the time have been a dangerous quagmire, wherein none dare venture who knew not the way, but which has of course since been drained and reclaimed by the building of banks and cutting of dikes in all directions. Mr Mason told us that the whole of the district shown on the plan was until the end of the sixteenth century a dismal, unhealthy swamp, the sparse inhabitants of which were fever-stricken, and the spot where the treasure was apparently concealed was in the deepest part of the basin, and in all probability a treacherous bog purposely chosen in order to defeat any efforts of Southwell's soldiers.

The allegation in The Closed Book that gold and silver objects had been sunk in the fish pond was no doubt in order to mislead, for, after all, it was not likely that the abbot should make so little attempt to effectively conceal what he wished to rescue from sacriligious hands.

"Depend upon it, gentlemen, we're on the right track at last," declared the rector decisively. He was an archaeologist himself, and was eager to see our splendid find of gems, just as he was eager to recover the long-lost treasure of the Abbot John.

The measurements on the plan which had so cunningly been concealed were given in paces from St. James' Bridge, about a mile to the south-east of the abbey, and Mr Mason suggested that having regard to the fact that Selby and his companions had the original plan in their possession, we should lose no time in going to the spot.

I glanced at my watch, and found it to be a quarter-past one in the morning.

Fred drew the blind aside and discovered that it was not a particularly dark night, although heavy rain-clouds had drifted across the moon. The suggestion to fix the spot was a good one, although it was arranged that as the land was Church property, and there was no reason for secret search, the excavations should be carried out on the morrow.

Together, the five of us, having borrowed two lanterns from the hotel keeper, left the house, and under the guidance of Mr Mason passed down the road beside the rectory, skirted the north wall of the abbey, and then out upon the broad, flat high road, past the dilapidated windmill, and on to St. James' Bridge, where we took another road eastward, flat, hedgeless, uninteresting like the first, and running straight as an arrow towards our destination.

Presently the rector halted and pointed out a distant clump of trees looming in the darkness as Thornbury Hall, while to our left lay the Decoy Farm. Beneath the uncertain rays of the lamp he carefully examined the plan again, and then led us through a gate into a large field sown with fen-potatoes, which we crossed carefully in the darkness for fear of falling into the dikes which in that country separate one field from another. At last we found the boundary, and discovered a single plank which gave access to the next field, with a crop of potatoes like the first. Then, having counted his paces carefully from the roadway, his face always turned to Thornbury Hall, he suddenly halted, saying:

"The actual spot is here, or within a few feet. According to the plan, it is one hundred and eighty-six paces due south towards Thornbury from the road anciently known as Guthlac's Drove—the road we have just left."

We lowered the lanterns, and groping about, examined the ground. The crop had certainly not been disturbed. We stamped just as we had done at Threave, but there was no hollow sound in the heavy fen clay.

"My suggestion is that we should send Barrett, the town policeman, to keep guard upon the place till morning, and then commence operations," said Mr Mason at last. "We shall recognise the spot by yonder old willow tree."

This suggestion we acted upon, and when we turned in an hour later the constable, Barrett, was keeping vigil in that lonely field, wondering no doubt the reason why the rector had found him on his beat on the Eye Road and posted him away in that unfrequented spot.

Chapter Thirty Seven
In which I Enter the House of Mystery

While we sat at breakfast next morning the constable, with his hand bound up and suspended in a black scarf from his neck, was brought to us by Mr Mason, and asked to report upon the result of his observations.

"Well, gentlemen, I met some rough customers last night," exclaimed the man through his brown beard. "All was quiet till the abbey clock 'ud just struck three, when I heard the sound of wheels, and a trap came up the road from the direction of Brotherhouse Bar. There was no light on it, and I heard it stop just opposite where I was on duty. Three men and a woman got down, and lit a lantern, and took out some spades and picks, therefore I crouched down and watched. Two of the men were tall, and the third, who carried the lamp, was short, and looked as though he were deformed, while the woman was slim and young, and dressed in dark clothes. I heard one man say, 'This must be the place. That house over there is Thornbury Hall. I recollect it is marked on the Ordnance map we looked at in the train. And there's Decoy Farm! Now, one hundred and eighty-six paces due south. This way;' and he led them into the field and continued straight across to the dike, over the plank, and then half-way across the next field, where we halted close to the old willow stump. 'This is the place!' he exclaimed, little dreaming that I was so near. 'It's quite a long way off the spot we tried before.' 'Are you quite certain of the distance and the direction?' inquired the other man, in response to which the first speaker quoted some kind of direction which he seemed to know by heart. The short man made some observation in a foreign language, but I didn't understand what he said."

"And what did you do?" I demanded eagerly.

"Well, the moment the four of them started to dig up the potatoes, I slipped out from behind the willow stump and demanded what they were up to. My sudden appearance upset their little game at once; but one man, the tallest of them, was inclined to be defiant when I ordered them off, telling them that the land was the property of the ecclesiastical commissioners, and that they would be prosecuted for trespass. He struck at me with the pick-axe he carried, whereupon I took out my truncheon, and next instant I saw a flash and found myself wounded in the hand. The fellow had used a revolver on me! This sudden action called forth the condemnation of his three companions, who declared that to fire on the police was highly dangerous. Then, all three, fearing that the shot had raised an alarm, threw down their tools and made their way back to the trap as quickly as they could, being followed by the cowardly fellow who had fired at me. I rushed after them, although my hand pained me badly; but they succeeded in getting clear away. Then I came back to Crowland and called up the doctor, who took the bullet out of my hand. I had a very narrow escape, gentlemen," added the rural constable. "I wonder what those people were up to?"

Mr Mason and Fred Fenwicke exchanged glances; but no one satisfied Barrett's curiosity.

"You see I couldn't well distinguish the face of the ruffian who fired at me," he said, in response to my inquiry; "but I heard the woman address him as Selby."

The woman! Could it have been Judith who had accompanied them, or was it Anita Bardi?

Barrett presently left to report the incident by telegraph to his inspector at Spalding, and the rector took counsel with us. A bold attempt to search had evidently been made, and had only been abandoned by the ill-advised action of one of the party. Although the constable had been the victim of a dastardly outrage it had certainly been fortunate that we had marked out the spot and set watch upon it. Our enemies had made wrong calculations at Threave by not having noted the second clause of the instructions; but here, with the aid of the plan, they had certainly hit upon the exact spot designated by the monk Godfrey.

Mr Mason had gone out to obtain assistance in our work of excavation, which we decided should commence at once, when a telegram was brought to me which showed that it had been handed in at King's Cross Station, and read as follows:

"Come to Grosvenor Street. Most important. Must see you immediately. If I am not at home go to Harpur Street; but if you desire to fulfill your promise to help me, do not lose an instant—Judith."

My first impulse was to read the telegram aloud; but my companions, being in ignorance of my intimate friendship with her, I resolved to keep my own counsel.

"I have to return to London at once," I announced, crushing the message in my hand. "You fellows will continue the search, and I will return tonight if possible."

"Private business?" queried Sammy, who had lit his morning cigarette airily, and stood with his hands deep in his trouser pockets, regarding me with some attention.

I responded in the affirmative; and, turning, told the maid to order a trap at once to take me to Peterborough Station.

Thus I was compelled to absent myself from the work of excavating in that low-lying fen field a mile beyond the abbey; and at half-past twelve o'clock I alighted from a hansom in Grosvenor Street, and, running up the broad flight of steps to the big portico, rang the bell.

"Yes, sir, her ladyship is expecting you," was the footman's response to my inquiry; and without further ceremony he conducted me through the fine hall, filled with magnificent trophies of the chase, and up the wide staircase to a small room on the first floor, wherein, white and haggard, she rose quickly to greet me.

"Oh, Mr Kennedy!" she gasped when the man had closed the door. "I'm so glad to see you safe and well!"

"Why Mr Kennedy?" I asked half-reproachfully.

"Well, Allan, then," she said, smiling. "But we have no time to lose," she went on. "I fear that something terrible has occurred; but exactly what, I don't know."

"How do you mean? Explain," I urged excitedly.

"You probably know what occurred down at Crowland last night!" she said. "They obtained the parchment plan, and at once determined to search for the treasure known to be hidden there; but a policeman discovered them and they shot him."

"I know," I responded. "And what occurred afterwards?" That was the first time she had mentioned the search for treasure, in any of our talks.

"They returned to London—all three of them."

"And the woman?"

"What woman?" she inquired, looking me straight in the face.

"The woman who was with them," I said meaningly, recollecting that her own telegram had been sent from King's Cross Station.

"I know nothing of her," was the response. "I'm speaking of my father, Selby, and the hunchback. They returned to London at seven this morning—to Harpur Street."

"Well?"

"I went there at nine o'clock, but found the house still closed, and could make nobody hear, although I know they entered there about eight o'clock. The blind is now up, and the bear cub is in the window," she added hoarsely. "There is death in that house!"

"Death! Is that the meaning of that strange sign?" I gasped. "Do you really suspect that some tragedy has been enacted?"

"Yes," she cried hoarsely. "I fear so. I've been there three times this morning and can make nobody hear. Oh, Mr Kennedy, you do not know the awful secret—the terrible—"

But she stopped herself, as though she feared to tell me all the truth.

"Is it that you fear for your father's sake?" I inquired, a new light suddenly dawning upon me.

"Yes," she cried, her white trembling hand upon my arm. "I do fear. Will you go with me to Harpur Street?"

"Most willingly," I said. "But if you fear a tragedy had we not better seek aid of the police?"

"The police?" she gasped, her face blanching in an instant. "Ah, no! Let us see for ourselves first. The police must know nothing—you understand. We must not arouse suspicion. I know they have returned, because at eleven last night, after they had left for Crowland, all the blinds were down, whereas now one blind is up and the sign is in the window."

I saw that she was nervous and agitated, and that her suspicions were based, upon some secret knowledge. She believed that some hideous tragedy had occurred in that house of mystery in Harpur Street, and invoked my aid in its elucidation.

"You will not blame me," she said in a hard voice. "I am culpable, I know, but when you have heard everything and are aware of the extraordinary circumstances which have brought me to what I am, I know you will forgive me and look leniently upon my shortcomings. Promise me you will," she implored in deep earnestness, taking my hand in hers.

I promised, then she rushed into another room for a moment, and reappeared in hat and jacket. We drove quickly to that short, dismal street in Bloomsbury, and on approaching the house I saw that the dingy Venetian blinds were all down save at that window where showed the mysterious sign.

Having dismissed the cab, we both ascended the dirty, neglected steps, and rang. The bell clanged loudly somewhere in the regions below; but no one stirred. I was in favour of calling an inspector from the nearest police station and telling him of our suspicions, but she would not hear of it.

"No?" she cried, terrified at my suggestion. "The police must know nothing—nothing at all. If they did, then I myself must suffer."

Her words were, to say the least, very curious. "No," she went on, "we must try and get in ourselves—force the door or something."

To force a door of that strong, old-fashioned character was difficult, I saw. The latch, too, was a patent one, with a well-known maker's name on the keyhole cover—nearly new. To force a front door in a public street in the broad light of day without attracting attention is well-nigh impossible; therefore, instructing her to wait patiently where she was, so as not to arouse suspicion of the neighbours, I waited my opportunity, and then got over the locked gate and went down the steps to the kitchen door in the basement. That, too, was securely fastened; but on examination of the window it struck me that the shutters were only closed to and not bolted. Therefore, I called to my love to go back into Theobald's Road and purchase a chisel, a glazier's diamond, and a putty-knife, and bring them to me as soon as possible.

She obeyed at once, and until her return I crouched down beneath the front steps in a spot where the passers-by could not see me. On her return, a quarter of an hour later, she dropped down the tools to me as she walked past the house to the other end of the street.

The door resisted all efforts, therefore I presently turned my attention to the window, at last succeeding in unlatching it with the putty-knife, working back the bolt of the shutters and crawling inside the dirty, dismal kitchen.

At that moment Lady Judith had ascended the steps to the front door; and, groping my way in the semi-darkness up the stairs, I gained the wide old-fashioned hall, and, after some difficulty with the complicated lock, opened the door to her.

Then, together, we went forth to ascertain what mystery that closed and gloomy place contained.

Chapter Thirty Eight
The Room of the Bear Cub

Judith, who was no stranger to that house of mystery, first led me into the front room, where I had once awaited her; but the rays of light that came through the chinks of the closed shutters revealed nothing unusual. It was neglected and dusty, but orderly as before. The room behind was a bedroom, in disorder, with the bed unmade; but there was no occupant.

In eager breathlessness we ascended the stairs to the room in which stood the stuffed bear cub, but found the door locked and the key gone. We looked through the keyhole, but could discern nothing. To our loud raps there was no response.

"We must break it open," I remarked, seeing no other way. And drawing back I rushed at it, throwing all my force against it.

Once—twice—I repeated the attempt, but in vain. At length, however, my love, in frantic haste to learn the truth, threw her weight against the door at the same instant as mine, and with our combined efforts we succeeded in breaking the cheap lock from its fastenings, and the door giving way, we went head foremost into the long, old-fashioned drawing-room, furnished in faded green rep of a style long since out of date.

The one blind being up gave sufficient light, and next instant our eyes fell upon a scene which filled us both with horror, and caused cries of dismay to break involuntarily from our lips.

Selby was seated in a collapsed position in an arm-chair, his head hanging listlessly upon his breast; while the hunchback, with hands outstretched and tightly clenched, lay face downwards upon the carpet behind the table.

I bent and touched their faces, one after the other. They were cold as marble.

Both men had evidently been dead some hours.

"But my father—my poor father?" wailed Judith. "Where is he? He must be in this house! Let us search." And she started off frantically from room to room, I following her in breathless amazement at this tragic discovery.

Yet although we searched the garrets and even the cellars, we failed to discover him. He was evidently not there.

Again we ascended the stairs to that room of horror, where the two men lay white and dead, a ghastly sight indeed; and as we re-entered she suddenly complained of an acute pain in her left arm and a curious sensation in the head.

Singularly enough I experienced the very same symptoms in my left arm—very similar, indeed, to those I had felt after examining The Closed Book.

"Ah?" she shrieked, "I know. I ran my hands along the rail on the stairs and felt a scratch. Look at my hand! Look—I—I'm poisoned!"

I glanced at her left hand and saw a slight abrasion of the skin straight across the palm. Then I glanced at my own, and discovered to my dismay that I had received an exactly similar scratch.

"What makes you suspect poisoning!" I demanded quickly. "Do you believe these men have died from the same cause?"

"Undoubtedly," she answered. But on quickly examining the hands of the dead men I discovered no marks there. "Ah?" she wailed; "you do not know. I am doomed to die, and no power can now save me."

I did not mention my own symptoms for fear of increasing her alarm, but merely said:

"If you really believe you have been poisoned secretly, I think I can give you something which may be of benefit. We must not, however, lose an instant, but go to the nearest chemist's."

"No medicine is of avail against this. I have fallen a victim, as I knew I must, sooner or later. In half an hour I shall be dead," she added hoarsely, gazing fixedly at the almost imperceptible scratch upon her delicate white flesh. "Ah! why did I come to this house of death when I suspected—nay, when I knew too well—the doom of those who enter here!"

"Come, Lady Judith!" I cried quickly. "Do not linger a moment. I feel sure that your case is not so utterly hopeless as you think. Come at once to a chemist's." And taking her forcibly by the arm I led her downstairs and out into the street.

There was no cab in sight, but I knew there was a chemist's in Theobald's Road, next door to the public-house where I had had refreshment on that first night of my return to London.

On entering the shop I seated her and quickly obtained a hypodermic syringe. Then, taking from my pocket the old green glass phial wherein the

Borgia antidote was still hermetically sealed, I broke it open, half filled the tiny syringe with the dark-brown fluid, and injected it into her left arm. It was, indeed, fortunate that I had kept it in my pocket instead of placing it in the case with the other objects.

"What is that?" she inquired; but, promising to explain all later, I administered to myself an injection of the precious compound.

She felt better almost instantly, she said, and I myself began to derive great benefit from it. The sharp pains in my limbs grew easier, and the drowsiness that had already come over me was dispelled. It acted like magic, and, whatever was its nature, it had, after lying concealed through three centuries, lost none of its potency in counteracting the effects of a powerful venom.

As we had descended the stairs my quick eye had detected a sharp steel point slightly protruding from the polished mahogany handrail. The colour of the wood was darker there, as though stained by some liquid that had been applied to the point from time to time. Was it possible that the steel point was actually envenomed with evil intent? It certainly seemed so.

Yet the mysterious death of those two men who had been my enemies was certainly not attributable to the same cause, for the skin upon their hands was quite uninjured.

I examined my own hand while I gave some fictitious explanation to the chemist, whose curiosity had been aroused by my actions. The skin was cut slightly for quite two inches across, like the scratch of a pin, and yet I had felt nothing until Lady Judith had directed my attention to it. The venom, whatever it was, had the effect of producing insensibility in the actual part lacerated. It was true that the little crystal bottle discovered at Threave had been stolen from Dover Street; but although the antidote had acted so successfully, I could not believe that the actual liquid from that bottle had been used to envenom us. There was some further and deeper explanation, for had not the woman I loved admitted that she was aware how those who entered that gloomy, dismal house were doomed, and that the sign of the bear cub was synonymous with death?

Presently, when Judith felt better, we went forth again into the street. It was our duty to inform the police of the mysterious tragedy that had been enacted in Harpur Street, yet she pointed out that in the circumstances it would be far better to allow the discovery to be made by others. Some passer-by would undoubtedly notice that an entry had been made by the kitchen window, a search would be instituted for thieves, and the truth would then be revealed.

"But will you not tell me all you know regarding that strange place and its inmates?" I demanded.

"Later on, when I am certain of what has happened to my father," was her response. "I shudder to think how near to death we both have been. You have saved my life, Mr Kennedy."

"It was my duty. I, too, was envenomed by the same secret means. We might both have succumbed, just as those two men have done, had it not been for the fortunate circumstance of my possession of an antidote."

"Ah?" she sighed. "Death comes sooner or later to those who visit that fatal house." Then she added, "Let us take a cab home. I'm unnerved by what we have just discovered, for it renders the mystery greater."

"Is it then a mystery—even to you?"

"Yes, even to me," she answered; and then lapsed into silent thought.

When, a quarter of an hour later, we entered the hall at Grosvenor Street, the footman handed her a telegram, which she scanned, and quickly handed to me to read. It ran as follows:

"Abbey treasure discovered at Crowland this morning by the rector and Kennedy's friends. Have been present at excavations. Arrive home at 4:30. Tell Kennedy.—Glenelg."

"Look?" she cried in wild excitement. "My dear father is safe after all! He has apparently been helping your companions to search, and the hidden treasure has actually been discovered."

I stood with the telegram in my hand, utterly staggered.

She refused to make any further explanation without her father's consent, and as it was then half-past three o'clock, I was compelled to await the Earl's return. In wonder whether any message had been sent me from my friends at Crowland, I took a cab to Dover Street, where the porter handed me a telegram from Walter also announcing the great find, and saying that he was returning to London with the Earl, and would meet me at Grosvenor Street.

Therefore, in hot haste, I drove back to Judith, and sat with her in the cozy little room she used as boudoir until there came a loud ring at the door, and the two men entered.

"Father!" cried Judith, springing up and throwing her arms round his neck. "We are safe—safe at last!"

"Safe?" he echoed. "How? What has occurred?"

"Both men are dead," she declared. "They are lying dead in that room at Harpur Street. Mr Kennedy has broken into the place, and we have both seen them."

"Dead!" gasped the Earl, gazing fixedly at his daughter. "Who could have killed them?"

"Ah! who knows?" she cried. "But I feared for you, knowing their deep cunning. Yet they have fortunately fallen victims, and you—whom they intended should die—have escaped."

"Really, Lady Judith, this is very extraordinary!" exclaimed Walter Wyman. "Cannot you explain matters? Who are these men who are dead?"

"Selby and the hunchback," was her reply. "Ask Mr Kennedy. He will tell you."

Walter then turned to me, and I briefly explained our gruesome discovery and our very narrow escape from death. He stood aghast, and then in turn told me how they had recovered the whole of the abbey treasure, corresponding almost item for item with the list given in The Closed Book. As soon as they had started excavating, aided by a dozen labourers, Lord Glenelg had approached, introduced himself, and to their amazement, had rendered valuable assistance. At first of course, they had been mistrustful, recollecting the midnight search of some weeks ago; but at last, assured of his lordship's good will, and that his interest was that of an enthusiastic antiquary, his friendship was accepted.

He had expressed a wish to Walter to meet me, and that was the reason the pair had travelled up to London, leaving the valuable treasure recovered in the hands of the rector, Fred, and Sammy Waldon.

"If, as you assure me, both men are dead, Mr Kennedy, I see no reason for any further secrecy," exclaimed the Earl, turning his grey face towards me at last, and standing with one hand tenderly upon his daughter's shoulder. "Judith would perhaps explain matters to you better than I can; but as she desires it, I will relate the facts as far as they are known to me."

Her sweet gaze met mine, and I saw that she was breathless and nervous, as though in dread of the truth being told. Her face was white and attentive; and she half-clung to her father, as though relying upon his paternal protection. She seemed apprehensive as if, even now, she would withhold her strange secret from me.

Chapter Thirty Nine
Contains Lord Glenelg's Story

There was a long and painful pause.

"Eight years ago I was living with my wife and Judith at the Villa Carracci, in the Val d'Ema, close to Florence, and first met the hunchback Graniani, or Fra Francesco, as he was then called, for he was then a monk at the Certosa Monastery at Galuzzo," said Lord Glenelg in a hard, strained voice. "He came to beg alms of me; our conversation ran upon books and ancient manuscripts, and I found, to my surprise, that he was very well versed in the study of palaeography. Discovering that I was a collector, he invited me to the monastery one day, and there exhibited the treasures of the library, including a very remarkable manuscript of Arnoldus. Away at Sienna there lived an English friend of this hunchback, named Selby, of whom he often spoke. One afternoon, when visiting the Certosa, I was introduced to this man, and found him to be a person whose past history was somewhat shady, and who was living in Sienna in strict privacy. It struck me from the first that the fellow, like lots of others one meets in Italy and elsewhere, had got into some trouble in England, and lived abroad to avoid arrest. On several occasions we met, and I could not help suspecting that there was some extraordinary bond of friendship existing between that hunchback monk and my dark-faced, oily-looking compatriot, who lived the life of a hermit, sometimes in Pisa, at others in Sienna, and frequently in Rome.

"My wife frequently gave alms to Fra Francesco, hence the lay brother was a constant caller, and was in the habit of bringing us in return presents of grapes, figs, and salads from the monastery garden. I, too, became interested in him, for his knowledge was several times of great assistance to me in my palaeographical studies in the Laurenziana Library and the archives of the Palazzo Vecchio. So, gradually, his connection with the adventurous Englishman passed out of my mind.

"After about a year a crushing blow fell upon me. I had been into Florence one morning making some researches in the archives, and on my return discovered my poor wife seated in her little salon stark and dead.

She had, it seemed, received Fra Francesco in the hall, he having called with a present of grapes, and she had given him a few lire. The grapes had been taken to the dining-room, and she had gone straight to her own boudoir and must have there expired without being able to call assistance. The medical examination was a searching one; but it was found that death was due to sudden heart failure. Fra Francesco explained at the inquiry that my wife seemed quite in her usual health when she had given him alms, and that she had told him to call again on the following Monday. Selby was in Florence, and called to condole with me on the day my poor wife was interred in the English cemetery. After that I took Judith, and we became wanderers, travelling about hither and thither across the Continent. People believed me eccentric because I had closed Twycross and my town house here and preferred life in hotels with constant change." He sighed, adding: "But they knew not that I travelled with one fixed object; that often when my friends supposed me to be thousands of miles away I was living here in secrecy, going forth only at night for fear of recognition. The object of this you will see later."

"Ah, yes!" interrupted Lady Judith, her face a trifle paler, "an object that is now happily accomplished."

"My daughter, here, was but a girl when my poor wife died," went on his lordship, speaking in that mechanical, reflective tone that he had used all along, relating a painful history only from a sense of duty. "For the first three years she was, on and off, at a convent at Angers, and then as my constant companion lived a life of continual travel—an existence which has happily ended this very day. Well, I need not describe our weary wanderings, our swift movements from one city to another, nor our constant subterfuges for disguise. It is sufficient for me to come to these present days.

"By careful inquiries and personal observation I was aware that Fra Francesco had, about a year after my wife's death, been forced to leave the Order owing to irreligious conduct, and that both he and the man Selby—who I had discovered was a chemist of considerable ability and had been lecturer at one of the London hospitals—were in possession of some profound secret. The pair travelled together very frequently, staying at the best hotels, such as the Langham in London, the Chatham in Paris, the Metropole in Vienna, Shepheard's in Cairo, the Métropole at Monte Carlo, the Grand at Rome, the houses of the first order in Bombay, Sydney, San Francisco, and New York. Indeed, the pair made a world tour, and, strangely enough, in several places where they went some person of affluence, man or woman, expired suddenly, the doctors attributing death to the same vague cause as that of my poor wife's disease—heart failure.

"Thus my suspicion became confirmed that this unfrocked monk and his shady companion had actually discovered some secret poison which, like the venom of the Borgias, while defying detection, could be used in the same subtle way and with the same deadly effect. The suspicion had been aroused by my discovering among my dead wife's papers a note written to her by Fra Francesco just prior to her death, which showed that she had, by some means, become acquainted with their secret discovery, and knew the reason of the death of a small landed proprietor named Bardi, whose estate joined that of the Villa Caracci. It was undoubtedly because of this discovery of their dastardly crime and fear of denunciation that my poor wife was secretly assassinated."

"Then you have watched these men for seven years?" I exclaimed, in utter amazement at these revelations.

"I have," was his hard answer. "I followed them everywhere, secretly noting how ingeniously and unsuspectedly they dealt death and were gradually enriching themselves without any fear of detection, for they were clever enough never to be associated with the actual fatality. Indeed, they could so regulate their poison, whatever it was, that death would occur almost instantly, or, if they so desired, not for several days, robbery, of course, being always the motive. Under a dozen aliases they made their dastardly progress, striking death in seven different instances within my own knowledge, without compassion or remorse.

"Among the persons who fell their victims were the well-known stockbroker Clement Harrison, of Wall Street, New York, whose sudden death in Paris you will probably recollect; a woman named Blacker, maid to the Duchess of Cornwall, from whom they stole a quantity of diamonds which the unfortunate woman had in her keeping in the Hotel Métropole in Vienna; a banker named Lefevre, who died suddenly in his offices in the Boulevard Haussmann; and a Polish prince named Lebitski, who expired mysteriously at the same hotel in which they were staying at Sydney.

"I enumerate these just to show you the progress of their atrocious crimes. From the last-named victim they obtained at least thirty thousand pounds in cash and securities; and yet, although I felt absolutely certain of their guilt, I was utterly powerless to denounce them, because never once had there been the slightest suspicion of poisoning. Indeed, in several cases, in order to satisfy the police, the viscera had been analysed, and all idea of venom utterly set aside."

"Then you dared not denounce them," remarked Wyman, listening as eagerly as myself to this extraordinary story.

"True. I felt assured that I was in possession of the startling truth; but in no case was there the slightest evidence that either of the men had anything whatsoever to do with the victim's death.

"Two years ago, however, the pair acted in a manner which, for a long time puzzled me. They suddenly separated while in New York, Selby returning to Liverpool and Graniani taking a North German boat to Genoa. They were evidently in possession of considerable funds; but both were sufficiently clever not to show it. Indeed, neither of them had ever betrayed signs of affluence, Graniani usually posing as a deformed man of easy circumstances, and Selby his paid companion.

"On parting from his accomplice, Selby spent a month in London, and then went out to India for the cold weather, staying with a military friend in Bombay. Nothing, however, occurred, although with Judith I had followed him. The meaning of this latest move confounded me until about a year ago he returned to London, rented that house in Harpur Street, and took a comfortable flat himself in Walsingham House, Piccadilly. He engaged as his housekeeper at Harpur Street a strange-looking little old lady named Pickard, and spent about half his time there, apparently in strictest seclusion. With Judith's aid I watched that house carefully and continuously," went on the grey-haired, rather sad man, "and was not long in coming to the conclusion that a stuffed bear cub was being placed in the window at certain times as a secret signal to some passer-by; but although I exerted all my ingenuity, and spent days and nights in that gloomy street, I utterly failed to discover its meaning. At last, after all those years of watching, I resolved again to approach this malefactor in order to entrap and unmask him. It was this sole motive, that prompted me to take part in the conspiracy—to learn the truth and rid society of the terrible danger. One night, therefore, I followed him from Walsingham House to Daly's Theatre, and having seated myself in the next stall to him, feigned to suddenly recognise him. At first he was puzzled to recollect who I was, but quickly remembered, and then we at once became friendly. Probably he anticipated that through me he might obtain introductions to certain wealthy men who might become his victims, and with that object gave me his address at Piccadilly, and invited me to call. I went, notwithstanding the great risk I ran. For aught I knew he might defeat me with that secret and terrible weapon which none could withstand, and certainly he would have done so without compunction if he had known how many years and how much time and money I had spent in tracking him down.

"But we became on friendly terms, and you may well imagine the care I was constantly compelled to exercise in order to conceal my knowledge of his years of travel and his dastardly crimes. Each time we met, either here or at his cozy flat in Piccadilly, I knew not whether he might suspect and attempt to kill me by his secret method. In the old days in Italy he knew of my love for codexes and manuscripts, and he also being something of an authority, our tastes ran in similar lines. Indeed, it was upon this study that I feigned to cement our friendship. I entertained him once down at Twycross, showed him the whole of my collection, and more than once went with him to Sotheby's to give him the benefit of my knowledge regarding his purchases, for he himself was forming a small collection. During all this time, of course, he made no mention of the house of mystery in Harpur Street."

"Yours was certainly a dangerous position," I remarked. "He would undoubtedly have envenomed you had he suspected."

"Most certainly. Like his unscrupulous companion Graniani, he would stand at nothing. A dozen times he could have killed me if he had so wished. He and his accomplice had, I feel convinced, recovered, from some old manuscript—in the Certosa, I believe—the secret of the Borgia cantarella. One afternoon he came to me here and told me in confidence of a most important palaeographical discovery made by his friend, Fra Francesco, who, he added, was no longer a monk at the Certosa, that monastery having been dissolved by the Italian Government—which was, I knew, the truth.

"The manuscript was nothing less than the noted Arnoldus of the Certosa, which had fallen into the hands of the Prior of San Sisto at Florence, and had been purchased by an English collector—yourself. Graniani had missed securing it, believing that it was not the treasured volume of the monastery, but a smaller and less valuable copy that he knew had been in the library. After it had been purchased by you, however, he discovered, to his chagrin, that it was the great Arnoldus itself, the book that contained some strange things in English written by an English monk named Lovel, who had ended his days at that famous monastery. Many strange and remarkable secrets were, he said, in that record—secrets regarding Lucrezia Borgia, her life, and the whereabouts of her jewels, all of which Fra Francesco had read years ago when, as a lay brother, he had had access to the manuscript. He was now about to obtain possession of it, and send it to England, so that the statements it contained might be investigated and verified."

"They stole it from my house at Antignano," I said quickly. "An Italian woman named Anita Bardi was the thief!"

"I know. Old Mrs Pickard went to Paris, met her there, and carried it to Harpur Street. That night he examined it alone, reading through the record; and afterwards becoming seized by extraordinary pains, he was compelled to send for a doctor. He showed me the manuscript at Walsingham House next day; but we examined it with gloves, for he declared that the vellum leaves had been envenomed. Afterwards, it mysteriously disappeared from Harpur Street."

"It passed again into my possession," I admitted, explaining how I had invoked the aid of my police friend Noyes.

"Selby had not finished copying the whole of it, hence our miscalculation of the spot at Threave," his lordship explained. "Of course, when Graniani returned to London and their scheme to obtain the treasure was placed before me, both myself and Judith announced our readiness to assist; first, in order to obtain the secret of that mysterious house in Bloomsbury; and, secondly, to obtain sufficient evidence to convict the men of their dastardly crimes. As participators in the conspiracy we were at length admitted there, and found it a gloomy, dismal place. The sign of the bear cub still puzzled us, and the reason of Selby's secret visits there were equally inexplicable. Judith did all she could to unravel the mystery, acting with utter fearlessness, although well knowing that at any time, if the faintest suspicion were aroused, she would fall the victim of secret assassination just as her dear mother had done."

"It was to avenge her that I have acted as I have done through it all," declared her ladyship. "I was determined to learn the truth about that pair of fiends and to unravel the mystery of that house with its secret sign. You sought of me an explanation of my conduct. Yet how could I give it without telling you the strange, tragic, and remarkable story which my father has just related? I promised you that you should know some day—and you have now heard the truth."

"I understand," I replied. "But not everything."

"Ah, no! you do not know everything," she sighed, stretching forth her hand towards me. "When you do, you cannot forgive."

"Forgive! What?" I cried. But her father hastened to calm her emotion.

"Yes," she went on hoarsely. "You may as well know at first as at last that I became implicated in the terrible secret of that house. At Selby's suggestion I invited there to luncheon a friend of his, young Leslie Hargreaves, a wealthy man who had met and, I believed, admired me. He went to Harpur Street to meet me and have luncheon on the very day you detected me at the window; but half an hour after his return to his chambers in Shaftesbury Avenue his valet found him dead, and notes to the value of nearly five hundred pounds known to have been in his pockets were missing! I suspected the intention of those men, and yet I actually allowed the sacrifice of his life! I shall never forgive myself for that—never?"

"But you were in ignorance of their real intention?" I said, excusing her. "Hargreaves was Selby's friend, you say. If so, you surely had no idea of treachery, inasmuch as you were friendly with these men, and they never sought to harm you."

"But I ought to have been wary," she wailed. "I ought to have saved his life. My offence is unpardonable before God—as before man!" And she covered her blanched face with her hand, sobbing in bitter remorse.

I bent towards her, and there, before her father and Wyman, strove to comfort her. What passionate, consoling words I uttered I know not. All I was conscious of was that she had at last utterly broken down. And then, when I assured her that I forgave everything, and that in the circumstances she was not culpable in the unfortunate death of young Hargreaves, she raised her head, smiled at me happily through her tears as I told her of my love, and there, before Wyman and her father, declared that she reciprocated the passion that was consuming me.

Then I knew she was mine—my own sweet love. Her eyes had filled with tears, and for a moment she rested her head upon my shoulder, weeping silently. She was thinking of that long and terrible past, and of how she and her father had at last avenged her mother's death and defeated the villainies of that dangerous pair of assassins. I knew it well. I held her hands in mine without uttering a word, for my heart was too full.

Chapter Forty
By which the Book Remains open

But *passons.*

I have perhaps related this strange episode of my eventful life at too great a length already. Yet you, my reader, may pardon me when you recollect that from out that musty envenomed volume, The Closed Book—which may be seen by you any day in the manuscript department of the British Museum, placed by itself in a sealed glass case—there came to me both love and fortune in a manner entirely unexpected.

Of the love I have already spoken. As to the fortune, we found the law of treasure-trove as elastic as all the others. You, no doubt, read the other day of the sale of the Borgia emeralds to the wife of an American millionaire through the medium of Garnier, the well-known jeweller in the rue de la Paix, and of the high price paid for those historic gems.

If you evince any curiosity regarding the treasure of the Abbey of Crowland, you may, if you search, discover the altar and certain other objects exposed to view in the British Museum. Two chalices, an alms dish, and a quantity of loose gems remain by amicable arrangement at Crowland as Mr Mason's share; while Fred Fenwicke, Sammy Waldron, and Walter Wyman have, of course, all equally participated in their great find. The bulk of the treasure is, however, still in my possession, and I placed aside one casket of ancient jewels intact as a gift to Judith on our marriage, the promise of which she gave me with her father's free and willing consent.

As regards the mystery of the house at Harpur Street, I telegraphed that same evening to Noyes, to whom we related the whole story, first obtaining his pledge that none of us should be dragged into the double tragedy that had taken place.

For the first time in his life the genial, well-trained police inspector betrayed absolute amazement; then, thoroughly practical, he left us hurriedly, hailed a cab, and drove away.

Next day the papers were full of the mysterious discovery, but neither press nor public ever knew the real secret of that house of death. Indeed, not until a month ago, after most exhaustive inquiries, in which the chief intelligence at Scotland Yard was engaged, did Noyes declare to us that the place had been used constantly by Selby during the nine months of his tenancy as a place to which to invite people, and, if it suited his purpose, to administer poison with an ingenuity unsurpassed.

One day he took me to the house in secret, and there showed me how murder had been brought to the perfection of a fine art. Not only did he explain the steel point in the polished handrail that had so nearly caused my own death, but showed me a similar hollow point cunningly concealed in the door knob of the drawing-room, which, on being turned, ejected the deadly venom like a serpent's tooth; an umbrella with a similar contrivance in its briar handle, as well as a silver matchbox which, being well worn, showed that it had been long carried in the vest pocket, and probably well used!

London regarded the death of Selby and the old Italian hunchback as one of its many mysteries, especially as the medical evidence failed altogether to prove foul play. Our theory, however, coincided with that formed by Noyes and certain other high officials of the Criminal Investigation Department. It was that Anita Bardi, daughter of one of the early victims of the dastardly pair, having been in the employ of Judith as maid for several years, and having travelled with her, had had an opportunity of watching the movements of the poisoners and had also overheard the suspicions entertained by Lord Glenelg and his daughter. She then determined to seek her own revenge for her father's cruel assassination, and with that in view had come to London. The warnings she had given me regarding Judith were, as the latter afterwards admitted, purposely uttered in order that I should dissociate myself from the dangerous affair. Being an accessory in the recovery of the case containing the Borgia ring and phial, she had undoubtedly possessed herself of them, had met both men on their return from their fruitless journey to Crowland, and had killed them by the very means they had themselves employed against others, afterwards locking the door, escaping from the house, and flying back to Italy.

This theory, indeed, has been proved to be the correct one by a letter, bearing no address and posted in Venice, since received by Judith.

The reason Graniani returned from New York to Italy two years before was evidently in order to search for the missing Arnoldus, known to have been sold with other volumes from the Certosa library and passed from hand to hand. Father Bernardo, who is now one of my best friends, was entirely innocent of the conspiracy, and has since told me that the reason he endeavoured to obtain repossession of The Closed Book was because of Graniani's allegation that evil would befall its possessor and—very Italian—his offer of a greatly increased price on behalf of an American collector. The hunchback had evidently followed me from Leghorn to Florence; and suddenly discovering the manuscript to be the actual Arnoldus, urged the prior to cry off the bargain and sell to him. Anita Bardi's visit to Father Bernardo was on a false pretext, because she was, of course, assisting Graniani at Lord Glenelg's suggestion.

Lord Glenelg has, as you know, recently returned to public life; but the secret inquiries instituted by the commissioner of police revealed the extraordinary fact that in no fewer than eight well-proved cases where there had been inquests regarding sudden death during the period of Selby's residence in Harpur Street, the deceased was known to have visited that house of mystery immediately prior to his or her death. And if these eight cases have been satisfactorily proved, how many others may there not have been?

After a long search, Mrs Pickard, the wizened old woman whom Selby had engaged as housekeeper, was found, and from a statement made by her to the police it seemed that the poisoner had an accomplice named Brewer—evidently the fair-bearded man who had assisted him in the assault on the valet Thompson, but who never came to the house. It was his duty to watch outside for the sign of the bear cub in the window, and then follow home persons who had been decoyed there, to ascertain that death really overtook them, and that they could not return and make an accusation.

The sign of the bear cub was the signal that some person had been secretly envenomed, and that a watch was necessary—a startling fact of which certain officials at Scotland Yard are now aware.

Happily for the personal safety of society, the formula for the manufacture of the venom has died with its discoverer, Graniani, and his accomplice; while the fact that the little crystal bottle of Lucrezia Borgia was found by the police empty in the grate of the front attic at Harpur Street, together with the poison-ring—now also in the British Museum, by the way—is sufficient evidence that the few drops of the fatal compound of the Borgias which we recovered are now also lost forever. The missing folio, which, however, contains nothing of great interest, I have since discovered in the Library of Trinity College, Dublin.

And of Judith—my heart's love—now my wife? She is not a woman of fulsome words. She has proved her love for me by deeds. Today she is seated beside me as, in the quiet of our country home, I conclude this strange chronicle. Here, as I write, the sun shines across the old-world lawn, where the high box hedges cast their long shadows, the mist has vanished, and the day, like all our days, is one of cloudless happiness and blissful hope.